TRAPPED
IN THE
MIRROR

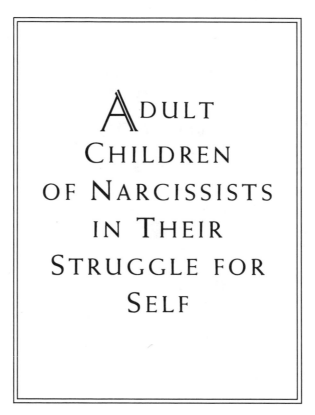

Adult Children of Narcissists in Their Struggle for Self

TRAPPED

in the

MIRROR

———

Elan Golomb, Ph.D.

WILLIAM MORROW
and Company, Inc.
New York

It is the policy of William Morrow and Company, Inc., and its imprints and affiliates, recognizing the importance of preserving what has been written, to print the books we publish on acid-free paper, and we exert our best efforts to that end.

Library of Congress Cataloging-in-Publication Data has been ordered.
Golomb, Elan, Ph. D.
TRAPPED IN THE MIRROR.
ISBN 0-688-09471-6   91-7669

Printed in the United States of America

First Edition

1 2 3 4 5 6 7 8 9 10

BOOK DESIGN BY RICHARD ORIOLO

To my mother,
whose last words
before an unexpected
death were,
"I have to learn how to assert myself."

Thanks to close friends, especially Lisa, Erwin, and Art, who helped me surmount my doubts when writing this book. Great appreciation to Harold Brody, the psychoanalyst who supported my struggle for self-definition and said in response to my questioning his words, "Life is too short for lying." Truthful words stay with you.

I appreciate those who trained me in psychotherapy, especially in observing the effects of insight. Thanks to Bernard Kalinkowitz, director of the N.Y.U. program in Clinical Psychology. It was he and the program that welcomed me to psychology.

Gratitude to all who told their stories. To Regula Noetzli, a literary agent who put great effort and insight into showing me what was readable and then into getting it published. Thanks to Maria Guarnaschelli, senior editor at William Morrow, who understood the book and wholeheartedly supported it.

CONTENTS

Introduction   11

1. How to Recognize a Narcissist and Narcissism   17

2. Who Is the Adult Child of a Narcissist?   25

3. They Make You Conform to Their Will,
   Even in Your Thinking   35

4. Anne and the Invisible Force   45

5. Suicidal Urges: John   55

6. Attraction to Narcissistic Mates by
   Children of Narcissists: Delores   71

7. No Right to Live If You Cannot Love:
   How a Narcissist Put His Inability to
   Love onto His Child   91

8. The Destructive Inner Parent: Victoria   97

9. A Life Devoid of Motivation: Nick   111

10. The Child of a Narcissist Who Becomes
    a Narcissist: Alan   119

11. Addictive Behavior in Children of Narcissists: Marie,
    Fat Is Dead—Obesity as a Protective Device   131

12. Raising a Child to Fulfill the Narcissistic Parent's
    Heroic Image: Mark, Unable to Respond to
    His Child's Dependency Needs, Requires the
    Child to Be Heroic   141

13. Changing from Weakness into Strength:
     How to Develop a Real Sense of Self   147

14. How to Find and Heal Your Self   169

15. What Do We Call Love? Where and How Do
     We Seek It?   189

16. People in Stages of Self-Development   197

17. Learning to Relate to the Narcissistic Parent:
     The Way It Is and How It Can Be Improved   223

18. Sending Home the Negative Introject   241

Epilogue   261

Index   265

INTRODUCTION

*T*here is a group of unsung victims whose number is very great. They often do not seek the help they need because they do not recognize that they suffer from a problem for which there is a solution. These are the children of narcissistic parents. I know their plight from the inside since I am one of them.

A friend asked me, "What are narcissists? Aren't they people who think themselves special?" The answer to this is yes and no. All healthy people regard themselves as special, unique beings capable of achievement and worthy of love, and it is no coincidence that this is exactly the way their parents saw them during their formative years. People who are relatively free of narcissistic traits (most of us have some) do not attempt to place themselves above others. They are unconcerned with such comparisons. They stay in touch with their feelings and try to do their personal best. Their standards are internal and realistic since they have a good idea of who they are and what they can accomplish (such objectivity is not insignificant). They are not free of idealistic wishes and dreams.

Narcissists are wholly different. They unconsciously deny an unstated and intolerably poor self-image through inflation. They turn themselves into glittering figures of immense grandeur surrounded by psychologically impenetrable walls. The goal of this self-deception is to be impervious to greatly feared external criticism and to their own roiling sea of doubts.

This figure of paradox needs to be regarded as perfect by all. To achieve this, he or she constructs an elaborate persona (a social mask which is presented to the world). The persona needs an appreciative audience to applaud it. If enough people do so, the narcissist is relieved that no one can see through his disguise. The persona is a defensive schema to hide behind, like the false-front stores on a Western movie set. When you peer behind the propped-up wall, you find . . . nothing. Similarly, behind the grandiose parading, the narcissist feels empty and devoid of value.

Because his life is organized to deny negative feelings about himself and to maintain an illusion of superiority, the narcissist's family is forcibly conscripted into supporting roles. They have no other option if they wish to get along with him. His mate must be admiring and submissive to keep the marriage going and his children will automatically mold themselves into any image that is projected upon them.

Here the tragedy begins. A narcissist cannot see his children as they are but only as his unconscious needs dictate. He does not question why his children are incredibly wonderful (better than anyone else's) or intolerably horrible (the worst in all respects) or why his view of them ricochets from one extreme to another with no middle ground. It is what they are.

When he is idealizing them, he sees their talents as mythic, an inflation that indicates they are being used as an extension of his grandiose self. When he hates them and finds their characteristics unacceptable, he is projecting hated parts of himself onto them. Whether idealizing or denigrating, he is entirely unaware that what he sees is a projection and that his views are laying a horrible burden on his child.

It is uncanny to observe how early the process of projection begins. Before the child is conceived, roles are already assigned in the narcissist's mind to the flesh of his flesh. The expected characteristics are confirmed by subtle actions of the fetus in the womb, and when the baby arrives the parent starts ratifying his projections through his interactions with the child.

For example, a narcissistic father was able to stop experiencing feelings of weakness as his own by finding them in the personality of his four-week-old daughter. He never questioned the validity of his perceptions. Such thoughts would occasionally reappear, only to be pushed aside and defended against by focusing on others' flaws, including those of his child. He buttressed his argument by judging her physical movements feeble and low in energy as well. Clearly, she was "biologically inferior." The baby's characterization stuck and her fate was sealed.

The mother duplicated her mate's view, unconsciously suppressing doubts and contradictory perceptions. Her thinking was influenced by the fact that her husband could only accept her when she agreed with him. She was in love with him at the time and very much wanted to please. It is worth noting that a person who marries a narcissist often does so to augment low self-esteem by amalgamating his or her ego with that of one who radiates greatness. They are excessively threatened by their mate's potential rejection and will readily give the required responses.

This child grew up according to parental blueprint. She became an overly compliant person, often turning to her narcissistic father to make her decisions. She took up her mother's profession and her mother's submissive role as the appropriate way to express femaleness and to relate to men. In doing so, she assumed the role that her narcissistic father could accept in a woman.

One hallmark of the child of a narcissist is that these children tend to take values wholesale from the parent rather than tailor them to fit their own personalities. Narcissists appreciate carbon-copy children, since any change or difference from their prototype is experienced as a criticism.

The young woman became the "perfect" daughter, obediently expressing her parents' nouveau riche values. She played tennis, took sailing lessons, spoke French, and summered in Europe. She was not outstanding in any of her acquired skills, probably because her participation lacked passion. Her whole self was not involved in anything she did. She was upset that no great talent ever emerged from her efforts. She was somewhat overweight although attractive, but rarely dated. None of the young men she encountered could measure up to her dad.

Still, she was remarkably agreeable, always smiling and nodding, suspiciously free of malice. In fact, she was rather boring. Inexplicably, this paragon of pleasantness came to be troubled by mounting feelings of rage. She was confused. Why should she be angry if all was so perfect in her world? She had never perceived anything damaging in the pressures placed upon her to become a polished showpiece. Such thoughts were taboo.

Her rage became uncontrollable. It took the form of world destruction fears in which everything was going to be blown up in a nuclear holocaust. This obsession reflected a projection of her repressed explosive feelings. Fortunately, these fears drove her into therapy. Her parents found it upsetting to accept that she needed help since this reflected upon their adequacy as parents. Their daughter had to be on the brink of insanity before she or anyone else in the family could admit that something wasn't right.

The offspring of narcissists grow up fulfilling their assigned roles. They may sense that they are in a state of falsehood, but do not know what to do about feelings of nonauthenticity. They try all the harder to become what they are supposed to be, as if their feelings of uneasiness come from an improper realization of their role. If their parents see them as miserably deficient, from the shape of their bodies to the power of their minds, that is what they become. If they were portrayed to themselves as great muckamucks, especially if they have innate ability to fulfill a powerful role, they become the movers and shakers of society.

At heart, children of narcissists, raised up or cast down by the ever-evaluating parent, feel themselves to be less than nothing because they must "be" something to earn their parents' love. Conditional love offers no support for the inner self. It creates people who have no personal sense of substance or worth. Nourished on conditional love, children of narcissists become conditional. They find themselves un-real.

The stories in this book concern the struggles of children of narcissists to free themselves from the web of their parents' distortions. Here we see the psychological reefs on which our lifeboats may be wrecked, not the least of which is our own unhappy narcissism acquired through identification with the powerful parent.

The people in these anecdotes often feel hopeless and paralyzed. Sometimes they break through to a sense of their true selves. Then they know freedom and joy. The journey is a rough one for all who undertake it. It is also the only trip worth taking.

You who recognize your story on these pages can take hope from the experience of the others, that it is possible to undo the illusions under which we were raised. Let us all work to rid ourselves of falsely imposed images in order to find our true identities.

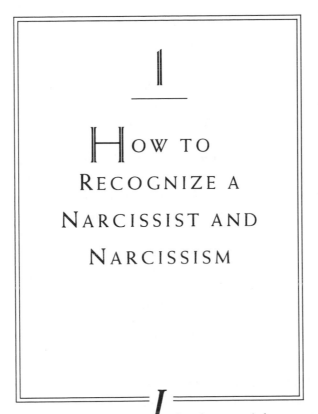

1

How to Recognize a Narcissist and Narcissism

*I*t has been said that narcissism is a common condition of modern society, that in the past there were narcissists but never in such profusion. Louis XIV, when he uttered his famous comment, *"L'état, c'est moi"* (I am the state) was expressing the quintessential narcissistic viewpoint of monomaniacal self-centeredness. The French Revolution was set off by his feelings of narcissistic entitlement. Louis's ego was so inflated that he felt it represented the needs of all France. If Louis ate, France should feel satisfied. Marie Antoinette offered her own narcissistic reaction to the starving masses begging for bread when she uttered her insouciant cry, "Let them eat cake." Since her belly was filled, their request for mere subsistence seemed ridiculous. These two comments are like bookends of similar design. They imply, "My needs are all; nothing and no one else counts."

A narcissist is interested only in what reflects on her. All she does or experiences is seen as a reflection of self. The name of this psychological aberration is derived from the ancient Greek myth of Narcissus, a beautiful young man beloved of the nymphs. The nymph Echo fell in love with Narcissus's beauty but he paid no attention to her increasingly mournful cries. To the gods looking down upon the play of men, unrequited love was a crime. They punished Narcissus in appropriate symbolic form by causing him to fall in love with his own reflection, ever reaching out to embrace an illusion.

Each time Narcissus reached for his adored image mirrored in a pool of still water, it would dissolve into numberless ripples. The narcissist, who is constantly trying to repair her injured self-esteem by adorning and admiring her gilded self, is also haunted by the terror of psychological fragmentation should she become aware that this self is not all she claims it to be.

The narcissistic character disorder is described in the DSM-III (*The Diagnostic and Statistical Manual of Mental Disorders*) as having the following characteristics: an inflated sense of self-importance; fantasies of unlimited success, fame, power, beauty, and perfect love (uncritical adoration); exhibitionism (a need to be looked at and admired); a tendency to feel rage with little objective cause; a readiness to treat people with cool indifference as punishment for hurtful treatment or as an indication of the fact they have no current use for the person; a tendency toward severe feelings of inferiority, shame, and emptiness; a sense of entitlement accompanied by the tendency to exploit; a tendency to overidealize or devalue people based largely on a narrow focus; an inability to empathize.

This list is extensive but not all-inclusive. We are said to live in the age of narcissism. Few of us are entirely free of its traits. It is in our label, "the Me Generation," and shows up in popular expressions such as "What's in it for me?" and "taking care of number one." Those who are philosophically inclined might ask which comes first, the narcissism of the individual or that of the society in which he is formed. There probably is a point at which the ills and emphases of a society and the neuroses of individuals living within it feed into a common stream.

If society worships such external things as how you appear to others, your status, power, and money, a person may acquire the belief that what she keeps inside, her emotions and the deeds that only she knows about, do not count. Yet the only real and lasting sense of self-worth that a person can have is the feeling of and for her essential self, the sense of being real, of doing what possibly she alone thinks appropriate. Having an appreciation of the subjective intangible is what we mean when we say that someone has "character," a rare trait today.

Applying the values of an externalized society to one's self causes narcissistic wounding. We use the word narcissistic to show that it is self-love that is harmed. When self-love depends on externals, on others' opinions of what you are and do, the self is betrayed. A woman who possesses great natural beauty was described by her boastful mother in front of company as "beautiful as a movie star." When she heard these words, the daughter cringed in shame, feeling herself to be worthless because she was only valued for her surface.

A healthy self has nothing to do with stardom. Psychological health comes from acceptance starting in early infancy of all that you are, good and bad, dirty and clean, naughty and nice, smart and stupid. In the adult, health is manifested by an accord between ideals and actions, by the ability to appreciate yourself for what you attempt to do as well as for what succeeds. It means recognizing that although you are not perfect you are still worthy of love.

In high school, coaches attempt to strengthen character by telling their charges to do their best and to ignore whether the outcome is win or lose. Our externalized society is so addicted to winning that such advice is but a weak antidote to the pressure placed on youngsters by hysterical parents, idealizing students, and the school board, all of whose egos need a win to contradict a basically shaky self-image.

To grow up to be a whole person, infants, toddlers, and children in their formative stages need the experience of genuine acceptance; they have to know that they are truly seen and yet are perfect and lovable in their parents' eyes; they need to stumble and sometimes fall and to be greeted by a father's or mother's commiserating smile. Through parental acceptance, children learn that their "is-ness," their essential selves, merit love. Self-love is learned through identification. Positive self-regard is the opposite of what the narcissist knows. He is "in love" with himself precisely because he cannot love himself.

As a child, the narcissist-to-be found his essential self rejected by his narcissistic parent. The wounds of the parent are a template for the wounding of the child. Each narcissistic parent in each generation repeats the crime that was perpetrated against him. The crime is non-acceptance. The narcissist is more demanding and deforming of the child he identifies with more strongly, although all his children are pulled into his web of subjectivity. How can he accept offspring who are the product of his own unconsciously despised self? His attitude is a variant of the Groucho Marx Syndrome, "I would not join any club that would have me as its member," here transposed into "I would not love any child that would have me as its parent." The child has rejection as its birthright.

The child who will eventually turn into a full-scale narcissist most often had a narcissistic mother. The reason why the maternal narcissist is more often likely to turn her child into a fellow narcissist is because the mother most often provides the predominant care that defines the baby's early world. If the father is narcissistic and the mother is not, the father's traumatic impact is attenuated at the time when the child is establishing a sense of self.

The narcissist-to-be turns away from a world he perceives as devoid of nurturance and love (since a mother's care gives the child its first version of the world). He withdraws into grandiose fantasies to shield himself from profound feelings of unworthiness caused by the fact that his mother does not really love him. Grandiosity permits him to believe that he is complete and perfect unto himself, thus shielding him from his secret sense that he is a ravening beast, ready to murder others in order to eat and survive. The food of this beast is admiration.

The narcissistic mother, caretaker of the child's earliest years, is grandiose, chronically cold but overprotective. She invades her child's autonomy and manipulates him to conform to her wishes. She rejects all about him that she finds objectionable, putting him in the anxiety-ridden position of losing her affection if he expresses dissatisfaction. She responds to his baby rages and fussing with anxiety, anger, or withdrawal. He becomes unable to cope with the ugly feelings that threaten to erupt and destroy the bond between him and his mother, the bond he depends on for survival.

His mother's grandiosity models a way out of his dilemma. She places him on a common throne, sharing the rarefied air of her greatness. By appropriating and embellishing the aura of specialness in which she has enveloped him he can create a grandiose fantasy about himself to escape to. This fantasy eventually crystallizes into a psychic structure we call the grandiose self. A new narcissist is born.

For all his air of self-sufficiency, the narcissist is full of interpersonal needs. He is more needy than most people who feel they have something good inside of them. If he is to survive, he must find a way to get his needs met without acknowledging the independent existence of the person off whom he wants to feed. To admit that a person is necessary to him gets him in touch with feelings of deficiency, which plummet him into intolerable emptiness, jealousy, and rage. To avoid this experience, he inhabits a one-person world. Either he exists and other people are extinguished or vice versa. In his mind, he is center stage and other people are mere shadows beyond the proscenium. This solution creates a new conundrum: "How can I get fed without acknowledging the feeder?" The solution is to dissect people and to turn them partially into objects, to make them inanimate. A person comes to represent a need-fulfilling function or an organ like a breast, vagina, or penis. There is no overall person to consider.

It is like living life in an automat in which various emotional foods are displayed behind little glass windows, with one crucial difference. In this automat the customer does not have to pay. He is entitled to eat. He remains aloof from people in his automat world. Since he is not psychotic and totally out of touch with reality, he is occasionally forced to recognize the presence of a benefactor. The emotional incursion of such an idea is warded off by demeaning the gift or the person who has given it. If a gift is unworthy he doesn't have to feel gratitude. Not to say that he does not at times proffer thanks. A narcissist can be quite charming when he wishes to impress, but his words are not deeply felt.

He usually does not see the need to go to such lengths with his family. They belong to him and are supposed to cater to his needs. His children are particularly crushed by his lack of recognition for their attempts at pleasing him since he is the main figure in their world. Adding insult to injury, they can always count on his criticism when what is offered falls below his standards.

Despite his bubble of grandiosity, the narcissist is remarkably thin-skinned, forever taking offense and feeling mistreated, especially when people appear to have eliminated the extras in their response to him. Less than special immediately implies that someone may be thinking the emperor is naked, precisely what he fears. He is enraged whenever the aching corns of his insecurities are stepped on.

He is wounded when the child he deems special fails to live up to expectations, reacting with a rage one might have for a limb that has failed to provide support. His children and his mate learn how to soothe him by propping up his grandiosity, and the special child learns not to let him down.

A narcissist tends to have transient social relationships since few wish to abide by her rules. She has quick enthusiasms, business associates but few friends. Her closest are other narcissists who keep a comfortable distance while exchanging gestures of mutual admiration. Neither makes emotional demands on the other.

In a mate, if she does not choose a fellow narcissist, she will cohabit with a person who feels inadequate and who needs to hide in a relationship. This suits her well since she doesn't want to recognize the existence of another being. Often, her mate is the child of a narcissist, already indoctrinated to regard exploitation and disregard as love. Others lured by the narcissistic aura are those in whom healthy childhood exhibitionism has been repressed. The period of healthy exhibitionism finds the little boy showing off his muscles to Mom, who is supposed to be properly impressed, and finds the little girl flouncing her new dress before Dad to court his admiration. If the parent puts the child to shame for showing off, the need for attention gets repressed into the unconscious. Repression means that the need is not satisfied and continues to press for expression in the adult without her being aware of it. The repressed adult may select an exhibitionistic mate to achieve vicarious satisfaction.

It should be understood that the narcissistic personality represents a serious malfunction, something that might be labeled an illness under the medical model. Since the medical model does not really describe human personality, a better measure of narcissistic tendencies might be the degree to which the individual is able to be truly productive and loving. A narcissist may be productive professionally but often is held back by his or her fear of being less than perfect. Such a concern can truncate creativity and certainly undermine relationships.

The grandiose narcissist in her automat world may not feel the emptiness of her life, although her narcissistic traits cause suffering in all those with whom she has intimate contact. She only comes to recognize that something is wrong (not necessarily with herself) when the environment no longer supports her grand illusions and she fails to live up to expectations of greatness. At this time she may become depressed and seek psychotherapy to relieve the pain.

The narcissist who hopes to change through analytic psychotherapy will find that treatment is not easy. The process must be arduous because it requires that she admit to human failings; that she recognize the need for other people, who have the choice to give or not to give (you cannot commandeer love). It means once more experiencing the feelings of being a helpless and manipulated child who sustained considerable damage at the hands of unloving parents. She will have to see the emptiness of a life compulsively controlled by the need for admiration and ostentatious achievement. The outcome of her struggle to uncover an authentic self will be the ability to lead an ordinary life, one with real joys and sorrows, not the fictitious pleasures of a mirrored image.

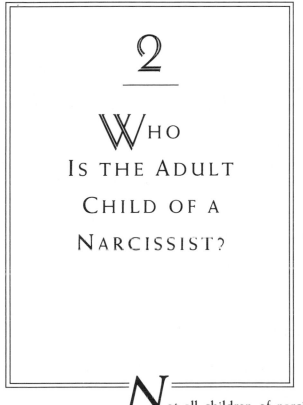

2

WHO IS THE ADULT CHILD OF A NARCISSIST?

Not all children of narcissists are identical but most share from a pool of common traits. The extent to which they manifest problems specific to having a narcissistic parent depends upon the degree of severity of the parent's narcissism and the presence or absence of ameliorating influences in the child's life. These would include loving grandparents who are frequently around, interested teachers or other adults who can understand the child's plight.

Unfortunately, one reason a narcissistic home can be so destructive is that narcissists tend to be very insular, having only a few close friends who are also narcissists, equally insensitive to the needs and feelings of children. Others drawn to a narcissist are themselves chil-

dren of narcissists, too mesmerized by the replay of their early childhood relationship to take an autonomous position with regard to her
children.

Nor would she allow it. The narcissist rules the emotional atmosphere of her home. She establishes an airtight reality from which her
children have little chance of escaping. Those children whose parents
separate can fare better if they live with the nonnarcissistic or less
narcissistic parent. This often does happen, as the narcissist rarely
wants the nuts-and-bolts responsibility of rearing her children.

She wants to be there on special occasions when she can make a
showy gesture. She will bring a present, rent a sailboat, tell remarkable
stories about her accomplishments and turn herself into a heroine.
Against this display, the daily ministrations of the other parent fade
into obscurity. Often, it is only as an adult, or when the grown child
becomes a parent himself, that the contribution and loving spirit of the
nonnarcissistic parent is recognized.

A child living in a home separate from the narcissistic parent is
only occasionally bathed in the icy sea of his or her parent's peculiar
world view. Even so, the narcissistic parent, who is loved, needed, and
identified with by her child, must have a profound effect.

The peculiar view espoused by the narcissistic parent is that her
child as an independent being does not count. Here are two examples
of how narcissistic parents could not relate to the real needs of their
children.

A young woman just out of college, living on an extremely limited
budget, asked her socialite mother for a vacuum cleaner for her birthday. Her mother agreed. When the date arrived, her daughter received
an expensive gift certificate to a fancy hair salon for "the works." Wild
with frustration (and able to express her feelings after several years of
therapy), she asked why she hadn't been given the gift that was promised. Her mother answered in the aggrieved tone of one who has been
unfairly attacked. "But that's what *I* thought you needed, dear." It was
impossible for the mother to understand why her gift was not altogether loving. The mother had given her daughter the gift that she
herself would have wanted.

In the second example, a narcissistic mother again pleased only
herself, being unable to appreciate the age-appropriate interests of her

children. She took her two youngsters to Paris, where she cooped them up all day in a hotel room while she went on a buying spree in the fabric houses. She returned in the late afternoon, to find two bored and angry children who demanded gifts for having been good. She felt unjustly attacked by the "little ingrates." Had she not brought them to this wonderful city of charm and culture which she had been out enjoying all day? They should have been able to appreciate it through her own experience, apparently through osmosis.

Osmotic expectations are extremely common in narcissists since they do not recognize the psychological boundaries between themselves and their children. The children should be as happy as they or, on other occasions, as miserable. If the child is happy when the parent is sad, it is taken as a sign of disloyalty and insensitivity.

The mother on her buying spree felt that her children should have been overjoyed knowing that their backsides would soon rest on wonderful Parisian upholstery fabric. How could they be so unappreciative of all the efforts she had made on their behalf!

The child of a narcissist is never seen as she truly is. Even before birth, the parent has attributed characteristics to the child which jibe with the fulminating needs of his unconscious. After birth, the child is maimed by endless attempts to improve her. She is found intrinsically unlovable and defective because she is born of a parent who feels horribly insufficient (although he can't admit it) and who unconsciously puts this label not on himself but on his child. The child can be attacked and corrected without the parent recognizing that he himself is the target.

The pressure from a narcissist to conform to expectations is like the water in which a fish swims, so relentless and uniform that the child is hardly aware of it. Struggles are infrequent while the process of shaping is going on. Of course, there are moments when the child feels mentally assaulted and may fight or cry, but even then she also feels bad, wrong, and confused. She feels what the parent indicates she should feel, since her shortcomings are a shameful disappointment to the parent. To be included under the parent's umbrella of grandiosity, the child must exhibit pure excellence in whatever the parent deems important. Otherwise she is pushed out.

Proper teaching involves the concept of improving functioning, something external to the self, not improving the inner person, which must be seen as intrinsically acceptable. Identification of the inner child with the behavior or the product of her behavior damages her self-esteem. She comes to believe that even if she does succeed she is merely gold over shit, the facade of beauty over true ugliness. The "successful" child of a narcissist feels like a fake since the true self is identified with failure.

Children of narcissists emerge from this crucible with a common and most serious problem. They feel that they do not have the right to exist. Their selves have been twisted out of their natural shape since any movement toward independence is treated as a betrayal and something that can cause the parent irreparable harm.

The narcissistic parent's philosophy of rationalized self-interest prevents the child from understanding why he feels guilty about having autonomous motives. The narcissistic parent's principle, "You don't count," means the child's effort to be seen as an individual is worthy of consideration, if only for trying to understand that her problems are felt by the parent to be an act of treason. The child's move toward autonomy is greeted by the parent's pain, resentment, and anger, from which the child learns that becoming a separate person is wrong.

A narcissist attempts to define his children's reality. He tells them what they are feeling and thinking, in contradiction to what they really do feel and think. For example, a father responded to his child who had just exclaimed, "I hate Grandma" (the narcissist's cold and narcissistic mother) by saying "You don't hate Grandma. Only a bad child could hate such a wonderful Grandma. You love Grandma." This statement created vast conflict and confusion in the child's mind. The child was experiencing what is known in the vernacular as "mind fucking." He was being trained to distrust the reality of his thoughts and to allow others to think for him.

Because the narcissistic parent contradicts his child's perception of his own feelings and thoughts, the child grows up confused and tries to establish relationships with people who think for him as a continuation of his childhood experiences.

The narcissistic press for symbiotic unity requires that the perceptions of the child and parent be identical. In the example given above, the parent is attempting to keep away his own feelings of rage toward his mother.

Since the child is the carrier of the narcissistic parent's perceived but rejected imperfections *and* grandiose fantasies, his self-image is disturbingly contradictory. He is a miserable failure who will never accomplish anything and must live his life in the shadows. He also is capable of total perfection and glory. His contradictory views of himself reflect the outer shell and the inner core of the narcissistic parent's self-view.

Whatever the parent feels is his or her problem is transplanted into the child. A narcissistic woman needs to be the most beautiful of all but fears that she is ugly. When this parent thinks that she lacks any other value, her child will be seen as an ugly failure and subjected to an endless campaign of reform to obtain some worth.

A narcissistic man obsessed with intelligence wants to be thought a genius, while secretly fearing he is an idiot. He sees idiocy in his child and persecutes the child into pretending to be a genius to cover up his idiocy. The entire problem has been transplanted. Ironically, the child may be extremely bright but can't fully use that intelligence nor take credit for it because he believes that he is only an idiot acting like a genius.

A child's sense of self-worth is damaged by false labeling. The more exaggerated his personal label, the less he feels his intrinsic worth. Like olives in a jar, he is summed up and his qualities exaggerated with little regard for the truth. With olives, the word *great* is used to designate very small fruit. The more a person's worth is exaggerated the smaller he feels. False labeling destroys one's sense of worth. All is for show. The narcissistic parent also feels imprisoned by the label he has placed on his child. He feels painted in turn by the image he has given the child and is always trying to raise the image's assigned value.

The child's inner self, which requires unconditional love, is treated as identical with his external behavior and his products. The child is subjected to a barrage of criticism which he eventually comes to believe. It isn't that his *paper* is well written—*he* is a genius. It isn't that he didn't understand a certain theorem in geometry—*he* is an idiot. The narcissistic parent frames his comments in such a way that the child's inner self is implicated. As a result, the child cannot be objective about what he does and cannot utilize criticism effectively. It hurts too much to take it in.

Consequently, he often has serious problems with performance. There are many ways of hiding. Some choose inarticulateness. Their thinking cannot be evaluated through the murk. Others cultivate the "fudge factor," a messy way of writing so that the teacher cannot read responses. The child can later argue that he meant something else. As an adult, he may act superior and throw out esoteric references as a smoke screen, counting on the fact that people tend to revere as superior that which they cannot understand.

Others fearing to try their wings are content to show early promise and to live with the belief that they could be great (and win their parents' love) if they ever applied themselves, which they dare not do. They might have a great natural tennis swing but they will never practice. The fantasy of approval for what they might do is preferable to the reality of possible rejection for what they can do.

The child who is continually warned about a dire end is being impregnated with the narcissistic parent's warded-off impulses and almost inevitably will eat of the forbidden fruit. A parent who repeatedly predicted that his daughter would "end up in the gutter" for being cute and sexy, by his verbalized lack of faith in her common sense put pressure on her to conform to his expectations by harming herself. Her promiscuity caused him pain and pleasure, which upset and gratified his daughter as well. She was unaware that her sexual acting out represented loving submission to his wishes as evinced by his prediction.

Many children of narcissists turn out rather paranoid. They develop hair-trigger sensitivity to anything that might be perceived as an attack, whenever someone commits an error, omission, or blunder that affects them. They are affected when they need not be, believing that people are deliberately out to hurt them. Life can be quite unbearable, as they always find themselves the targets of other people's bad moments. Repeatedly attacked by the narcissistic parent, they have come to believe that they were to blame for his or her moods. The experience of being a target is later extended and generalized to the responses of spouses, friends, children, rude cab drivers, people who squeeze them out of seats on subways, and the drunks who call out dirty names as they walk by.

Having learned to accept without question the opinions of the narcissistic parent, the child often transfers this onto the world in the form of a pervasive or specific-to-certain-situations gullibility. She can be manipulated by someone who speaks with authority even if the supporting evidence is lacking. She may fall prey to the seductive power of cults, wherever love is promised for surrender.

Her choice of friends will tend toward the narcissistic, people who demand uncritical acceptance. She assumes her familiar role at their feet, the one who listens without being listened to; the one who laughs but doesn't get to tell a joke; the one who calls but never is called. She arranges her life around their schedules. Friendships are frustrating and unfulfilling, not unlike the relationship with her narcissistic parent, but she does not know any other way. She is in the grip of a compulsion psychologists call transference, still trying to win the narcissist's love.

She does not know how to protect her interests since she was called selfish by her parents if ever she put her needs ahead of theirs. Loving meant total selflessness, giving the loved one whatever he or she wanted without resentment, competitiveness, or jealousy, even if giving harmed the giver. She was to make the other person happy. Children of narcissists can be a remarkably unselfish breed.

All children need love to survive. If there is no real affection, the child will interpret what attention the parent does offer as love. If all the child receives is criticism, then criticism is interpreted as love and the behavior the parent criticized will be repeated. If the child was only attended to for being slow, sloppy, lazy, careless, etc., all passive-aggressive traits, then these will be retained into adulthood. That is how maladaptive behavior can become ingrained and cause all kinds of difficulty in later life.

Since children of narcissists feel so bad about themselves, they often develop characteristics of the skunk, objectionable behaviors that drive people away. By being offensive, they avoid the pain of getting close.

As painful as early rejection and loneliness can be, the skunk person prefers to control the rejection. To bring this about, he becomes such things as an obnoxious interrupter, a borrower who forgets to repay, sloppy, unkempt, or smelly. He commits a thousand offenses and by doing so and getting rejected for these, preserves the hope that his real self might be loved if ever he eliminated the provocation. He defers seeking love until the future.

Bombarded by evaluations and labels that are not appropriate to him, the child of a narcissist does not know what is real and what is not.

He does not know who he is and is prohibited from experimenting through trial and error to find out. The child who was constantly told "You're no good," ends up feeling just that. He is what they say—bad, ugly, stupid, and an embarrassment to others. The narcissistic parent who so often suffered from shame for personal shortcomings in the eyes of his scornful parents looks at his own child with disgust and subjects him to the scorn he once knew. He masters the trauma of his own early experience by taking the active role and doing it to another as helpless as he once was.

The child is raised to mockery, nasty laughter, a finger pointed in accusation, expressions of disgust and rejection. The outcome of so much shaming is that the child shrinks away from contact. He seeks invisibility to feel safe. Grown up, such a person will live behind and through people but never out front for himself. The exposure of his inner being is too threatening.

He grows up feeling unlovable, since he has been taught that not having been loved is his fault. At best, his acceptance was conditional. A straight-A student whose grades are boasted about at a party by his narcissistic mother feels like a gilded bird in a gilded cage. It is not *he* who is appreciated.

The narcissistic parent lives on within the mind of the adult, even in the absence of the real parent. This inner parent is known as an introject. It keeps reinforcing childhood roles and behaviors acquired for survival. The introject still threatens to withhold love if the child departs from its program. There is no place to run to, no geographical hiding place to get away from this harsh inner voice. The child of a narcissist grown has the job of rooting out the influence of the inner parent by careful examination and analysis.

A final and tragic irony is that the child of a narcissist may himself have acquired many narcissistic traits, up to and including being a full-blooded narcissist. Some common features might include: self-centeredness, the compulsive need to be right and to have other people submit to his views, an inability to take criticism, the desire for perfection in self or in others he is close to, hypersensitivity combined with the continuous feeling of being mistreated, an exaggerated need for acclaim and support, and an even more desperate need for reassurance that he is loved.

In a home where the narcissistic parent was sadistic and his spouse or child the victim, the child of a narcissist may emulate the sadistic role since this is what was perceived as powerful. Children do not know that there are possibilities other than those demonstrated by Mom and Dad and so sometimes select the role that appears to be less hopeless. The adult child may victimize his spouse, children, friends, and employees. He may even victimize himself, attacking his own weaknesses with the hateful savagery of the internalized narcissistic parent.

It is extremely painful for the child of a narcissist to discover that he has become what he hates, that he has incorporated from his narcissistic parent the very traits that hurt him the most. We do not like to see such things in ourselves. Sometimes, the child of a narcissist develops a blind spot about his behavior, not unlike the parent who also cannot see the truth. Nevertheless, if the child of a narcissist wishes to achieve autonomy and self-respect, such traits must be greatly reduced and interpersonal sensitivity developed.

In the stories that follow, we shall see how various children of narcissists have struggled with these issues.

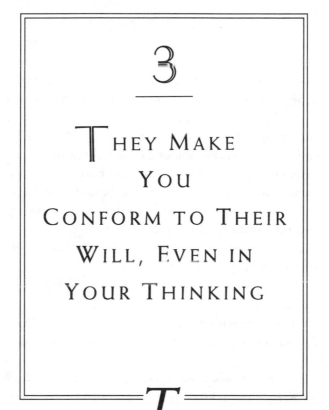

3

THEY MAKE YOU CONFORM TO THEIR WILL, EVEN IN YOUR THINKING

*T*he power of the narcissist's influence permeates everything with which the child has contact. It becomes automatic for the child to conform to the parent's viewpoint in order to avoid disapproval. A narcissist disagreed with tends to either attack or withdraw. Either response would threaten a child. The habit of agreeing with the parent becomes ingrained. Even a grown child with some intellectual grasp of the parent's dictatorial and twisted approach can still find herself abandoning her own perceptions and goals and joining the parent. This collusion is a kind of emotional flashback brought on by parental pressure.

The childhood habit of conformity has been reacti-
vated. Once the child has shifted from her own point of
view to that of the parent, she may feel quite out of touch
with her self without understanding why. Having abandoned her own position, she finds herself in a no-man's-land.
Her mental paralysis is seized upon by the parent as an
opportunity to extend his control. The parent calls the shots
and the adult child goes along in confused submission, like
a prisoner of war who has been partially brainwashed. She
gives the desired responses as long as she is prompted by her
jailer.

For those adult children who have developed a fairly
autonomous self, submission occurs mainly in the presence
of the narcissistic parent. For those who have not developed
sufficient autonomy, this submissive behavior will go on
throughout life, in response to both the negative inner parent and the pressures of the real parent.

The following story is an example of a short-lived regression to the experience of confused submission.

This piece was written with my father in mind. I imagine him looking
over my shoulder saying, "What the hell are you doing? You know you
can't write."

The story given below is my own, that of a person who has been
working on herself for a long time and is reasonably aware of her
parent's difficulties. It shows how I succumbed to the narcissist's pressure, although I recovered soon afterward and gained insight into what
had happened.

Imagine being raised in a room in which all the walls are distorted.
Instead of being rectangular they are trapezoidal, and they continually
change their shapes ever so slightly. The only window is a narrow slit
set high up and containing distorting glass. Whatever can be seen
through this glass appears hazy and indistinct. This is what happens to
your perception of reality when you live with a narcissistic parent. Not
only do narcissists see things idiosyncratically, at deviance from reality,
which is common in all disturbed people, but they insist that you see

things this way too. They insist because every difference in your perception is experienced as an attack upon themselves. They methodically wipe out their children's attempts to develop their own perceptions.

The following is an example of what happens when I regress into allowing myself to be manipulated by my father. He and his wife were in Florida for the winter months. In his last phone call to me, he said that my eighty-eight-year-old Aunt Sara, who lives in an old-age home, was failing. He said that she was "giving up" and no longer cared to live in a body that refused to obey her, that she had sunk into herself and would not respond to speech or touch. My father said that when the will to live is abandoned, death often follows. He said that I "would of course want to see [my] aunt while she is still alive." I agreed to come as soon as possible.

Aunt had been struggling with progressive Parkinson's disease for the last few years. Now she was unable to speak except for occasional bursts of sound when she was excited. She was confined to a wheelchair, strapped in against her will. Aunt Sara had always been a cantankerous, rebellious sort and so had fought the necessity of learning to use a walker properly, picking it up with two hands, pushing it ahead of her, and advancing step by step. Parkinson's had made her unsteady on her feet but she wouldn't give in to it. She would stagger along wildly, clutching the offending walker over her head in one hand. As one might expect, she had several nasty falls, resulting in blackened eyes, black-and-blue chins, and, eventually, a broken rib. The old-age home refused to take responsibility for her if she insisted on walking about as she did, so she was unwillingly strapped into a wheelchair. On one occasion, she was discovered sawing away at her restraining straps with a knife she had secreted from the dining hall. Unable to walk, unable to speak, unable to write, and eighty-eight years old, she lived in a chronic, bottomless despair.

Paul, her henpecked husband, as despised as he had been needed, had died seven years earlier. This had made it imperative that Sara go into a home. It is not unusual for all members of one family to be narcissistic to some degree, and so Aunt Sara had the narcissist's hatred of her husband because she depended upon him. The efforts of the slave must not be noticed while he gives royalty its due. When it came to mates, Sara knew that she could have done better.

Nevertheless, she was not a consummate narcissist like my father. She was capable of affection and concern, and had demonstrated these to me, her niece, in the many years we had lived in kitty-corner apartments in the same building. As a little girl, I and my dog had visited Aunt and Uncle almost every night, while she fed me sugar cookies, her stand against my tyrannical mother, who wanted to control my every move. This made me uncomfortable at the times when I was feeling loyal to my mother. I accompanied my aunt, who brushed my hair, gossiped with me, and was a fixture in my life. No, I could not let her die unacknowledged. I made reservations to go despite an extremely busy schedule that would only allow me to stay the weekend.

My father exists in a rigidly structured routine in which the central, controlling factor, as one would expect with a narcissist, is himself. He has embarked upon a writing program that has consumed most of his time for the last ten years. His schedule is as follows: up at eight, exercise for forty-five minutes, breakfast served by wife (who has already eaten), write until lunch, eat lunch, write until four, stop, go for a half-hour run, return and take a nap, get up and have dinner served by wife (who has already eaten); watch TV and read at the same time, or lecture to wife on political topics. Father's wife goes to bed before him. He reads until 2:00 A.M. and then goes to sleep. The next day the routine is repeated. Time spent trying to please wife by meeting her needs: nil. In order to be with him, she must type his manuscripts, cook and serve his meals, listen to his political analyses, making only slight attempts to disagree with him on minor points, so as to maintain the illusion of being a separate person. She is shy about asking for what she wants, especially for nonsexual affection. He needs to think that all he does is fine with her. Naturally submissive, she sometimes complains about his selfishness, but mainly accepts it and goes on.

When Father's wife expressed a desire for such things as pleasurable outings, her ideas were dismissed as the workings of an immature mind. He scorned her as though she were a child, his characteristic way of demeaning a woman. He was engaged in more important things than the frivolous pursuit of entertainment.

When his wife railed against his rigidity and his unwillingness to deviate from his program for her, he refused to speak to her for days. He has threatened to leave her. One wonders how he would survive without her services. Typically, she practices an unconscious self-censorship, choosing to view him as a superior man above petty needs and vices. Her need to lose herself in a partner fits in with his own need to obliterate the differences between them.

Father's rigid schedule is not entirely a concomitant of his narcissism but also represents an attempt to remain organized despite some brain damage received in a car accident many years before. Yet his schedule is pursued with all the self-centeredness of a narcissist. It follows that although he lives a mere twenty minutes from his older sister languishing in a nursing home, he sees her but once a week for an hour. A day-care worker was engaged to spend a few hours a day with Sara, to stimulate and amuse her. "That is enough socialization for her," Father had declared. He thinks himself quite dedicated and loving for that once-a-week break in his work schedule.

I arrived at the airport in Florida at 1.00 A.M. and was in my father's apartment by 2:00 A.M. True to form, he was waiting up for me. His wife sprang awake unnecessarily. She emerged from the bedroom to ply me with food in the intrusive way she employs to show her egoless love. All I wanted was to end the social chatter and go to sleep. I was exhausted.

Early next morning, I got out before anyone had awakened, to run and take a swim. I dallied a while at the beach. This was my time alone. When I returned to the apartment, my father's wife snapped, "Where were you? You were away so long." The slave resents another's freedom without recognizing the source of her pique. "Swimming, running, like always," I said. It was my morning routine whenever I visited them. She knew that.

My father spoke. Now we have the moment of the body snatchers, the moment when the daughter surrenders her personhood in order to become an acceptable extension of the all-knowing one. "When would you like to see Sara? Today or tomorrow?" I could write a scenario around what I should have answered. I could have said, "I want to see her on both days for several hours. You and I can do things together during the time that's left over." If my father objected to driving me, I could have said, "I'll borrow your car or take a taxi or a bus. I don't need to disturb your schedule." But that's not what happened. My father said, "Let's go today. The day is already shot as far as doing anything else. Tomorrow we can take a real trip to the Everglades or the Monkey Jungle." His wife looked happy at the prospect of an outing. "We can bring your Aunt Betty." "Let's do that," I said.

A fog was settling around me. I felt as though I were observing my actions from a great distance, moving my arms and legs as if drugged or as if moving upstream in water. My center and purpose were dissolving. I was being steered by outside forces. At the back of my mind I had the idea that tomorrow I would renegotiate. I put the issue off. It was impossible to cope. I even began to anticipate the pleasure of a trip to the Everglades. The blinders were on now and I was looking in the desired direction. "OK. Let's go see her today." So it was decided. Everyone was happy. Father had his 2:00 P.M. lunch, keeping everyone waiting as usual, and we were off to the nursing home.

We parked in the lot in front of the handsome Spanish-style two-story building. The seeing-eye automatically opened the doors to let us pass through into a beautiful inner garden, profuse with flowering plants and huge, ancient banyan trees. Everywhere there were people, the elderly with canes or wheelchairs, their attendants and guests. But Aunt Sara was nowhere to be seen. We went inside and took the elevator to the fourth floor. Upstairs, the wheelchairs were lined up against a divider topped with plants in front of the entrance to the dining room. Eating was probably the bright spot in their day.

The old people all looked terribly frail, expressionless, almost transparent. I didn't know where to look for my aunt. Was she lying comatose on her bed? Father was scrutinizing the denizens in their wheelchairs. He approached one who was terribly out of it, her head drooping on her chest. What a sorry human specimen.

It was my aunt. I had forgotten that my aunt had stopped dying her hair jet black. Aunt had always been such a pretty woman, nothing like this huddled, gray rag doll. My father put his hands on his sister's head, gently, with a kind expression. The head raised itself up and looked about. It was Sara. All kinds of feelings welled up. Pity, horror, and deep love. "Sara," I exclaimed, and gave her a huge hug and a kiss. Tears filled my eyes and spilled down my cheeks. Sara's eyes also filled and she had a big smile on her face. Her eyes were opened wide with excitement. We held on to each other's hands as she was wheeled down to the garden. Now Sara was rooted in time. She knew the hour and the day. An event was occurring to mark it. She was relating.

We found a nice spot under the shade of a banyan tree and drew up wire garden chairs. "Which side do you want me to sit on, Sara? Which side is your good ear?" Unexpectedly, Sara spoke, sarcastic and wry as ever. "Who knows? You choose." Everyone crowed with pleasure. Sara's speech was a triumph. I sat on my aunt's left side. A few more words, however, and my aunt's vocal chords stopped responding. But the joy of being together remained. We tried writing. Here, too, my aunt's hand held out for a few words, then trailed off in a spastic scrawl like the EKG markings of someone having a heart attack. She wrote *Paul* in tiny, controlled letters, the name of her dead husband. Perhaps she missed him after all. So many years together, he attentive, she rejecting. He had given her his life. "I know, Sara," I said. She wrote *Art*, the name of her dead brother.

Here we have another aspect of the narcissistic relationship. When Sara was put into an old-age home, her narcissist brother, my father, no longer accorded her the rights of someone in full possession of her faculties; or perhaps his need to dominate simply increased. One right of the elderly is to attend funerals; sister following brother, friend following friend, until no one is left.

My father had declared that Sara was not to know of their brother Art's death. "It would kill her," he said. She was treated like some kind of idiot, unable to figure out why her brother had never sufficiently recovered from a long illness to call or write. I had thought Aunt Sara should know her brother's fate. She needed to be at the funeral like everyone else, to share the healing words of the mourners: " . . . so sad . . . I remember . . . we are left . . ." I had been dragged into the conspiracy against my will. The lies were already told before I had been consulted.

I wrote the word *gone* next to Art's name. She did not seem to understand, as there was no visible response. Perhaps she could not read my handwriting. By writing this, I had crossed my father, contradicting one of the laws of the narcissist, namely: "I know what's best for you even if it includes depriving you of your humanity and your human

needs, including the right to know and to make up your own mind."
Art-gone. What would my father think? It had just slipped out and it was
too late now to take it back. I hoped that Aunt Sara would know that
I was trying to relate to her as a full human being.

Now Sara's handwriting was extinguished. But we were still together. We had communicated for a while and I knew that there was
still a brain and a heart. Sara was sitting, smiling, very present, not the
idiot child amidst normal children. We looked around. There was not
a person to be seen. No wheelchairs or walkers, no nurses or aides, no
strolling elderly people and their guests. Time had flown. Everyone had
gone inside to eat. It was time to part.

My father dictated a final message for me to write to my aunt,
some kind of instruction for her to hold on to in the intervening
months—something about the way she should think or live. But I
wanted to leave a message of my own and I didn't want my father to
read it. He had a way of demeaning the purity of feelings with his
manipulations. He was a spoiler of other people's sentiments, probably
because he was incapable of real feeling himself. Perhaps he was jealous.

I wrote, "Take good care of yourself, Sara. I shall write to you." I
wrote, "I love you," and tucked the piece of paper into my aunt's
restraining belly strap. The last moments to see the prisoner. Sara was
wheeled to the door of the dining room. I feared that the aide would
pin the note to Sara's mirror where my father would see it, and that he
would later say something to me about it.

I kissed my aunt good-bye, not wanting to let go of her small
hand. "Good-bye, Aunt Sara," I said, thinking that perhaps it was for
the last time. My father's narcissistic glue continued to paralyze my
will. It was easier this way, not to have another encounter with inevitable mortality. Hide your eyes. Have fun instead.

The next day we went to the Monkey Jungle; my father, his wife,
and her sister, my Aunt Betty, wife of the now dead Art. In the car, my
father dominated the conversation with his version of the fight they
were having with the co-op board. His wife waffled, taking first one
side, then the other. She was incapable of holding a position since it
might cause someone to dislike her. She found this intolerable. My
father was infuriated that her loyalty to him was not absolute. He
produced an extremely loud, strident, and remarkable torrent of words.

A musician friend who played the trumpet had once said that my father had mastered the art of circular breathing so that he could take in air even as he was speaking. No one could interrupt him. If anyone tried, they were angrily told to wait until he had finished. We were his captive audience, his slaves. I felt stung by the sharpness of his tongue even though I shared his opinion of the board's pusillanimous behavior. Most of me was in a deadened state, even as I went through the motions of joining in the chatter. It was his show now.

Monday morning I took an extremely early cab to the airport. Something inside me felt wrong, but what was it? My father kissed me a tender good-bye, asking me if I had had a good time. "Of course," I said, not wanting to hurt him. "I'm glad that I came."

At the airport, I got into a fight with an Eastern Airlines employee. There was only half an hour until flight time and there was a huge line at the ticket counter. "I already have my ticket," I said. "What gate do I go to for La Guardia?" The woman, walking down the line, counting, kept her back turned and said nothing. "What gate do I need?" I repeated. Still no response; her head remained averted. I tapped her on the shoulder with my ticket holder. "Please tell me what gate to go to." She whirled around, saying, "Don't you strike me." "I was just trying to get your attention," I said. "The next person you do that to will strike you back. She won't be nice like me," she said. I was boiling. "You're not nice. In fact, you're quite rude and if you keep this up, I am going to report you." The girl spat out, "Gate twenty-three." I set off at a run, thinking that the girl had been spoiling for a fight. But so was I. Why was I so angry?

On the plane I calculated: I had spent $290 for the ticket, $45 to put my car in long-term parking, $21 for cabfare back to the airport, $12 for the Red Top jitney upon my arrival. That made a total of $366. A lot of money to see my aunt for one hour.

It hit me hard. I had been entirely co-opted. The trip had been almost in vain. Rage and then depression flooded me. How could I have allowed this to happen? Although I was angry at him, it wasn't even my father's fault. He was just being himself, like a force of nature. I had gone into the lion's den without a whip, into the desert without a compass. I had been emotionally unprepared and as a result, once the force field had been turned on, I had reverted to the little girl's posture

I had always taken, the role my father imposes on all women, that of thoughtless, frightened obedience. Poor Sara, with her one-hour visit. If not today, then tomorrow, her chin would be back upon her chest. I could not afford another trip soon. This one had been spent with monkeys. Perhaps the next one would be too late.

In this story, we see the interaction between the narcissistic parent and a grown child, one with considerable ego strength and awareness. Nevertheless this child, myself, succumbed to her father's egocentric philosophy and once more entered the distorting trapezoidal room. I forgot how to exert my will, lost my intention and purpose, and was incapable of reviewing my options. For a brief spell, I entered the obedient limbo of the inauthentic life whose main reward is not to be attacked or rejected by the narcissistic parent. Once away from him, I soon recovered. Unfortunately, not soon enough to have a full visit with my aunt or to make a proper farewell.

Next time, I will go down to see my aunt without telling my father that I am there. To confide such a plan to a person who is hypersensitive but blind to the needs of others when he will surely disagree causes unnecessary difficulties for both parties, since the narcissist must always be right.

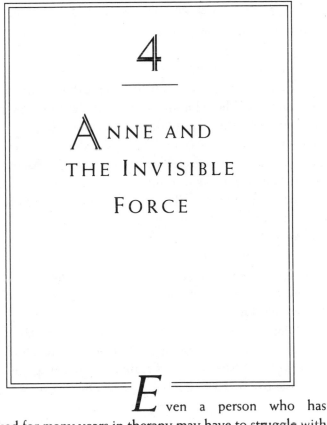

4

ANNE AND THE INVISIBLE FORCE

*E*ven a person who has worked for many years in therapy may have to struggle with the invisible force that is the emanation of the negative inner parent continually trying to control the adult–adult child's actions. The child part of the adult mind refuses to surrender its wish to win the love of the internalized narcissistic parent. Despite abundant evidence to the contrary, it continues to believe that such love is possible. It is this desire and belief that keeps alive the power of the negative inner parent.

To please this inner parent, the adult must be what the

narcissistic parent seemed to require. An adult might suspect that she is falling under the power of the negative introject any time her behavior seems to be veering in a direction counter to her adult aims. It is a likely explanation for otherwise inexplicable feelings of inadequacy and inferiority, especially when attempting to accomplish something. The negative inner parent undermines adult effectiveness in the same way the narcissistic parent undermined the child in order to "accept" her.

There is an ongoing war between the adult finding her way in life and her childish part still under the sway of the negative introject. The adult part can prevail if the person learns to recognize that the messages of this inner parent are wrong. These messages tell the person that she doesn't have what it takes to make it in the real world. The inner parent withdraws its support if the adult persists in her efforts. This leads to severe anxiety, depression, and feelings of abandonment.

If the person believes the messages of her negative inner parent, she surrenders real life for the reward of living according to childhood rules and the fantasized satisfaction of parental love.

Due to the undermining of her ego, the child of a narcissist is easily discouraged by real-life difficulties. The negative inner parent distorts reality to prove its point about the person's inadequacy and the person believes its message. In Anne's story, we see a woman struggling with the invisible force, the power of her negative introject. The outcome of this struggle will depend upon her skill in detecting the workings of the invisible force and her determination to root out its influence. Every child of a narcissist must develop his or her will if he or she is to recover.

Anne and I speak about her inability to finish the projects she has started. She is full of despair, aware that this problem touches every aspect of her life. The symptom of incompleteness even appears in our interview, as when she interrupts a painful recounting of how her mother failed to help her at a time when she was sick to admire my earrings, completely forgetting what she was talking about. Her light-hearted prattle and myriad time-consuming, seemingly unavoidable chores cover up what is really going on. Anne is not allowed to achieve if her objective is of personal benefit.

She takes me downstairs to see her daughter's playroom, a huge finished basement looking out onto a lawn. Every inch of the room is strewn with toys or some parts thereof, games, puzzles, and objects to climb on or into. The chaos is striking. The whole room looks like a Mattel toy showroom after a saboteur has thrown a bomb. Anne says sadly, "I keep meaning to clean it up, but all I do is keep looking at it." Each day, looking at the disorganized playroom without doing anything about it reinforces the message she gives herself of her impotence.

The overabundance of toys hints at other issues. If the child is inundated with things, it may indicate that Anne cannot set limits. If she cannot say no, she will feel angry and frustrated at things getting out of hand. One can easily picture her daughter amidst these mounds of toys, so many that she cannot develop an attachment to a favorite. If one gets broken or a part is lost, she moves on to another, overstimulated yet unsatisfied.

Another reason for offering so many toys is that such a profusion will keep the child from developing a favorite and leave the mother as number one. A parent who so much fears the loss of her child's affection suffers from profound insecurity.

I ask Anne about her giving. She says that she was deprived in childhood and she is trying to keep her child from knowing that terrible feeling. I do not ask her of what she had been deprived. I suspect that it wasn't just toys.

She feels guilty any time she thinks of her own needs. If she wants to go for a run, she will do something for or with her child instead. She lets the child "consume" her and resents the child for doing so. Her fury explodes into yelling. Then she becomes depressed at being a bad mother who is out of control, which leads to more indulgence of the child as atonement. She cannot see where and how to break the cycle.

Anne may feel trapped in her pattern but she is trying to change.

She is in therapy. Her healthy side looks at her sick, compulsive side and shakes its head in amusement. She says that her "sick side" is in the grip of an "invisible force."

What exactly is this invisible force? It is the irrational influence she conceals with various rationalizations as she flits from one uncompleted project to the next. The invisible force is what holds her back and prompts the most peculiar behavior. Take her most recent attempt at a career. She has been a nightclub singer, a teacher in the public school, an athlete, all of which she was good at and abandoned. Then she entered the field of real estate.

She received her license and survived the initial anxiety of learning how to sell property. She found that she enjoyed selling, liked meeting new people, and derived a good deal of satisfaction from showing people houses they liked. She had absorbed the narcissistic viewpoint: If they like *it*, the thing I sell, then *I* am OK. All was going well and monetary success was on the horizon when she started sabotaging herself.

This sabotage involved not getting her customers to their destinations, an integral part of the business of selling real estate. Suddenly, she could no longer read a map and began to get lost, even on roads she knew quite well. Feeling more and more helpless, she would hand the map over to the client to extricate them. The idea that she had displayed incompetence made her believe that her customers would not trust her judgment about the property she was showing. In her embarrassment she would grow tongue-tied and forgetful.

Ultimately, she grew to believe that selling was a lost cause. It was difficult for her to see that it was her unconscious that was getting her lost. It was her unconscious that caused her to hand over the map in order to create an image of incompetence. It was the invisible force that told her to quit rather than to fight it out with herself.

After a long period of struggle, she became totally exhausted by the worry and stress of her self-defeating game. She hated going to the office and had trouble getting up in the morning. It seemed to her that there was something physically wrong, and a doctor's exam confirmed it. Stress had made her quite anemic. It became necessary for her to quit the job.

It is not surprising that Anne was married to a man who felt insecure about his own abilities. In order to feel adequate, he needed to be the main breadwinner. His wife's potential for earning could threaten him. He felt better if his wife merely dabbled.

One might expect the unhealed child of a narcissist, under the compulsion of the invisible force, to marry someone who would hold ideas about her nonfunctioning in some ways similar to those of her parents. Since her husband found Anne's potential for earning threatening, she was convinced that he could not accommodate her movement toward greater independence and feared that she would lose him if she continued.

Through the childhood experience of her parents' rejection, Anne had become well versed in the art of submerging herself. The expected abandonment by critical parents and a suppressive husband sat in the back of her mind, creating overwhelming anxiety. Her thoughts were not clearly organized. She just knew that everything she held most dear was in danger if she continued to develop her job skills. It was a relief to fail and get it over with rather than to continue, all the while expecting the earth to open and take away the support of her husband and the pleasure of her family.

Longing for parental love creates the invisible force. Love causes us to learn what the parent needs from us. It places the parental figure in our psyche as a governing body, setting standards for behavior and granting love as a reward for doing what meets with its approval. The need for love makes the child malleable clay in the parent's hands.

When the parent is a narcissist, the course is extraordinarily difficult. Most of the child's natural behaviors meet with disapproval. The child is always trying to please yet never finding out what is effective and acceptable. The ante is always being upped. The child becomes confused, angry, and depressed, alternately trying and giving up, yet remaining in the parent's sphere of influence. He does not learn to please himself.

Let us look at Anne's upbringing. She got a double dose since both parents were narcissists. Neither was able to accept her as a person. Her mother used her as a handmaiden. Anne was required to be charming and lighthearted as she attempted to meet her mother's needs for support and company. Anne's compulsive gaiety emerges when she speaks of her various self-destructive activities as if she were telling an amusing tale. Her laughter indicates that the child within her has been obeying the immolative laws of the inner parent telling her to destroy herself. If the inner parent is happy, she is happy.

At times during Anne's childhood, her mother would attack her for no apparent reason. Anne remembers one such occasion in which her mother flung a hairbrush at her with such force that it left a raw gash in her head. Anne understood her mother's rage as the result of some flaw within herself.

Her father also was controlling and physically abusive. Although he did not admit his attraction and never acted openly sexual toward her, he had strong incestual leanings. His daughter was very attractive. Her hourglass figure and huge, laughing eyes had the boys flocking around. Her father couldn't stand her interest in other men. He needed her to remain his exclusive possession.

Anne's needs did not count. Her parents defended their fief in her by verbally attacking and demolishing her interest in each young man who came along. Cowed by their violence and still seeking their approval, she accepted that the boys were as unworthy as her parents claimed.

Her father was a self-made man who needed to flaunt the brittle power of money. He was an accountant with many clients in the underworld. His own tough, lawless attitude showed an identification with the gangster mentality. The only boyfriend of whom her father approved was also a shady character. He could accept someone whose personality was like his own. If Anne had accepted the gangster, she would be symbolically choosing her father. If she chose a different type, her father would take it as a personal rejection. Despite his attempted influence, Anne resisted and did not marry the gangster suitor.

Her latent healthy side craved a relationship with someone who would care for *her* and not merely use her as an embellishment to his causes. She did meet that someone, a fine young man who understood her entrapment between two narcissistic parents. He advised her to leave them, not so much to please him but so that she could "become a person."

The two young people shared deep feelings. Anne did not know what to think of her experience. After a lifetime of manipulation, she was confused by honest dealing. Her father probably understood better than she the importance of their union. He didn't like it. One day, he called her over and told her to get rid of the young man saying, "That one is evil!"

Who could be more evil than one who threatened his hegemony over his daughter? He reinforced his comments with a hard slap in the face, humiliating Anne as he had always done. Humiliation leads to the selflessness of surrender. Confused and numb, she said farewell to her young man. She had to believe that her father was right.

As Anne spoke to me of this time in her life, I could sense her love for the young man. He was the one she had wanted to marry. She loved him still. He had given her the strength that helped carry her out of her crushing parental home. He had cared about *her*.

Anne spoke to me out of emotional need, as a former member of a shared psychotherapy group in which we listened to one another's problems and offered our solutions. She asked me the question that haunts children of narcissists: "Did they want to hurt me? Did they want to ruin my life?" And in this instance, "Why did they reject every man who ever cared for me?" The narcissistic parent does not want to hurt his child. He does not even see that there is a child to destroy since he lives his life by looking in the mirror. He needs to destroy any "obstacle" in his path, any situation that threatens his security. This includes the developing autonomy that helps his child to grow away from him. The child is felt to be a part of himself. If the child separates, he will be hurt and possibly destroyed. So he holds on as long as possible by extinguishing the spark of separateness.

The narcissist attacks separateness in everyone with whom he must have a relationship. Either they fit into his ego-supporting mold or they are extruded from his life. Narcissistic rage and aggression are based on fear. His entitlement to absolute control over others must go unchallenged. The child's natural growth sets off the parental alarm signals. The child is blamed for his emerging individuality as if it were a crime. He is made to feel that there is something wrong with such development.

Anne's father frequently called her a "nothing," especially when he saw that she did not exist exclusively for him. One time, she had injured a tendon while dancing at a party. Her father paid her a condolence call in a rage, since her injury was material evidence of her unfaithfulness. After visiting for a brief period, he yelled, "You are nothing," and stormed out. In gist, he was saying, if I can't have you, you don't count.

Anne's mother also treated her as a nothing. She needed her children to be valueless, dependent, and helpless so that they would always be at her beck and call. She also needed them to fade into the woodwork when she didn't want to be bothered by them.

One of her grown sons now holds a job but is otherwise totally under the control of his wife. The other son "faded away" into drug addiction. The mother is now widowed and well off. She is unwilling to do much for Anne, who is treated as a traitor, probably for the crime of moving far away. Her addict son has the run of her house. He has his own key and permission to use her apartment whenever she is traveling. Once, he brought a fellow addict and a puppy that soiled her rugs. He ransacked his old room and other closets for things that he could sell and left the place a filthy mess. Anne's mother complained to her about his activities but let him keep the key. He is an extension of her royal, pampered, baby self and is therefore allowed to eat and soil wherever he wants. She is pleasing herself by indulging her son and does not realize that she is destroying him in the bargain.

If Anne asks to borrow her mother's apartment while the mother is away so that she and her family can enjoy an affordable California vacation, she is told, "I'll see," or "Do you really need it?" Anne and her family are unimportant. Her request is an inconvenience. Anne is hurt that her mother shows no interest in Anne's daughter. When her mother visits, she does not spend five minutes talking to her grandchild. Anne's raw pain over her mother's behavior indicates that she still does not accept her mother's limitations. She doesn't recognize that her mother's self-absorption is nonnegotiable. If she were to show interest in her grandchild, it would only be an act.

As we talk about these things, Anne scratches her head in the age-old gesture of one trying to understand the incomprehensible. She cannot grasp that her parents' destructive treatment has little to do with her. The trap of obsessive doubt ensnares many children of narcissists, sometimes for life. They keep trying to understand, trying to find the key that will release the as yet unseen parental love, instead of breaking away and leading their own lives.

Although the overall picture of narcissism can be readily understood, small details of parental behavior are inexplicable. There is no rational explanation for what a completely self-centered person will do. What they themselves say about it later bears no relation to the original motivation. They often surrender to overpowering impulses based on distorted, one-sided, and limited perceptions. The adult child of the narcissist must wean himself of the compulsive need to understand the finer points of his parent's behavior. He must steer himself away from the pool of Narcissus before he falls in and drowns.

Let us return to Anne and the invisible force. She completed college and immigrated to Buffalo, where she met and married her first husband. He was a kind-hearted tyrant who demanded that she accede to his eccentric lifestyle. People imprisoned by the invisible force are more comfortable with emotional prison walls than living in a free environment in which they continue to feel paralyzed.

She continued to live according to the parental edict: "Be nothing." She has many ways to be nothing. One is to be unreliable. She cancels appointments at the last minute. She forgets to show up and is always late. Such behavior makes the symbolic statement, "Don't expect anything of me. I don't exist." Her weight went up and came down, a roller coaster of obesity. Fat is another way of hiding. A fat body reassures her inner parents that she is a good little asexual girl not at all interested in sex and boys. During adolescence she became addicted to diet pills, believing herself too weak to control herself without them. Pills became her support for all kinds of social interactions. Her ego sagged as she increasingly attributed her accomplishments to the power of the pills.

The child of a narcissist is not supposed to see her own power, which would threaten the inner parent. Recently, Anne had to take thirty-seven college credits in an extremely short period. She gave herself no praise for getting through. Credit to the self interferes with obedience to the law: Be nothing.

She has assimilated some of the narcissistic ideas of her parents, for example, that only perfection is acceptable. Accordingly, her fear of criticism keeps her from trying out for the acting career she has always wanted. Perfectionists are afraid of being seen and judged. She finds it difficult to lose weight and to exercise although she loves sports. Narcissism demands that she remain ageless and perfect. To take care of one's body is to note the ravages of time and to resist them as best one can. If Anne remains a "fat baby," she is ageless and safe. Time is the worst enemy of narcissists because it is an even greater force than they are. Even they must defer to time. The narcissist is too weak to admit to vulnerability.

But Anne is getting there. She remains in therapy and continues to struggle with the unconscious pressure on her to be passive. The war is not over yet. There are temporary defeats but no final surrender. She tries not to punish herself with depression each time she falls. She picks herself up with a laugh and starts again, saying a slow farewell to the internalized narcissistic parents who have coalesced into her invisible force.

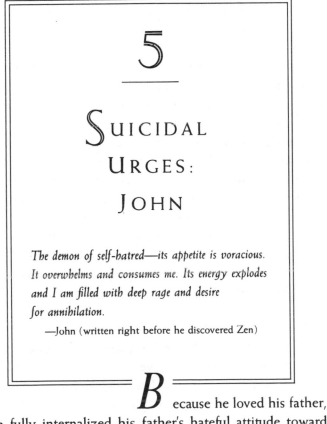

5

SUICIDAL URGES: JOHN

The demon of self-hatred—its appetite is voracious.
It overwhelms and consumes me. Its energy explodes
and I am filled with deep rage and desire
for annihilation.

—John (written right before he discovered Zen)

*B*ecause he loved his father, John fully internalized his father's hateful attitude toward him. This created a powerfully self-hating negative inner parent (negative introject). A child's need to believe that his parent loves him, no matter how he has been treated, caused John to read parental mistreatment as a kind of love. If it was harsh and hateful love, that is what was merited by his unworthy self.

John's father had high academic and athletic expectations but treated John as a shabby failure who "didn't have it." John lived a life of horrible conflict. One part of him

resisted his father's pressure to conform to wishes that would
have obliterated him as a person. The other part secretly
agreed with his father's condemnation and deferred to the
negative inner parent, attacking himself with a deadly hatred.

Any time his environment shifted so that his minimal
emotional support and appreciation diminished further, the
negative inner parent would call for suicide. Suicide offered
resolution for several needs and motives. It was an act of
spite against those who had failed to help, mainly his father.
It was an indirect plea for help for one who could not find
the words. In a negative way, suicide was a request for love
from the negative inner parent. If this introject would have
John kill himself, then by following its edicts and making
the attempt, he is trying to please that internalized need
system. As a result the negative inner parent should love him
for acting like a "good boy."

This is one logic of the unconscious. It shows that
suicide is always a motivated act, but the motives vary except in cases of severe physical disorder where it is only to
end a life of pain.

John sprawls before me on his bed smoking cigarettes and speaking of
the past. We are old friends. I have seen him through many stages,
during which he often clashed with various authority figures or threw
in the towel on his latest endeavor or interest. He would get fed up,
bored, and start to bail himself out despite unmistakable signs of success. My telling him about the theme of this book sent him deeper into
history. He alluded to his childhood as a source of black humor. His
stories offered a sarcastic depiction of violence and rejection, but never
before had I heard him speak of his suicidal past nor felt his emotion
when speaking of the almost grotesque mistreatment to which he was
subjected.

We are sitting in a room that is dark and austere. Since his wife's
recent and abrupt departure and the removal of her bric-a-brac, dolls,
exercycle, and TV, it has reverted to the monastic cell it actually is.

John is a Zen priest living alone atop a Zen meditation center. It is as if the marriage never happened and perhaps it should not have, even though the union had several positive elements in its favor, such as friendship, fun, loyalty, and a shared love for Buddhism. The missing element was sexual passion, the same lack that quickly damned his first marriage.

When choosing a mate, John seems unable to seam the rational and sexual sides of his nature. Since only one side is represented, sooner or later the unmet needs of the other begin to build tension until there is an eruption that blows the whole structure. After the marriage, which occurred primarily to please his second wife, she grew fatter and fatter until he was totally turned off and unable to respond to her sexually. But sex between them had never been very satisfying to him, and she may have gained weight to protect herself against the ultimate abandonment she expected from this enigmatic man. She could blame his rejection on her weight rather than on some more essential flaw. John followed the script and did develop an attraction to another woman in the Zen community, which came to his wife's attention in the most unexpected manner. She fled.

John has more than once thumbed his nose at societal restraints, including the restraints of conventional monogamy. He walked out of graduate school halfway to his master's degree. Once, as a kid, without asking permission, John, his brother, and his sister, Delores, ate the cake they found cooling on a shelf in the kitchen. Their mother had baked it to be served to her social group the following Sunday. They enjoyed every bite of it. I asked his sister for an example of John's antisocietal position and she said that John led a hand-to-mouth existence, never trying to secure a reasonable and constant salary. I remember his cooking for a health food restaurant and coming to work in pants so torn that his buttocks were half exposed. His sister called this "commonplace hippie" behavior, but I remember it as causing a minor scene when he came out to speak to a customer. The seeds of rebellion are planted deep but John does not recognize them when they flower. He does not see the repetitive elements in his life pattern.

Childhood was spent in the West. His family on both sides are old Western stock, sturdy, intelligent, and cantankerous types who came over on the first waves of migration from England when the United

States was still "the colonies." A famous general is in the family tree. John is proud of his heritage.

In the earliest memory of his father, the man is advancing before him, a hazy figure whose feet make crunching sounds on the gravel. John trails behind listening to his father's footsteps. The resounding crunches are very pleasing to his ears. They suggest that his dad is big and substantial. John knows his father only through indirect epiphenomena, like the trail of a jet in the sky after the plane has already passed. It is hard to know a person who is disguising his image and on the run. His father does not speak. John's own footsteps on the gravel are inaudible.

His father has always been out of reach. He doesn't speak to any of his three children, two boys and a girl. John is the youngest. Delores, the oldest, is away at prep school. John is starved for knowledge of his father. He sneaks into his bedroom and opens bureau drawers to smell the familiar odor of his clothing. He tries on his father's shoes and fantasizes about his father's life.

He has nicknamed his father the Sphinx, not for wisdom but for silence. John's own self-image is limited by a shortage of paternal male qualities to emulate. He knows that his father is a minister with a distaste for his work. His father's mother pushed him into the ministry so that he could replicate the image of her adored father. Needing one's children to fulfill personal expectations regardless of their own interests suggests that she was narcissistic. Her other son also became a minister but was better suited to the profession.

John's father suffered from a stammer as a result of his mother's shifting him from left- to right-handedness when he was young. Although making righties out of lefties was not uncommon at that time, child "improvement" is the hallmark of the narcissistic parent. His stammer was suppressed by a special training program but would put in an appearance under stress. This did not make pulpit work any easier.

Since flying was his love, Father moved his family to a new ministry on several occasions to get closer to a flying field. He also did not hit it off with his congregation. When John was about ten, his father left the ministry for flying. Now he no longer had to fake his role as leader of the flock, to give stock sermons while surreptitiously glancing at his watch to make sure that he got to the golf links on time.

He loved to teach flying, to be around it and to do it. After he left the ministry, he became even less available to his family because he was always down at the field. Occasionally he took John along. John says wistfully, "I loved flying and wanted to be a pilot." He needed to have something to share with his father.

John remembers an early drawing he made of his home with a green lawn in front, his bike leaning up against the house, and a small plane circling overhead. He says, "That was Dad, up in the sky." He was perhaps eight or nine when his father would take him to the airport and park him in a "crashed out, ancient plane" on the edge of the field. His father would tell him, "Try and start it up," and leave to go up into the sky with other people whom John assumed were his students. John says, "He didn't want any kids around." John received none of the special recognition, attention, or training that would usually be accorded to the instructor's son. He would play for a while in the crashed plane and then just hang out, waiting for his dad, yearning to be up with that glamorous figure. He spent an inordinate amount of time alone. He says, "I was used to it. I could amuse myself."

While his father was still living at home, he obviously didn't enjoy the company of his children. He was always clearing them out of any room he was in and sent them to bed as early as possible. Boys were "too noisy." They weren't "peaceful."

John and his older brother, Timothy, were not at all friendly with one another and fought all the time. John says that "Timothy was full of anger and he . . . worked me over good." Fighting probably was an outlet for their frustration as well as having the unconscious objective of forcing their father to intervene and pay them some attention. Their father would pull on his belt as if to say, "OK, boys, now you're gonna get it." It wasn't much but it was better than nothing.

John remembers only a single moment of tenderness with his father. Significantly, it occurred after he was beaten. He had been smoking under the house when spotted by a plumber, who turned him in to his parents. John had been smoking cigarettes stolen from his parents for years. It was a point of pride that he enjoyed inhaling while his friends were still holding the smoke in their mouths.

When John's father heard of his smoking, a habit that he of course shared, the belt came off in earnest. There was no discussion, no concern for the inconsistency that allowed him to punish his son for something he himself did. Five or six blows were administered to John's posterior. He lay weeping on his bed when he felt his father's hand gently rubbing his back, attempting to soothe him. Love, at last. Did John form some association between abuse and love? He has certainly lumbered into an inordinate number of mistreating relationships in his life. His girlfriends, of whom I have known three, were selfish, self-centered, and demanding; they also were attractive and distant. I remember one who would not say hello because she was washing her hair at the kitchen sink right in front of me; another would not go with John to visit his sister because she didn't like the area. For John, love and warfare are related, not surprising for the son of a bellicose narcissist.

The silence of the Sphinx extended to John's mother. She had no inkling that her husband was planning to leave them and had thrown a surprise birthday party for him just a few days prior to his departure. Things had not been good between them for a long time. One day soon after the party, her husband threw a few things, including his presents, into a bag and departed for good. The only clue that ten-year-old John had of his father's approaching flight was seeing him sitting on the side of his bed with his head in his hands. John knew better than to inquire about what was bothering him.

John's father is a narcissist. He had little interest in his wife and children. During World War II, although a minister, he vanished into the RAF, leaving his wife to fend for herself. He was still a minister at this time but his interest went into flying. His wife was left with their baby daughter since her husband always did exactly what he wanted and others had to live with it. Intelligent, talented, and extraordinarily self-centered, he avoided human contact and responsibility by escaping into the sky. To people outside the family, he appeared likable and easy to get along with. He was so different at home with his children that John felt that it must in some way be his (John's) fault.

His father left his family and moved to Portland, Oregon, where in addition to flying, he taught mathematics at a local high school. He remarried a woman who had kids of her own. In his teens, John joined them for a while and found his father taking off as usual because he had people he wanted to be with and they were not his family. His wife shed bitter tears. Mostly his father's friends were fans of flying, mathematics whizzes, and athletes. John attended school knowing that his father wanted him to be a letter man and a big man on campus. To be accepted it was necessary that he be good at scholastics and sports but he was good at neither. For a while, he played a halfhearted game of football, but he "couldn't stand banging up against people." With his large and muscular frame, one can easily imagine him as a star athlete, but obviously he was unwilling to conform to his father's conditions. He would not sell out. Instead, he sank steadily and progressively into the mire of rebellious failure. Perhaps failure was closer to the role that his father unconsciously envisioned for him.

He watched with rage and despair when his father took a young student under his wing, treating him as a friend. The boy was what John was supposed to be and in his place. As an ultimate sign of buddyship, his father and the boy played golf together. John could not mobilize himself to work at sports or academics. He was unable to concentrate or study and classes were intolerably boring. He was turned off, inattentive, and cutting up. He did very poorly.

His feelings of resentment toward his father found their way into the classroom, into problems with authority. Reports of his poor conduct could not help but reach his father's ears. Perhaps John unconsciously wished to humiliate him. John felt little sense of belonging since, due to his father's changes of living place, he had attended several schools. Overall, what sent John into a tailspin was the lack of relationship with a father who knew and cared for him.

Although terrible report cards reflected only his rebelliousness and depression, John irrationally believed that he had been correctly assessed. He joined the teachers in their negative view and felt horrible about himself. The report cards reinforced what he had already discerned from his father's treatment, that he wasn't worth bothering about.

John remembers the time he broke the code of his father's nonverbal gestures and really "knew" his father's opinion of him. He had just uttered a dirty word when his father entered the room and overheard him. His father's look conveyed the message, "You're nothing but shit." The shoulders lifted in disgust gave the message, "I'm finished with you. I give up." John was later to hear these words spoken to his face. He internalized his father's evaluation and believed it true. Every child does this. He took all the blame for how he was treated.

He believed himself utterly stupid. His brother's grades were excellent while his were abysmal. His father's wife's kids also got high grades. As an adult, John's mother told him that his IQ had tested exceptionally high, way above the A-student stepsiblings with whom he was to live. But his younger years were lived as an angry dunce. At one time, he and his brother cut school eleven days in a row. Three points per day were taken from each of John's grades, leading to a long string of F's, while Timothy's grades were left untouched. This was one more proof that he was inherently marked and doomed.

When John was about thirteen and still living with his mother, she made another unfortunate choice in the man she remarried. John describes Ralph, her husband, as "brilliant but driven," one who could be the "sweetest man on earth," or explode in rage. Once, he threatened John's mother with a knife and "threw her good stuff into the woods." When the couple fought, his brother, Timothy, and he would huddle outside their bedroom door with a baseball bat ready to save her life. One night their mother slept in the woods to hide from Ralph. The man was extremely threatening.

Yet John has no conscious anger at the destructive male figures his mother introduced into his life, nor is he angry at her for doing so. He speaks understandingly of Ralph's "problem," the fact that he had a high-pressure job and took his tension out on the family. I asked John if Ralph drank. After a pause, he answered yes. The role of alcoholism as a partial explanation for Ralph's conduct has been underplayed. John has been inculcated into the family pattern of denying the seriousness of drinking in its men. No foreigner to drugs himself, he has turned to chemical solutions as a means of escaping from psychological pain when no human succor was available.

John never blamed his mother for becoming involved with men who could not adequately parent her children and whose problems made her inaccessible to them as well. It was as natural for him to be without a father's love as it may have been natural for his mother to be without a reliable and intimate husband. Her own father had been hopelessly narcissistic so she was used to being ignored and abused. If one were to compare Ralph's mistreatment with the sporadic availability and total self-involvement of John's father, Ralph was an improvement.

Even before high school, John was already disconsolate. His mother was too busy keeping her own head above water to notice his psychological condition and he had learned not to speak about such feelings. Communication about despair was avoided by the entire family. They tended toward a manic hilarity, partying, drinking, the young ones smoking dope, all running from their troubles. A positive aspect of his mother's personality was that she was not a worrier. She gave John the gift of independence, was loving and trustful and not overprotective. She supported the development of his adventurous spirit. At the age of seven, he would bicycle ten miles from home. She gave him freedom but would not share his burden of pain. He was very much alone.

At around twelve, he was beginning to get into his "suicide head." His thoughts were filled with obsessive self-loathing. There was little to hold on to and nothing to hold him back. He was out of contact with the family who could have cared and, as usual, failing at school. He desperately craved attention but could not request it in words. He used a symbolic gesture to signal for help.

His first suicide attempt was kept secret. He tried to drink Clorox but could not get it down. Immediately after abandoning this method, he sawed away on his arm with a blunt knife but survived. No one ever learned of this practice run. The idea of suicide became an imaginary door out of his misery. It was a bitter comfort, always open for his departure. Suicide expressed the hatred of one part of himself for the other. The part that hated had identified with his scornful father. It found the rest of him unworthy and declared that if someone is not worth loving, he is not worth keeping alive. The negative inner parent enjoyed the idea of immolating the inadequate child within. Psychologically, the walls were closing in.

In the seventh grade, unruly behavior and irreconcilable conflict with Ralph landed John in the formalized hell of military school. The only relief was that he could smoke openly. There was much physical abuse. Officers passing by would gratuitously smack students on the head, school rings turned inward to leave a painful goose egg. Students were punished by having to lean against a wall supported by their thumbs until they collapsed. They had to do innumerable knee bends. Bigger boys attacked the small and all ganged up on John because he was an unrepentant free thinker. Military school was an exacerbation of the abuse he was used to at home.

Again there was no one to turn to, no one who could understand.

His father had disposed of him and was disinterested. His mother was overwhelmed by her problems with Ralph. In military school, the idea of suicide became a fixation whose impulse was periodically dispelled by the violent treatment he received from others. They did the punishing for him.

After a year in military school, he returned to his mother's home. He was there for half a year when he went joyriding with a friend, another defiant and lonely boy. The only problem was that his friend had stolen the car they were riding in. They were caught and arrested. John was given the option of a reformatory or going to live with his nineteen-year-old sister in Los Angeles. He chose the latter. At least it got him away from Ralph.

His sister was trying to make it as an actress and dancer. Modeling provided subsistence. She received no help from either parent. They had cut her off for having refused college. She and her mother paid John's tuition at a private school. Their father made no contribution to his children's upkeep.

If John had been behind in country schools, city private schools chosen by his sister were so much more advanced that he felt hopelessly outclassed. The kids already had years of a foreign language and he had none, and so on. He felt unable to live up to his teachers' or his sister's expectations. Still unable to concentrate and apply himself, he got another lousy report card. He still gave undue respect to grades. Once more, he had been branded inferior.

At fourteen, he made his second attempt at suicide by throwing himself in front of a moving vehicle. He escaped injury but his sister realized that he had more serious problems than she was able to cope with. Still, no one asked him what was wrong. His sister also had been raised in her family's conspiracy of silence and was unable to relate to the intensity of his self-hatred. She had the family rules down pat: Act upbeat, strive hard, and look good for the world to see; do not complain or make demands. She could no more relate to John's suffering than she could recognize her own pain. John had again been forced to take the nonverbal route. The suicide attempt was a symbolic gesture announcing, "Hey, someone, help me. I'm desperate and going under."

He didn't get much help. His father remained distant and breezy on the phone. He showed no desire to reach out to his son and John's ego was too fragile to allow him to make a direct request. He couldn't have taken further refusal and so veered off the topic. His mother was too busy with Ralph; his sister had her career. He was summarily shipped off to an aunt in Portland.

It was painful to live with his aunt and uncle while his father lived nearby with the "good kids." His father had always favored other people's children over his own. John was apprised of the fact that his father's stepchildren were straight-A students in the high school where their mother was a teacher. Any comparison between John and the stepchildren put him in an unfavorable light. He continued to believe that they were receiving something from his father that he was not, loved because they got good grades. This was a self-destructive fantasy. His father was no more available to this family than he had been to John's own. He was still totally self-absorbed and hanging out at the airport. That's who he was and couldn't be otherwise.

In school, fifteen-year-old John continued to act out his despised self-image, unconsciously hoping that someone would see through it. He was still the rebellious "bad boy," the "tough guy" who was incapable of learning and who played hookey. He received yet another disastrous report card.

Report cards were always the event that tipped the balance of his relationship with himself, sending his self-esteem into a downward slide. John needed the scholastic world to evaluate him favorably and it failed to do so. His ego was shredding with no one to know it. He resolved to die, bought several bottles of over-the-counter sleeping pills, and went out to the beach of a nearby lake. He waded in to a depth where he could reach down and bring the water up to his mouth. Cupping the water in his hands, he took all the pills.

His mouth was dry. He felt nauseated. He vomited, then began hallucinating, hearing voices. Time passed. His aunt and uncle came searching and found him by the lake. It hurt him that it was they and not his father who had been looking. When they saw his disordered state, they assumed that he was drunk and John did not inform them otherwise. It was a kind of crazy pride that kept him from explaining, from asking them for help. He returned home, where his father was waiting, not the least bit interested in finding out what had motivated his son. The child was condemned—again. The first words out of his father's mouth were: "Pack your bags, boy. I'm washing my hands of you." According to his father, he was an incorrigible waste to be dumped.

The next day, or perhaps it was that very night, he is not sure, John was on a train back to his mother. The thing that troubled him was the enforced separation from his girlfriend. He didn't even realize how much it was going to hurt him to be without her.

Back with his mother, it was just the two of them. Ralph, her second husband, was gone. She was divorced and living in a different rented apartment, on the road five days a week working in sales. With this schedule she left John alone and he was increasingly morose. He sat on the couch, which was his bed, shades drawn to make it as dark as his mood. He played songs on the guitar and wrote many cards and letters to his girlfriend. He wrote the poetry of desperation. A few alienated friends joined him in making music, singing mostly sad songs. He ached for the love of his girlfriend, for someone to touch him in his solitude. His loneliness became intolerable. Something had to give to break the hideous tension. He saw no other way but to kill himself. This time the attempt was very serious.

He got hold of the barbiturates that his mother kept for head-aches. He left himself an out in that the attempt was staged at school, where there was a possibility of rescue. He took the pills, fell unconscious, and was taken to the hospital where his stomach was pumped. Then he was placed on a psychiatric ward.

Although most of the people there were far sicker than he, he liked it. There was no social facade to maintain. Everyone was straight-forwardly desperate. They were real. He made friends with another suicidal boy and entered into the turning point of his life. For the first time, he was able to communicate with honesty and depth. John had never known that it was possible to emerge from the prison of psychological isolation and be understood. He acquired a new perspective.

John's friend was determined to die. He got hold of a razor and sneaked onto the elevator, away from surveillance. He cut his wrists between floors. John says, "They put him further back." He never saw his friend again. Even so, his healing had begun.

His father flew in for the weekend to visit him in the hospital exactly once. It was an obligatory gesture. John was not comforted by his cold demeanor.

Once out, his mother sent him to a "fifty-dollar psychiatrist" who was short on sympathy. He told John that he was "bullshitting" when he spoke of his fights with his brother. John saw in the psychiatrist yet another rejecting male and quit therapy for good. He never had much luck with father figures.

He was out of school for the rest of the year, accompanying his mother on her selling rounds. In his final year he played hookey a lot, as usual. The only exception was Miss Nunnamaker's class.

He showed up drunk in her class and instead of sending him to the dean, she told him, "Go to the lavatory and get yourself cleaned up." He felt that she was genuinely concerned about him, not just with the rules. He was inspired to work in her class, history, a subject which he did not really enjoy. He got an A. It was his gift to her. He had responded to a small degree of kindness. Perhaps he was ready to believe that someone might find him worthwhile. He knew that he had made his last suicide attempt although he was "still capable of the notion."

He went to college and did extremely well. His father was "too busy" to attend graduation. He went to graduate school in English but quit before completing his master's thesis. Pulling in the reins at the last minute became a pattern. He allowed himself to demonstrate ability but not to complete the course. On one level, success might mean trying to please his rejecting father. On another, it might mean replacing him. He was trapped in a limbo of indecision about what to do with his life.

He floundered through many jobs. The unconscious taint of his father's appraisal, that he was a "hopeless fuck-up," probably followed him and had its influence. At eighteen, he had a first marriage that failed after producing in its second year a son who was called Little John. The marriage split up in its fourth year and his son was left with his mother, who soon remarried. John kept in touch with his boy, even more as time went on. At the time of his birth, he may not have felt capable of full-time fathering. His own experience of fathers had never been anything but destructive. He may have feared the kind of father he would be with such models and fled from too intensive and damaging a contact.

With his discovery of Zen, John made his first real commitment. It is suggestive that he characterized his father as "unknowable in words." A Zen meditator looks beyond words to an ineffable reality within the quiet void of mind. John says, "The authority of Zen is in the silence." Perhaps he was trying to understand his father, the Sphinx, by looking into silence. Perhaps he was trying to be like him, the former minister.

His father has played a striking role in John's life. John knows so much about him and yet has not yet been able to create a unified picture. He keeps the bad father in one compartment of his mind and the good father in another. He says that his father is "incapable of making enemies," and forgets the years of rage when his mother supported a family of three children without assistance. He calls his father a "gentle man . . . with sweetness in his character," and suppresses all the memories of being cruelly rejected, overlooked, and scorned. By keeping away the negative images, he can continue to idealize a man who could be generous with his friends when full of the bonhomie of drink or without it.

John visited his eighty-year-old father in the hospital where he awaited a dangerous operation for an aneurysm. John was in his early forties and uncomfortable to find his strong and silent father terrified. His father told him, "Be careful with Little John. Otherwise you'll lose him." In these words, John believes he heard an apology for all the years of rejection. But words are not enough, especially where a narcissist is concerned. The words of a narcissist can mean very little.

And so it is with his father. The old man uses easy, Western endearments, calls John Honey, tells him, "I love you," giving a twenty-dollar bill as a Christmas present to a son who can really use a hand. Endearments had been reserved for his girlfriends, never for his kids. As an old man, he first used affectionate terms but still refused to offer financial help and spent only limited time with his children. This father was unwilling to help his daughter set up her own business, even to cosign a loan. His claim of insolvency was an obvious lie. He gives his money freely to cronies and buys expensive presents for women he wishes to impress. His children still do not count. Let them struggle. Let them sink. It is not his problem.

John needs to see his father as he is. Parental idealization misconstrues reality and is destructive to his development. If his father was "not capable of hurting a soul," then John's wounds are his own fault.

He must see that his father was incapable of love, rather than see himself as a born loser. He can throw off the role of the deficient child who is not worth saving and come into his own power. It was not his fault that the paternal well was dry. It is time he learned that he is worthy of love.

There is hope for John if he knows that he chooses to limit himself. He has to express his anger in ways that are not self-destructive, to learn that he can love without losing his soul and can be loved in a different way.

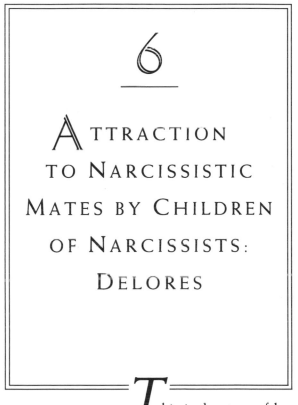

6

ATTRACTION TO NARCISSISTIC MATES BY CHILDREN OF NARCISSISTS: DELORES

*T*his is the story of how our early experience with a narcissistic parent, particularly one of the opposite sex, can lead us to choose similar types to love. How else can we account for our choice of suffering? Despite our complaining we repeat the problem.

We loved our narcissistic parent although we may only remember pain. Adults often do not stay in touch with their childish longings and satisfactions but develop an association between the pain and love once felt. If our parent forgot his appointments and holidays with us, we choose a forgetful lover. If the parent did not help out at home, we end up with the household chores. Some of the similarities between then and now may be exact. Some will follow a general pattern. Like a lover who does not earn sufficient salary at a job different from the one held by a parent who was a poor provider. Or a lover who does not touch us with affection but is sexual in the same way we felt our parent to be.

We look at our past with hatred and do not see its resemblance to the present. It isn't pretty or fun to know that we love a person because he mistreats us in specific ways. It is painful to realize that we are with a narcissist to get the love that we never received from our narcissistic parent. We do not want this man for himself but need his loving to prove our parent's love. We have chosen a life without easy pleasure when better is available. If only the past would loosen its hold on us.

Delores is my oldest and dearest friend. While we lived in San Francisco, we had known each other through many years and extended helping hands over life's rough terrain. Because our fathers were supremely narcissistic, we have trodden similar psychological mine fields and emerged with related battle scars. We offer each other the understanding that we never found in our families.

I asked Delores to participate in this book as an example of a "woman who loves too much" and she agreed. Almost immediately, we ran into a characteristic snag since she barely had a moment for a formal interview. We could talk only between spurts of activity when she was in the throes of exhaustion. Delores is a whirling dervish, dancing in a high wind. Her phone is forever ringing; she listens to other people's problems, giving instructions to the workers of her booming interior design business. As the child of a narcissist, she has strong doubt but stronger determination. Her bravado borders on arrogance. A talented person who likes to direct projects, she is also the child of an unreliable narcissist and allows other people to cheat her.

She is ever planning her next party, event, or dinner, imagining and inventing, purchasing or considering purchasing. A business in home design grew out of her life since she is always reaching out for new experiences and drawing people to her. Once she talked me into buying a water bed, with the consequence that I slept on the floor for years until I found a buyer.

Delores told me a recent dream that showed her fear. She is climbing a mountain, going higher and higher until she reaches its peak. Before her is a drop off to emptiness. Filled with anxicty, she must go down or fall off.

In this dream, Delores saw fear that her business will fail, that she will run out of ideas and be cheated of success. My interpretation of the same dream had a different slant. The idea that achieving great heights can be dangerous may relate to the grandiosity it stimulates. Narcissism lurks within the psyche of every child of a narcissist since we had such a parent to identify with. Rise too high and you can become narcissistic. Getting out of touch with people is like a death.

Delores is five years older than her brother John, of the chapter on suicide. They have the same father, cold, haughty, self-centered, interested in flying his plane and getting away from his family. Delores spent her first five years without him because he was flying in England for the RAF. He had left his family for a voluntary enlistment right after Delores was born, which shows how little he cared for his wife and child.

During his time away, Delores was raised by a somewhat narcissistic mother who focused on appearance, permed and bleached the baby's hair, and put her on interminable diets. Delores grew up with a fantasy about what her father would be like, kind, sweet, and physical, like her uncles who cuddled her cousins on their laps. But when he returned from the war, it was different.

He was cold and offered no physical contact, attempting to rein her in and to remove the privileges she had had with her mother. He responded to her assertiveness with dislike. In her teens, she and her father argued when she neglected to call him sir, for which he slapped her in the face. In some peculiar way, a slap from this oblivious man meant he cared for her. He gave the same aggressive response followed by a token of affection to her brother John. At the close of her father's living with his family, he left them flat, providing little subsequent contact and no financial support.

By the time of his departure, Delores was in her midteens, a scornful person who didn't want him to be around. Cynicism covered the memory of her early years of pain, when her hopeful gaze was met by his coldness. She secretly blamed herself for his response, thinking she wasn't lovable, nice, acceptable, or pretty enough to please him. His slap was one of the strongest responses he had given her. Although she resented it, one must infer from her subsequent choice of men that she unconsciously marked it as evidence of his love. In this way, abuse became part of her model of being loved by narcissistic and abusive men.

Tortured relationships with men formed the centerpiece of our lives and the frequent subject of conversation. Delores and I would talk about our boyfriends' behavior and try to help each other out. Men are the emotional center for many women, but not always because they are upsetting. Men usually are valued because they offer a woman security and pleasure, friendship, intimacy, the support of a helping hand.

But not ours. They were very difficult to get along with. We couldn't get close to them and be nicely treated. We focused on them in an obsessive, addictive fashion and kept trying. The worse it got, the harder it was for us to let go—up to a point. I chose men who were intelligent, self-centered, and unwilling to make a commitment. Delores chose men who were intelligent, dependent, and very abusive.

The negative traits that attracted us were no accident, although we were unaware of our pattern. Each fell for her "ideal" man and was blinded by love. Suffering took a while to penetrate. Unavailable and ungiving intellectual workaholics were like my father. Abusive, intelligent, and demanding men who gave nothing and took everything were like her father. Our unconscious goal was to turn these men into loving, giving, and available partners. It was like trying to carve Mt. Rushmore with a toothpick.

We stood by each other through incredible pairings and did not shame the other for it. Our conversations were funny as we caricatured the latest mishap and absurdity to which we clung. Laughter diminished the importance of the latest men who were sandpapering our souls. We never felt secure with the guys who turned us on and stimulated a painful yearning. Eventually, we got rid of our current disasters but never spoke of the inevitable ones to come.

My men would usually vanish on their own as soon as I pressured them to get close and make a commitment. Delores's men would immediately move in and weather her attempts to get them to change their abusive patterns until she gave up and asked them to leave. Her asking was soft and tenuous. They responded with anger, smoked a joint, and generally ignored her.

With Delores, the repetitious element of abuse took many forms. Men promised her the world and secretly expected it from her. Delores had her way of promising back. Her suffering had a kind of sweetness and excitement. You could hear it in her voice when she spoke to her hypersensitive mates, high and soft, as if singing a lullaby to a baby. She chose her words carefully so as not to set off their nitroglycerine tempers.

Her father also had an explosive personality, demanding attention and consideration and giving none back. As an old man, he visited without telling his kids that he was coming. Summoned to his side, they had to procure his favorite cigars, feed him on schedule, and drive him to his motel on command regardless of what was going on.

Some of Delores's men have included the following (I am omitting others no less difficult): a Coca-Cola addict, hopped up on caffeine and sugar and constantly generating fights. Ten minutes after I met him, we had an angry repartee about the effect of liver on your health! He had escaped from a career in science to a backwoods hermitage without running water where he made oddly shaped candles that reminded me of the works of Charles Addams. He met Delores in a co-op where he sold candles and she sold the paintings she was doing at the time. Delores put up with his tantrums and tried to make him stop his Coca-Cola. He proved unregenerate.

I first met Delores with her husband, Jay, a charming and extremely irresponsible man who abused her with his "meditative" lack of interest in the practicalities of life. Irresponsibility had been a central trait of Delores's narcissistic father, who was unavailable when he was needed and later refused to support his family. Delores's husband was an otherworldly baby who held on to her for dear life. She could not entrust him with the smallest task. He lifted his huge eyes to the heavens when asked to contend with a task in "gross reality" and usually would mismanage it. He was a follower of Eastern religion and left the concerns of the world to God, guru, and wife, in that order.

Jay was paid a subsistence income for barely working in the firm of his wealthy, disapproving, and rejecting father. Jay was used to being bailed out by his mother, for whom Delores served as a substitute. Despite talent and artistic pretensions he only dabbled at drawing and photography. His work had an otherworldly, vanishing perspective and was presented to visitors to entertain them and gain self-esteem from their appreciation. He had no interest in developing his abilities to generate income.

After Delores had their baby, she had two children to take care of, Jay and her son. Her dreamer husband would leave the house in unmatched socks and shoes tied with string. A religious "fool" is above such things as appearances. Sent to buy milk for his child, he would return hours later in an elevated state having purchased a rare and holy book. The milk had been forgotten and the book was expensive. Delores did not dare let him take their son shopping for fear that he would forget and leave him in the supermarket.

The only material thing that concerned him was that Delores should not be long out of his sight. He became hysterical when she came home later than expected, saying that he feared her being mugged. Probably he was afraid that she would meet another man and leave him. Which she did.

He was one of a long line of baby men who, with Delores's encouragement, glued themselves on. Glueyness kept them from walking out as her father once had done. She could control these men by "giving" to them as she had done with father and brother.

A few boyfriends after her marriage came a spate with a revolutionist carpenter who liked his beer and was charming and unreachable. As long as she catered to him, went dancing, and smoked grass, everything between them was fine. On her birthday, he used magic marker to write "Al loves Delores," in huge black letters on the school wall opposite their apartment. But did he? His revolutionary feelings were expressed by ripping off society. It was but a short jump to abusing the woman with whom he lived.

Why is Delores attracted to opportunism and lawlessness in men? Many of her men have followed this pattern, leading quasi-predatory lives outside the mainstream and finding their easiest victim in her. She was drawn by their ability to survive in unconventional ways. So much oppressed was she by the numerous strictures of her mother and father that their defiance seemed to spell freedom. She didn't see it as inevitable that they would also take advantage of her. Like other women who "love too much," her addiction to abuse is unknown to her. Where better to find abuse than from an angry rebel who is looking for reparations?

There were various kinds of violence in her "love" relationships. A spoken word can be as hurtful as a blow. Until I interviewed her for this book, Delores had never spoken to me about her physical mistreatment, since the victim may consider such behavior to be a humiliating thing. She may also secretly think that she deserves abuse, which is why it and the relationship continue. We only discussed verbal violence except for the one "accident" when she and her boyfriend were working on their apartment and his hammer "somehow" flew through the air to hit her in the head. She said that it felt as if there was something peculiar about this but didn't dwell upon it.

She didn't make a connection between the present and her past with a father who had been violent as well. In speaking of her love misadventures, she is like the woman who tells a friend, "I don't think my husband loves me anymore." "Why?" asks the friend. "Because he hasn't hit me in a month."

I asked her more about violence and she spoke of cursing and yelling, pinches, shoves, and slaps. Her current man once pushed her to the floor and threatened her with a chair leg; another time, he attempted to strangle her for asking him to contribute more to household upkeep. Angry, terrified, disgusted, she nevertheless eventually went back to him. In his savage passion she saw a sign of need and love. She felt regret when battered by his cry—"Don't abandon me." Claiming to be depressed by him, she finds a million reasons for remaining and does not see how his mistreatment fits into her childhood experience of what she learned to call "loving."

Delores has always placated men, starting with an angry narcissistic father who ignored her individuality. He did not appreciate her physical beauty or ability to dance and disregarded her need for affection and attention. Romantic partners followed suit, transgressing against the principles which she does little to make clear. Delores's principles would include a fair exchange of services, in which one party is not to assume the financial burden of the other. It would include being mutually pleasant and responsive. She would have her men be reliable and true to their word, but in this respect she is like her narcissistic father and does not present a reliable and verbally trust-worthy image of herself to them. Their unreliability is complained about and accepted. Hers is excused and overlooked. Delores does not set limits and is terrified of using the word *no*. Not only do her boy-friends take advantage, but also her son, who is dependent and unde-veloped. Boyfriends, son, friends all try to parasitize her since her behavior teaches them to take from her without constraint and to ignore her needs.

Her mother's having to placate her father and the way he treated his daughter taught Delores that a woman's role is to make the man comfortable by acceding to his every wish. I have heard Delores com-plain in a weak, ineffectual voice that seems to say, "Ignore me, I don't mean it." To me, she speaks of confusion, anger, and pain, but her man does not hear much about it until her positive feelings for him have been completely exhausted.

Her series of boyfriends included many surly ripoffs, drug users, name callers—demanding, insensitive men. They were a series of emo-tional hair shirts of whom Delores said, "I loved them all but I didn't like any one of them." It shocked her to speak this thought aloud although she claimed to have always known it. Often, we do not pay attention to our thoughts until something brings them center stage. Apropos of this, our talking together did not set off vast insights since so much is invested in remaining the same. Addiction to our painful quest keeps many children of narcissists locked in unhappy relation-ships. I would say that Delores's primary insight from our discussions was learning that she encouraged people to take advantage of her. In our last phone call, she said she was taking a weekend course on how to make demands.

In our discussions, there were many questions and denials, such as, "How can I be choosing a man to love me who resembles my father when my father loved me so little?" Delores doesn't see how a healthy supportive love affair and what she actually seeks are different. Cutting through our defenses and fantasies takes more than logic. If we cannot correctly see ourselves, we need to submit ourselves to the insights of someone whose vision is more trustworthy. We must break eggs to make an omelette and we must give up the ancient pleasures of courting the narcissistic parent if we want to learn to live a different way, enjoying a person who sees and accepts us as we are. When Delores read the final chapter in this book, she resolved to fire the dependent and unreliable workers in her shop and to find people who would do the job.

Although liking a person is usually based in part on a realistic appraisal of how she or he treats us or on objective characteristics that attract us, loving also comes from a deeper and sometimes irrational place. The experiences of childhood can cause us to love someone who doesn't treat us well at all.

Delores's childhood was broken up into three sections: the time before her father came home from the war, the time he was home again, and the time after he had left for good. Life with a narcissistic mother also affected her later relationships with narcissistic men. Her first five years were spent with a mother who gave dancing lessons to support the two of them. Mother was a feisty woman who encouraged Delores to be creative and free-spirited. She was not the kind to dwell on unhappiness or unpleasantness but would activate herself in a kind of manic defense against depression.

Mother's narcissistic traits kept her from accepting Delores for herself. Mother's love was conditional, in the narcissistic fashion. Delores had to meet her need for social status since Mother believed that this would lead to happiness.

She had been a model once and Delores had to be equally popular and beautiful. Mother's scrutiny sensitized Delores to the least of her physical imperfections, like having a "pigeon" breast (protruding breastbone). Delores was encouraged to think about ways to hide her flaws and enhance her good points with makeup, dress, manners, and charm. Before going on a date, she had to pass muster with her mother. The only acceptable words, to be heard with relief, were, "You look beautiful." Such training led to a career in interior design—Delores could put people into fantastic settings that changed the way they saw themselves.

In Delores's mother we see the previous generation repeating the choice of a narcissistic mate due to having had a narcissistic parent of the opposite sex. Delores's mother was the daughter of a narcissistic father, an arrogant man who despised everyone as beneath him. He nicknamed his wife Nummy, short for numbskull. His daughters obediently called their mother Nummy, as if unaware of what the name signified. By denigrating her, they courted Dad's approval and sullied the image of women. Many children of narcissists come out hating themselves and their sex.

Delores's mother told a story about her own father. It was the height of the Depression and he was preparing a tire for repair by soaking the inner tube in a tub on the dining room table. His daughter was expecting a suitor and asked him to remove the tub so she could use the room to entertain him. Father flatly refused. No one else counted.

Daughter grown up, she met her future husband and was immediately smitten, enchanted by his looks, fine manners, and excellent profession. He was a minister who knew how to "woo the ladies." She claims to have had no inkling of his narcissism but we all have unconscious radar that tells us the kind of person we are with. Delores's mother had found a man like her father, one who would soak his own psychological tires on her dining room table.

After they were married, he quickly showed his colors. He was disinterested in her family and separated himself from their doings. He was not interested in their outings at the beach where her family had a house, didn't want to "schmooze" over lengthy dinners, and didn't like his work. His charm with the ladies was strictly for strangers. All he wanted to do was to get family obligations over with and return to the safety of the flying field where he gave lessons. Flying took him away from demands that he give his family interest and love.

After he returned from the war, two more children were born, both boys. The family moved several times to new towns to be nearer the airport. His congregation expected a generosity of spirit that Delores's father did not have. His boys were neglected and growing up angry, having been treated by Dad with disdain and dislike. Mother got the short end of the parental stick and probably resented her mothering duties without support and appreciation from her mate.

Delores says, "I had no use for him and his meaningless rules." But when Delores was eleven or twelve, the family took their meals in miserable anxiety. They would all sit down to eat. Her father would hastily consume a bit of food, push back his chair, and mumble, "Gotta go." It was over and he was off. No talking and sharing. The family hated feeling abandoned and began to gobble alongside him so as not to be the ones that he left. Delores still hurls down her food in a self-generated race to finish quickly.

It was an unhappy family trying to put on a good face. Delores's mother liked to play and didn't want the burden of raising her children without help. She saw salvation in Delores's tractability and increasingly turned to the young girl for help. Delores lacked confidence in her ability to do it but, to get mother's approval, replaced her at baby-sitting.

One time, Delores was sitting in the backseat of the family car with her two rambunctious brothers, who were increasingly out of control. Afraid that she might not be able to manage them, panic drove her to act the charade of control, which calmed her brothers. The unspoken consequence of her success was to turn her into a performer, a person who could act a role that others would believe. Assuming such a role helped her mother, who was resistant to the burden of her children's miseries. Delores fell into the pattern of acting like an adult to cover childish fears. But covered fears are not outgrown. They smolder behind one's defenses.

Fear of separation rules Delores's life, much of which had its basis in her mother's narcissistic isolation as well as her dad's abandonment. Separation anxiety often has its origin in the period around age two when the child needs to practice separation by coming and going from his parent. The child returns periodically for "refueling," which means to feel the parent's happy greeting assuring him that all is well. A favorable response shows that his independent action is acceptable and that the parent will be there when needed.

Two of the parental reactions that can undermine the development of autonomy are if a parent can't let go or if a parent lets go too quickly. Often there is a combination of these two with the parent listing from one side to the other.

Delores's moderately narcissistic mother probably clung to her child at first as an extension of herself. Once the child started to separate, mother hastened the process because she was unable to tolerate the coming and going. Feeling deserted by her husband, who went to war, the actions of her child exacerbated such feelings, so she prematurely disengaged from the child and demanded full autonomy of her. A child who is afraid that the parent will not be there upon her return becomes an adult who is afraid to let go of her partner.

Delores gives evidence of such thinking in her early teenage babysitting. She felt deserted by her mother when left in the car with her young brothers. It flitted through Delores's mind that her mother was not coming back at all. This relatively adult fear of being left can be a repetition of the early childhood trauma she experienced over her first move into autonomy.

Evidence of a problem with unreliable parents is passed on to the following generation. Delores's son had phenomenal powers of observation. I remember when he was about two and a half and reminded me to take my sweater (which I was about to leave behind). It was hanging on a hook in conglomeration with other sweaters. "Elan," he said, "you forgot your sweater." When I asked him about this memory for the book, he said, "I had to be totally observant because I was afraid that Mom would leave without me. I had to keep my eye on everyone. I knew where all my backup people were, you and Elsa and Rose, in case I got left."

We replay our traumas with our children. A woman fearing that she will be forgotten by her mother and her dad raises a child who fears that she in turn will be forgotten. Imparting similar fears to our loved children reassures us of our parents' loving motivation.

These problems show up with our mates and friends. Delores, who feared that her mother would disappear, became an adult who cannot bear to be alone. She does not feel connected with her "significant other" if he is physically absent. Having considerable beauty and charm, she rarely lacks for companionship. The gaiety of her surface denies the anxiety that lies beneath. More than just liking male company, she has to have it.

Fear of solitude is shown by the immediate replacement of one departing live-in lover by another. She promises herself (and her friends) to live alone for a while but cannot. The speedy choice of her next man is helped by his dependency. She plummets from man to man, a chain of men, with few intolerable moments of emptiness between. Her choice of dependent men is fed by her unmet and early need for an unavailable mother and father.

As she grows fed up with the current man, she is grooming the next. Her new man comes in the back door as the old one goes out the front. In response to the power of her conviction and his need for merger, the new man thinks he is the one who will last. For her, he is a need-dependency-user man, a repeat of what led to the demise of the relationship before. A man with a healthy ego takes longer to establish his commitments since he looks before he leaps.

Delores is like two people. Her first analyst said that she was like "stones and water." On the surface she is a leader and trailbreaker, on the underside she is fearful and clinging, a woman who accepts provocative abuse and is incapable of calling a spade a spade or a punch a punch. People who know her well but are not predatory find it difficult to believe in the huge disparities between her actions and attitudes. Delores herself has not integrated the strength that she possesses. Having learned self-abnegation from her father's cold response to whatever did not concern himself, she thinks that the price for assertiveness is desertion. Fear of abandonment supports her choice of addicted, clinging men.

And yet, there is another side. The men she is so crazy for are secretly "boarders" with whom she plays the role of submissive victim. This means that there is a power she keeps restrained. If and when she wills it, she can show them the door. Despite increasing financial independence her choice of men remains the same, as does the role she plays with them. For a long while, she enacts the game of the little girl with her narcissistic father, trying to get this self-centered man to love her fully. When she tires of it and sees that the relationship is going nowhere, she declares it to be over in a breezy and irresistible way. The man who has been seeking a permanent berth and reveling in her undemanding approach believes that he has made it into heaven. He is shocked to learn that this is not his survival train's last stop.

Delores's ego has grown stronger as she sees herself capable of earning money. She feels the power of ownership, bought a hot tub and a dishwasher, has with limited finances landscaped her lawn. Her home had been creative but rudimentary. Now, even her sheets and pillowcases match. But even with her increasing power, she remains with David, her latest man, perhaps the most violent, dependent, demanding, addicted, and ungiving of them all. David may be closest to the model of her narcissistic father and she calls them look-alikes, short and dark, slouched over with sardonic and disapproving expressions.

Delores claims to not feel "that way" about him anymore. Six years have gone by and he remains the same, refusing to produce sufficient income and unwilling to leave. If pressed to break it off, he throws a tantrum and she caves in. He accuses her of having destroyed his life, which plays on her sympathy. He says that first she took advantage of him and now wants to cruelly throw him out. For good measure, he adds the threat of suicide.

David doesn't try to please Delores sexually. When I asked her why she didn't get a different lover, she said that her work took all her energy and she didn't care much about sex. In this rationalization there is the unstated pleasure in her pain. She said that despite all the negatives, there is comfort in his companionship.

I was there at the outset of their relationship and saw how unconscious paths are followed, how Delores got embroiled even though she knew better. It was like eating an apple in the Garden of Eden. "Just one bite and I'll eat no more." Once eaten, there's no turning back.

I was visiting Delores that afternoon. As we were together in her car, she saw David tooling around her neighborhood on his bike. They'd met the previous day and perhaps he hoped to run into her. Delores and I were coming back from shopping when she spotted him. I saw his dark hair and the pure, soulful expression of an angel. Although I too was taken in at first, I later learned that his choirboy act was a cover for a satanic ego. He held on to her hand through the open car window, and looked at her with melting eyes.

He invited us to visit him right away and we accepted, following his bike in her car. It was the first time that Delores had seen his place, a small cottage set among trees in a quiet neighborhood, college digs in an idyllic western town.

We entered the living room. Before us, a kitchen, two bedrooms, and a bath. On the inside of the front door was a space-age poster with physics formulas on it, some kind of insider's joke. Also he had an incredible collection of books and records, esoteric odds and ends, all declaring "herein lives a head."

From our freewheeling conversation, he appeared to be extremely intelligent. I later learned that he had been valedictorian of a large western high school. His level of education and plans were not discussed. Delores didn't care about his major and when or if he was going to graduate. She wanted to know if he was going to be fun!

I was interested in such things and concluded that he was one of those young men who hang out at a university for an indefinite time, sometimes taking classes but never completing the degree. Time limits, degrees, vocation have nothing to do with the leisurely experience of getting an education. He is a college "lifer," considerably younger than Delores and considerably older than his classmates.

Our time together was very pleasant until we were interrupted by the knock and entry of his landlady. She was very angry because she claimed that he owed her a considerable sum of money. His roommate was gone and he persisted in paying only half the rent. How long the roommate had been gone, we do not know. How hard David sought replacement is a moot point. He occupied the house alone. He felt that looking for a roommate was enough to abrogate his responsibility, that the landlady was an irrational pest who wasted his time. He treated her with a combination of annoyance and boredom. Why didn't she take her petty problem and disappear?

In the car on the way home, the drama we had witnessed alarmed me. I babbled my anxious thoughts to Delores. "He's a freeloader of royal proportions. The world is owed to him. He thinks only of himself and has no conscience about extortion. Don't get involved." She agreed with me wholeheartedly. She usually agrees with the wise counsel of her friends—and then goes straight ahead, propelled by forces that have little to do with her ability to think.

That night, Delores had a premonitory dream in which her unconscious mind was attempting to save her. A vampire bat was buzzing around her throat and she was extremely frightened. We discussed the dream. The vampire bat was this new man who was looking to feed. A classic vampire plot shows a heroine who succumbs to chthonic forces and sleeps while they consume her.

I left Delores at the end of my visit thinking that she had resolved to nip the relationship in the bud, for that is what she told me. Years later I recognized that when Delores spoke of a relationship that made her unhappy, it was not with the intention of withdrawing. She was ventilating her unhappy feelings so that she could continue with the man.

David moved in by inches; first his cartons were stored in her garage and then loose items in her house. Little by little came the man himself. He was working sporadically and beneath his native capacity. At first, he drove the local bus—when he got up in time. Delores sometimes joined him on his route before she went to work, giving it a party atmosphere. He often went to work late and took absences, not wanting to disturb his precious mental tranquility with trivial obligations. He had a roof over his head and didn't need to make the rent.

He pushed away the stresses of tawdry reality by smoking a lot of homegrown grass, something Delores overlooked when trying to understand his lackadaisical behavior. She had a way of turning a blind eye to addictive behaviors that caused her trouble. Her own drug use made her insensitive to its effects on others and led her to deny its consequences. She smoked pot quite often and did acid occasionally as part of the custom of the hippie culture.

She was at the beginning of her painting business, achieving a degree of fame through paintings of prehistoric beasts, friendly dinosaurs that munched on leaves and toothy tyrannosauruses. She sold these paintings at fairs. David would take off from driving the bus in order to accompany her. He would help her set up her display and then hang out. His companionship pleased her. She only became dissatisfied when she realized that he did not want to work hard and would let her foot the bills. He didn't always come up with his share of the rent and food money. He ran up phenomenal phone bills to a large family that was far away, saying high-handedly that he would pay for his phone bill when he had the money. He never thought of depriving himself at the moment. Delores was supposed to take up the slack.

He showed how much he loved dependency when he squandered a twelve-thousand-dollar inheritance from his deceased aunt. Delores begged him to use the money to learn a skill, bookbinding, in which he was interested, or the cooking which he loved. Instead, he bought himself toys, including a synthesizer that he never learned to play since lessons were not part of his budget. Practice was too much like work. He preferred to doodle in music, free-form and stoned. His inheritance was quickly spent.

Delores was horrified, infuriated. Her ethic of work made her hate his profligacy. At least he should get good at the synthesizer. Her pressure on him to use his money wisely was responded to with infantile rage since he wanted to remain on an eternal vacation. Grass made this seem to be a feasible approach. On one of my later visits, I asked him what he intended and he said, "I'm waiting for my ship to come in." But his ship had already come and he had sunk it. In private Delores told me that his current ship was the S.S. *Delores*.

She stayed with him. Or rather, he continued to live with her, responding badly to any request and often sabotaging what he did when forced to comply. He broke her rules, rejecting her needs in a callous manner. If she asked him to feed the dog, he strewed her fine, hand-thrown plates around her backyard. A thousand requests would get something accomplished but she would pay for it.

He lived by the motto, "What is asked for will not be given." His memory for literary fact was phenomenal, for personal requests imbecilic. It was shades of her narcissistic father. Sex was poor since he refused to do what she asked and didn't remember her requests. If she put his hand where she wanted it, he would resist and remove it as soon as she stopped holding it. He was rigidly and obstinately unprogrammable. She didn't look forward to sex with him and put forth the rationalization that they were like an old married couple. However, the real issue was that David would not give.

He hated women. His father had died of alcoholism and his large family was held together by a controlling mother who would beat him to the point that he feared for his life. All the world now consisted of strong mothers who would pay for his suffering.

Years went by. David claimed to be extremely depressed, as if depression accounted for his nonfunctioning. Perhaps he was depressed at functioning so poorly, but as an addictive person, his primary motive was hanging on to the host. Friends asked Delores what she was doing with a man who was not only predatory but not nice. He didn't compliment her for the things she did around the house. His mouth was often compressed in a thin line, eyebrows raised in disdain. His attitude was, "With such petty things do you occupy your life." And he used those things. He ate her food, listened to her records, used her phone, slept in her bed. She hated and loved this abuse. Like many children of narcissists, she is addicted to the prickly, miserable, ungiving, self-centered meanness of the unloving narcissistic parent.

David had been abusing her financially for a long time, like borrowing her son's car, which she had just refurbished in order to sell it. He then used the car for months! Even more fantastic was Delores's inability to ask for it back. She could only approach him with a supplicating murmur. "David, please, I need the car." For a long time nothing happened. Repairing his own car would take money that he lacked. He further ran down her car and reduced its monetary value.

Delores's fury was mounting beyond containment. Perhaps she had developed the sense that she could survive without him when she told him to come up with more money and laid out his areas of insufficiency. She pushed him too far. How he hated aggressive women with their endless demands! His big hands went around her throat, pushing her against a wall with her wind cut off, out of breath, feeling strangled. It was no joke.

When he let up on his grip she was injured. Her neck was painful. A vertebra was out of place. Terror penetrated her denial. For once, she couldn't bury her emotional experience and told her friends, who panicked for her. They knew that she would forget her terror, and they saw real danger in the couple staying together. Later, he blamed his violence on her PMS! When Delores told me of this event, she said that he had hurt her before this time as well.

Her friends got her to put him out and change the locks. They asked her to go for an order of protection from the police, which she kept putting off as her mind started to bury the incident. One could feel her fear and the memory of his violence seep away. It was scary to watch this happen. When she had to go on a business trip and her plants needed watering, who did she ask to do the job, which necessitated that he have the key? Her friends did not know of this. By the time she returned from her trip, David had once more ensconced himself in the house.

David remains with Delores. Little has changed except that time has moved on. He has been destroyed by his unwillingness to stand on his feet. Growth usually needs to occur within the appropriate developmental periods or it doesn't catch up. She still thinks of getting rid of him but turns most of her energy to business. Sexual affairs can be carried on in distant cities on business trips while he remains in his ignorance at home. She considers trading him in for a new man, but remains with the pleasure of his abusive ways. He gives her very little and she continues to get something emotional from it.

When Delores first got into painting, she did a magnificent work showing a unicorn with two heads. The head looking forward into the future was a unicorn with a powerful horn. Looking backward was the head of a traditional woman, wide-eyed, vulnerable, sweet, and pretty.

The unicorn is a phallic beast, narcissistic in that it needs no one and others need it. Its horn is a symbol of masculine power, like the symbol of the narcissistic male as distinguished from the female helplessness to which Delores was raised. At work, with friends, she can be aggressive and even ruthless. She can use people, getting around them with her charm. She accrues power and radiates a narcissistic luminescence.

The backward-looking maiden is transfixed by her past. It is the submissive female who chains her man with her own enslavement. It is the delicate woman who cannot raise her voice or say no. Her true love is the narcissistic and vanishing father of childhood. She never gave up her need for him because she is not in touch with the feeling. She is unconscious of the origin of her replay. Blindly and compulsively, she chooses men who feature the most narcissistic and worst traits of dear old Dad.

These two heads looking in different directions are unaware of each other. They operate in different spheres and from different aspects of her personality. The forward-looking head denies the influence of the past. The backward head is too caught in its dream to integrate. Each represents an extreme.

To heal the rift, Delores needs to slow down and to take a look at both. Her current lifestyle is probably too successful to make her want to deal with the suffering that her backward head is causing her, or to look at the suffering that the forward head is causing others. Perhaps later. She is a formidable lady and quite a remarkable one. As her brother once said to me, "Our family matures late."

Delores and I are trying to learn to treat ourselves and others well. We remind each other of our need for love, knowing that the only one who can move us toward love is ourselves. We must learn from experience in order to change, although the hardest thing to change is one's definition of love. We want to love a different kind of person and to experience his generosity as love.

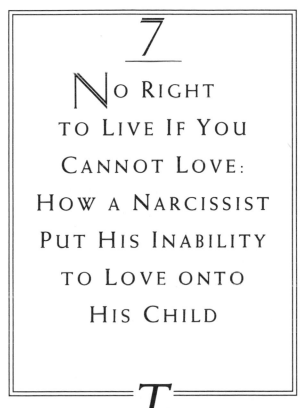

7

No Right
to Live If You
Cannot Love:
How a Narcissist
Put His Inability
to Love onto
His Child

*T*he narcissistic parent puts
what he feels is unacceptable in himself onto his child, but
the child does not realize that she is a repository, accepting
instead whatever the parent feeds her as the truth. A child
presumes good intentions since the alternative is too frightening to consider. In this story, as in the story of John, a
child is forced to deal with her parents' critical lack of love.

Here we have Elan, a girl of eleven staying in the country with her
mother. Her parents are recently divorced. Her mother hates her ex-

husband with great intensity. She is a hater by nature, and additionally is on the rebound from twelve years in the service of his narcissistic grandiosity. She received no thanks. His philosophy was to verbalize only fault. If you couldn't appreciate yourself, you were out of luck. Neither mother nor child was capable of doing this.

Typically, even though both parents had full-time jobs, Mother came home to do the cooking, cleaning, washing, ironing, and serving. Father read his newspaper. He had been trained to do this by his doting and narcissistic mother, who demanded that her boys be "geniuses," thereby creating in them vast feelings of inferiority and a need to overcompensate. Elan's mother remembers her mother-in-law weeping when she saw her son, the college graduate, washing dishes after his wife had cooked and served. She had stated to herself, "I too am a college graduate." But her need to create bonds through dependency due to abysmal self-esteem, which made her expect rejection, had kept her serving. Now it was over.

She was enjoying her first weekend away from work in many months in the log cabin that she had acquired with her ex-husband. Her dealings with the little girl were extremely unstable and change-able. Even though she loved the child very much, her pressure-cooker personality led to constant verbal explosions of rage, to endless criti-cism, and to an insistence that she do for the child what the child wished to do for herself. She did not want her child to be independent because here, too, she saw in that the potential for abandonment.

Reeling from the blows of both parents' criticism and caught in her father's egocentricity, the little girl had become extremely compli-ant. All she wanted was to be sheltered from the endless rain of blows to her ego. The child needed to find value in herself and some purpose for living. Her escape route and salvation was nature. Communing with animals, her mind sailing on the wings of birds, her senses drunk with the scent of flowers, lulled by the buzzing of bees, she was free.

She was an artist, creating an ecstatic and loving world to go to. When one finds a child of a narcissist who is relatively intact after surviving a horrendous childhood, one should look for the making of art. Art heals.

She was what was, for her, an approximation of happy when old Mr. Etzel, the proprietor of the general store a quarter of a mile away, came limping down the road. They had no phone. From a distance, he called out a breathless message. "Your father just called. Your grandmother's died and the funeral is tomorrow." He heeled around and started back up the road.

She didn't know how she was supposed to react. She had no good feelings for this grandmother, who took an interest only in her grades, which were never good enough. What was she supposed to do? She looked to her mother for guidance.

This was her mother's first vacation in a long time. She didn't want to drive straight back to the city. Besides, she had hated her mother-in-law and could express her hatred through the little girl without quite recognizing that she was doing so. She did not allow herself to recognize the effect that the child's actions would have on the child's position in her father's family.

She told her daughter, "You do not need to go back today. There'll be enough time to be with the family tomorrow night." The girl accepted her mother's decision with a feeling of trepidation. Why would her father have called if he did not expect something of her?

And yet the city was so far away. Whenever she was with one parent it was as if the other resided in a foreign country. Her father was distant in any case. He kept poor contact, calling infrequently, and was always at least two hours off the appointed time of his visits. She would sit looking out the window experiencing waves of mounting hysteria, not knowing if he would come at all. She needed him so and her mother did nothing to relieve her anxiety. Her mother's focus was on hating her ex-husband, not on comforting her child.

He had treated his daughter as one who counted for very little and her mother had seconded the motion. She obliged them both by feeling so. A worthless person does not give her own opinion much respect. She buried her anxieties about what her father might think if she did not come immediately. Her mother had often helped her to shirk responsibilities in the past.

The next evening, she entered her grandparents' apartment. She walked the long, dark hallway into the interior rooms. At the end of the corridor she saw her aunts and uncles sitting on packing crates. The mirrors were covered with cloth. She saw her father at the same time that he saw her. He walked toward her. Was it grief that was constricting his face? His expression seemed to hold something else, something vaguely ominous. He seemed angry. He steered her back down the hall to its darkest point, out of earshot of the relatives. What he had to say was private, between the two of them. As she walked she noticed the familiar old bronze vase atop the bookcase and the two charming Chinese painted lamps with streamers and dragons. Then she remembered her mother saying that after he moved out, her father had sneaked in and removed these objects from their home when no one was around. Her mind was empty, vague, and disquieted.

Her father was grasping her shoulder with his bony fingers, piercing her eyes with a pained and accusatory stare. He was speaking. ". . . you have betrayed me." The child attempted to pay closer attention to what he was saying. He was speaking about her not attending the funeral. She had committed a crime. She would not be allowed to blame her mother for staying away. That he held her responsible for being a poor grandchild, although he exaggerated and she had been abetted by her mother's resistance to her going and unwillingness to drive her there, also touched upon her readiness to feel guilty.

He spoke in conspiratorial tones. His voice was grieving yet angry. "Your grandmother always loved you." This must be part of her deficiency, since she was unable to feel that love. "Your not attending the funeral was . . ." He was searching for the perfect weapon. She felt the knife poised above her with the satisfaction of one about to be immolated. ". . . it showed that you really are . . . unable to love anyone." Satisfaction came from serving her constant role as victim, which met his need and hopefully made him happy.

The knife struck. She felt a fierce pain. Then went numb. The truth was out. Something inside of her gave way, the thin gray thread that bound her to other people. Her true self tumbled to the bottom of a deep well, leaving only a feeling of emptiness. Now she understood her father's endless attempts to correct her, her mother's rages and accusations. She had lost her shaky standing as a human being since the coin of love is the only real interchange between them. Love generates love and she was bankrupt.

From now on, she would shun close contact. She would stay deep inside herself, looking out at the world as if through a periscope. Where were her feelings? Gone. Her father had declared it so. Her self lay in shambles at the bottom of the sea. Hope for the future was eliminated. All the years of questioning and torture now made sense.

Years later, after many years of psychotherapy, she comes to a realization. Amid tears of joy she sees that she loves. She has always loved. Her father, confronted by his mother's deathbed, found himself unable to feel for the person who had been closest to him. How could he avoid accusing himself of heartlessness—unless he could put the fault onto a scapegoat. His daughter was to be sacrificed. He was safe.

The person who could not love was really he.

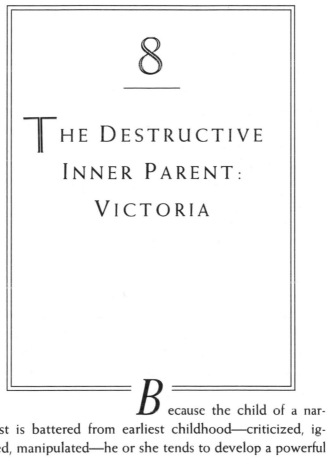

8

THE DESTRUCTIVE
INNER PARENT:
VICTORIA

*B*ecause the child of a nar-
cissist is battered from earliest childhood—criticized, ignored, manipulated—he or she tends to develop a powerful
negative introject, an inner representation of the rejecting
parent. The introject embodies the demands the child is
supposed to meet in order to gain parental approval. We
have seen strong examples of this negative introject in previous chapters, as when Anne could not drive her customers
to their destinations. The introject also embodies parental
rage at the child for failing to meet his standards, as when
John grew utterly depressed for not getting good grades.

Because the introject is so harsh, it can never be fully integrated into the personality as a normal conscience. It leads a person like John to make a suicidal gesture for doing poorly at school. The negative introject always feels like a foreign, attacking entity. Its cruelty comes from the unmitigated hostility of the parent as well as the anger of the child at his frustrations.

Internalized anger and harsh inner rules need to be softened and balanced by the experience of parental love. This is how one develops a reasonable conscience. But for the child of a narcissist, love is in short supply. Therefore, the negative introject remains destructive and takes up the parent's cause from inside the child, hating him and telling him not to do and be.

A person raised by nonnarcissistic parents also has internalized rules and consequences. He feels "signal anxiety" when contemplating an action that goes against his value system. If he transgresses, he may suffer a degree of guilt and even some mild depression. This self-imposed punishment keeps his behavior under the control of his system of morality.

Anxiety, guilt, and depression are kept within reasonable bounds since his conscience is modeled on his parents' reasonable attitudes. Normal parents basically accept their child even when he does wrong. They condemn the bad behavior without rejecting the child.

Conversely, the negative introject acts from within as a punishing enemy. It creates such severe anxiety that it paralyzes, produces such powerful guilt that the individual feels totally worthless. Depression, guilt, and inner conflict tear the person apart.

Since the desire to reform and control was an important motivation on the part of the narcissistic parent, this becomes part of the intentions of the negative introject. When a person suffering from a powerful negative introject falls in love, the loved one is reacted to as a part of the self. When we fall in love, there is a merging of ego boundaries and a sense of oneness. This brings into play the aggression of the introject, which starts criticizing and reforming the loved one, who now is subject to one's personal self-hatred. The sudden switch from total love and acceptance to hatred and rejection causes the loving persons to doubt their own sanity. They will painfully come to doubt their ability to love. Such is the story of Victoria.

Victoria is excited. A new day has begun and her changes are unmistakable. Arrogance is giving way to sympathy, irresponsibility to order. She is less selfish and greedy, more considerate. She is beginning to like herself. To herald these changes, she has developed a sexual relationship with a man. This is after a five-year hiatus of cloistered lesbianism. Lesbianism can be a healthy sexual choice or the result of self-deprivation. In Victoria's case, having had a mother who called her inadequate and kept her from her dad resulted in a lifelong inhibition of her heterosexual urges. Victoria fears that no man would want to be with her.

The previous six months had been full of agony as the probe of therapy opened the trapdoor to her obsessive self-loathing. She had been drowning in it, had undergone a major psychological house-cleaning, and now it was over. Relief seemed to be in sight. Seemed to be.

To top off the list of changes, she had begun to take care of her body, that aspect of herself that she had always treated as an unacceptable burden. Before, she had only abused it, would binge on sweets and ignore nourishing food, get fat and take diet pills to slim down, smoke cigarettes, drink alcohol, and trip on psychedelics.

If she exercised at all, it was because she was forced to. She hated being confronted by her image in the mirror, seeing all that jiggling flesh. Suddenly, when the self-hatred abated, she discovered her body. She was like a baby exploring its toes. She entered into her body and moved it around. She liked breathing hard after exercising, feeling the ground solid beneath her feet. She liked to stretch and pull her muscles and was beginning to feel alive all over. She started having orgasms during sex. Her orgasms were not as good as other women's, of this she was sure. But they were orgasms.

All was going rather well until the arrival of Kali, which is what she named the feeling of driven hatred for weakness in others, especially in those she was close to. She didn't only hate their weaknesses, she hated them for having it.

Kali is the Hindu deity of world destruction. She is a terrifying vision with a blackened face and a necklace of skulls draped around her neck. Half-devoured human bodies fall from her mouth. Kali is not a pleasurable identification.

Victoria felt that her own self was lost, buried in the goddess and carried along by her wrath. Her Kali-self attacked people she cared for, wounding them over and over. She hated herself for harming but was drawn with the same addictive power that she felt toward all destructive passions in her life. Once in the vortex of rage, she had to explode.

Her words were meant to expose faults. They were uttered with utmost scorn. She unleashed lethal words. She demanded that her target change his or her behavior on the spot to become more effective. She rationalized that she was a surgeon cutting out rotting flesh, only the surgery was not elective.

Most of all, she hated her boyfriend for his weakness. It is no accident that she had chosen a man who could not fight back, since that was the trait she despised the most. After knowing him about half a year, they decided to take an extremely exotic trip. This destination represented the need of both to get away from ordinary life. Victoria especially sought freedom from her narcissistic mother's control by delving into the esoteric. The hope that one can leave behind what one carries within one's mind is usually quickly dispelled.

Her Kali-self was a constant during their long vacation. In Bangkok, her boyfriend insisted that they stay in a hotel described in his travel guide. He liked to be guided by authority. The hotel turned out to be inadequate, perched on a noisy intersection where the beeping of taxi horns and ringing of bicycle bells was deafening. Standing in the center of their room, they had to yell to be heard over the roar of the traffic.

Victoria didn't want to stay. Her boyfriend did. He always resisted change since the known was less frightening than the unknown. She spoke to him scornfully. "Look at what you've chosen. This place stinks. Only an idiot would put up with it. I'm leaving and if you don't come, I'll go without you." She rose. He got up, silently trudging beside her. As they walked the unfamiliar streets she continued her attack. She hated him because he so clearly manifested her own fears. He was supposed to be the strong one, but he wasn't.

She got him to ask directions of a passerby who knew some English. Almost immediately he got confused over what he had heard. Victoria called him stupid. After stammering out his befuddled directions, he fell back into sullen silence. She knew that she was turning him into a helpless baby. He never fought her directly but withdrew. Her mood of despair deepened when he insisted on having lunch in the same restaurant they had gone to for breakfast. Why was she with such a ninny? She wanted to claw his bland face. She resorted to ripping words instead.

He did not make love to her that night. He had not made love to her for weeks. He went to bed early. She sat on the bed berating him for his low energy level, which made it necessary to get ten hours of sleep. The more she nagged, the sleepier he got, sinking away from her into oblivion. Once he was asleep, she felt abandoned and was conscience-stricken once more.

She became cold with fear. Wouldn't he eventually leave her, the only man who had ever offered a commitment? His leaving seemed as intolerable as his staying. She hated his submissiveness.

He demonstrated the same low energy, slinking away from conflict, that she had once manifested in her own family, a hive of manic aggression. Then she had been the one who passively succumbed. It was her mother who reviled her for being a shy introvert.

Her mother was the classic narcissist. She had what it takes to be the center of attention: an extremely beautiful face with porcelain skin, blond hair, a fine figure, brains, ambition, and extreme feistiness. Despite the above, she was unbelievably insecure.

Like many insecure people, she was grandiose. She needed to be worshiped as a supreme being. Victoria and the rest of the family, her sister and father, deferred. The main focus was her mother's looks. Victoria still believes that her seventy-year-old mother is more beautiful than she.

Her father's role was to run interference for his wife, to see that her glory was properly heralded. He was her exclusive possession. His eyes and words were for her alone. He would tell his daughters, "Girls, your mother is a knockout, the greatest, a killer, the best-looking at the pool, etc." Looks were the most important thing in the world. But what about his daughters? Didn't they have looks too? They were not about to hear about it from him.

Victoria worshipped her mother, who "got it all," but held on to the secret, disloyal wish that her father would beam a few words of praise her way. Her mother's unwritten law determined that he was to make no contact with this daughter. Victoria and her father were to be the mother's slaves and to relate only through her. As a result, Victoria did not sufficiently develop her heterosexual identity. In our culture, the father defines the female role. It is through her interaction with him that the child learns how to be a woman. But Victoria was allowed to relate only to her mother, who continually attempted to renovate her into an acceptable state. As her mother's possession, she was not to have the pleasure of men. This is one foundation of lesbianism. Being raised by an emotionally withholding mother who turned her from men also led her to seek the love of women.

Her mother had been raised by a destructive mother, a paranoid who hated and rejected this child. Victoria's mother had to deal with intense self-hatred. Instead of openly questioning her own worth she unconsciously placed her feelings of inadequacy onto the one nearest, her daughter. From the safety of her remove, she could hate and reject Victoria's faults without ever recognizing that she herself was the subject. Victoria had been raised to believe that she merited her mother's scorn. She saw herself as disgusting, "more a toad than a woman."

She surrendered to her mother, the "all-knowing one." She swallowed the pain of personal attack and palliated her misery also by oral means, bingeing herself senseless. In grade school, she was already "a little fat girl." She felt as she looked, awkward, incompetent, and hopeless. The appetites of her body were out of control. As her physical appearance changed, she grew frightened. She no longer recognized herself. Could those be her thighs? Was she inside that increasing mound of blubber? When the body loses its natural shape, the mind also grows distorted since body image and intactness of mind are intimately connected.

Amidst the fusillade of her mother's attacks, she began to hear the distant babble of hallucinated voices, like the sound of a radio when the pointer is between stations. That terrified her. She was saved from a full descent into madness by her older sister's uncharacteristic willingness to listen to her problem, reassuring her that she was not alone. Her sister and she were usually isolated from one another. Victoria was her mother's emotional property and her sister was her dad's. It was rare that Victoria could share what she was feeling with another being. Instead of communication, there was only the terrible force of her mother's verbalized hatred presented under the guise of love. There was not one thing in her life that Victoria could hold on to, not one thing about herself that was worthy of respect.

Food became the center of her existence. Food represented love. The availability of food meant security. She spent her entire allowance on candy bars and crammed them into her mouth, six at a time. She made midnight raids on the refrigerator to wolf down ice cream out of the plenteous supply that was always to be found.

There is a double message to a child who is a compulsive eater when the family keeps ice cream and other high-calorie foods on hand. Double messages were the rule here. Victoria's mother would tell her, "You must diet. I want you slim," and then provide the fattening foods her daughter found irresistible. The covert message, of course, was that Victoria should eat, that fatness was acceptable, even desirable. But why would her mother want to do this to her? The answer was obvious. Victoria was turning into a beauty. Her mother could not accept a rival.

Like the Wicked Witch in Snow White, she needed to hear her mirror say, "You are the fairest of them all." Along with the intention of improving Victoria's appearance, which represented a projection of her own fear of ugliness, there was also the opposite need, to maim and undermine her rival. Her improvement campaign drove Victoria into the shadows. Victoria had intimations of her own beauty but also believed the opposite about herself. She accepted the destruction of her looks as the vehicle to her mother's acceptance.

Let us follow the history of Victoria's mane of blond hair, her glory. It was so long she could sit on it. Everyone admired this hair, her most beautiful feature. Her classmates regarded it as a communal treasure. She felt that the color and length of her hair gave her value. In a family that worshiped looks, her hair was her most important feature.

She was an undisciplined child, a chatterbox whose main comfort in life was talking to her friends. She repeatedly got low grades in conduct. When she was in about the fourth grade, her mother decided to make a federal case of it, and threatened to cut off the hair unless her conduct mark improved. Victoria was panicked and told her classmates, who shared her fear and banded together to write a communal letter begging her mother to spare the hair. Even her teacher got involved, not wanting to be the lead agent of a massacre. He upped her grade in conduct.

Presumably the grade was not good enough, or perhaps her mother was already set on the punishment for other ancient crimes, for the hair did come off. Her mother wielded the scissors, snipping until the uneven strands were shoulder length. It no longer fell beneath Victoria's waist, no longer rested beneath her buttocks when she sat. She felt very diminished and depressed. She believed that she had somehow deserved the punishment.

A second assault was made on her glorious blond hair like a halo around her face (it was glorious again since hair will grow back) when she was about fourteen. Her parents had gone out. A self-conscious and overweight Victoria had sauntered into the kitchen to make herself a sandwich when a group of boys from her class happened to pass by. They looked in the window, catching her in the act of eating. Because of her weight problem this so embarrassed her that she covered up by acting sophisticated, and invited them in. Usually, she was not so accessible.

The boys had made themselves at home in her living room when her parents drove up. They were astonished to see male heads go sailing by the window in the usual hyperactive way of adolescents and jumped to the incredible conclusion that their reclusive daughter was in the midst of an orgy. They resolved to catch her in the act. Their latent violence was ready.

Her mother took the front door and her father the back. At a given moment, they exploded into the house. The boys scattered and escaped but Victoria was their actual prey. They pursued her into the kitchen as she fled before them.

Not a single question was asked. She was thrown to the floor. They shoved and kicked her until her mother spotted the kitchen shears hanging on a hook. Instantly the blond hair came off in ragged hanks.

Later Victoria contemplated her mangled head in the mirror. Her once beautiful hair stuck out at odd angles. Her usual sense of having something special about her appearance was gone. She had already forgotten their absurd accusations of illicit sex and connected the incident with her sin of eating a sandwich. At least that made some kind of sense. She had broken her diet, hadn't she? Victoria attempted to find order and justice in her parents' actions. She didn't want to think that she was living with irrational tyrants. That would be too much to assimilate. She withdrew further.

Victoria tells one final hair story. She was about to leave for college and felt extremely insecure about her appearance, although she had managed to diet down a bit. Her mother came up with a new suggestion for improvement that involved reshaping her hairline. She was to shave her forehead to create a widow's peak instead of her own natural hairline. So she shaved her forehead, convinced that she was ugly without heavy makeup and all the subterfuge of illusion. Acceptance depended on this elusive beauty. She was living her life on thin ice.

Now let us look at the other depredations orchestrated by a narcissistic mother on her daughter's body. Preoccupied with Victoria's weight, she mocked the girl's overeating and despaired of her ever being slim. While harping on her diet and on self-control, she bought an abundance of extra-large and shapeless clothing for her and stuffed the refrigerator with high-calorie desserts, which were forbidden to her child. Such behavior belied her stated desire that Victoria be slim and seemed to endorse obesity. Victoria accepted her mother's verdict that she could not master her problem.

At puberty, her body ballooned out, sprouting breasts that were rapidly becoming huge. Her mother stuffed those breasts into long-line bras that were boned to the hips. Rather than disguising their size, the bras made her breasts stand out like battleships. Her protruding belly was constricted by a rubber girdle with holes in it that tortured her flesh by creating rubs and puckers and leaving her stomach dotted with small red marks that faded after a few hours without the girdle. She concealed her breasts and belly beneath a billowing man's shirt or walked around in a long coat regardless of the season. Boys had begun to show an interest in her breasts and this rather frightened her. Nothing in the way her father had treated her as a child had prepared her for the sexual desire of men.

By then her mother, who was a nurse, had introduced her to diet pills to help her control her eating. With the pills came the implicit message, "You are weak and will have to depend on outside agents to keep yourself in line." The stage was set for further addictions, the first, of course, being diet pills. In time were added alcohol, sugar, tobacco, and diet shots. Victoria was to be a person propped up from the outside, always seeking a new crutch to lean on to help her to control her unruly self.

In junior high school and before any of the other girls, her mother introduced her to makeup in order to correct her "fish eyes," till then a deformity of which she had been unaware. Her mother said Victoria had fish eyes because her lashes were too light. Now she felt even more like a freak, first because of her fish eyes, which needed correcting, and second because she was the only girl in her class in makeup. All she really wanted was to fit in with the rest of the kids.

Her mother encouraged her to enter summer stock as she had done in her youth. Her mother's many instructions were directed at helping her daughter create a dramatic mask to hide behind. Victoria was being induced to develop the defenses and attitudes of narcissism. Off she went to summer stock in her heavy makeup and men's shirts. Theater helped her develop the art of seduction. She used her manner and appearance to gain the interest of men but quickly discarded anyone who tried to get too close.

She developed a crush on a pathetic bearded alcoholic in the company. He represented Victoria's discarded self. They drank together and kept their masks in place. She acquired beautiful diction, a clipped, stage English, and the same imperious manner she had always admired in her mother. If anyone had asked her how she actually looked and came across, she wouldn't have had the foggiest notion. She was all affectation and no substance. Her true self was in hiding.

Her mother engineered one final and major attack upon her body, the most devastating and irreparable of all. Victoria had returned home from her first semester at college. She had been very erratic, strung out on amphetamines and unable to concentrate. Overeating had been the only means of bringing herself down. She would steal other girls' diet pills and add them to her store. Hoarding them increased the magical power that kept her from coming apart.

When she came home for school break, the young woman was huge, monstrous and passive as a stone. She refused to leave the house and chance being seen by someone she knew.

Her mother had a brainstorm. As usual, her method of helping focused on appearance. Why did she continue to think that direct work on appearance was the answer to psychological problems when such solutions had never helped before? Narcissists do not ask such questions. They are like the surgeon who announces, "The operation was a success but the patient died." Lack of humility is the mark of a shaky ego. It leads to the inability to learn from mistakes. One must go on doing the same things as proof of one's infallibility. In addition, the mother was still projecting her own ugliness onto her daughter and felt compelled to ameliorate it.

This time she focused on her daughter's breasts. They were too large and in need of "remediation." A breast operation would change those "cowlike udders" into "nice, high, girlish breasts." Fat was to be sucked out of each breast from the bottom. Victoria went along passively, as usual.

She emerged from the operation with two ugly scars, like the toothless grins of old men. That is how she presented their image to me although I have never seen them. She said that a lover later reacted with concern, which confirmed the worst of her fears. She was deformed. Her scars would be in her mind any time she had to disrobe to make love with a man. Wouldn't his face fall in disappointment when he saw? By virtue of distraction, the tire of fat she put on around her middle actually helped disguise the scars.

Despite her powerful self-hatred, she managed to graduate from college and then from graduate school. She became a social worker who was a psychotherapist. Many children of narcissists go into the psychological helping professions, being well schooled to be sensitive to the needs of others. She was neither a success nor a failure at her work. Believing herself a failure, she would never stick long enough at practice-building to get anywhere. She read signs of her inadequacy in the usual difficulties of getting started.

Programmed to be an underachiever by her mother, she took far too many breaks to establish patient trust. She was sabotaging herself and rationalized it by saying, "I just had to get away. I am too sensitive to the noise and ugliness of the city." Each time she returned from a lengthy trip, a significant number of patients would have left. Unconsciously, she was still clinging to her mother by having an unsuccessful professional life.

Still, Victoria never stopped studying and learning, partly out of an exaggerated insecurity fostered by her mother. She was always broadening her understanding of psychotherapy. She would call her mother for a booster shot of self-doubt, describing her latest project or course of study. Her mother would respond with predictable scorn, saying, "Why would you want to study a peculiar thing like that?" Or she would plant the seed of doubt by asking, "Do you really think you can do it?" She reminded Victoria of her rightful place in life, somewhere beneath her mother in all things.

Though her lifestyle was nominally hedonistic, Victoria was fulfilling her narcissistic mother's edicts. She neglected and undermined her profession, health, appearance, and desire for a male lover. Everything constructive was avoided. All that remained were the secretly addictive and destructive pleasures condoned by her mother. She still had the glamour of marvelous red hair and blue eyes, an elegant face, and theatrical expression. Beneath her glamorous facade, Victoria felt despair.

Let us fast-forward through the years. A first therapist who limited Victoria by accepting her as the lesbian that she didn't want to be was replaced by a second who saw other options. Thus far, Victoria has not been very happy with either women or men as lovers. She has always played the Kali game against them and hated herself as a result. A person who hates herself cannot much love her partner. Sexual pleasure has been limited with partners of either sex. The man is never considered strong enough or thought to have an adequate penis. The female lover is thought devoid of the necessary organ and pleasure with her deemed unimportant. Sexual confusion reigns.

Is it only Victoria's self-evaluation that says any orgasm she has is not good enough or is she truly holding back? Victoria has sex with her boyfriend, a man who, like her father, accepts peace at any price. She reviles him and hates herself for persecuting him. She is in her mother's role, acting toward him as her mother did toward her father, as her sister did to her boyfriend. She is acting as she vowed she never would.

She wants the impossible, that her submissive boyfriend will stop her. She wants him to release her from the maternal introject (inner parent) of her Kali rage. She wants to set free the man in her female-dominated father. She wants to be a woman who can be sexually close to and satisfied by a man.

Homosexuality can be a neurotic sexual choice but it doesn't have to be. Victoria's sexual orientation is ambivalent and unclear. Raised to be her mother's possession, she accepted not being with men. Now she fears the rejection by men because she feels inadequate. Although attracted to men, she is separated from them by scornful arrogance, the concealing mask she copied from her mother.

She believes that she has never had a satisfactory orgasm with either a man or a woman. However, it is hard for a person with a poor self-image to assess her own experience. She desires to be sexual with men. Motivation has a lot to do with what we become. If Victoria can undo her conflicts over sexual pleasure and her fear of a man touching her, she may come to enjoy a sexual relationship with men.

With her current boyfriend, at times she attains a measure of objectivity and knows that her behavior is unjustified. Often she is overwhelmed by the urge to criticize and she feels no mercy for her victim. After her Kali fit is over, she feels horribly guilty and ashamed.

To free herself, Victoria needs to know in her guts, not merely in her head, that what she hates in others is the weakness she finds in herself. The desire to hurt the weak directly expresses her identification with her mother, who attacked her for weakness. If her boyfriend is timid, so was she. If she hates him for spending too much time in the bathroom, so did she. Her parents hated her for being a bed-wetter and a pants-wetter. (They had traumatized her by starting toilet training far too early.)

What she does to others is a replay of what was done to her. Her boyfriend is a mirror for her weak and despised inner child, closely connected with her true self. If she can find compassion for her own weakness and timidity, she will become kinder to him and her true self will begin once more to grow. Kali-hatred cannot exist with compassion.

Finally, when her mother criticizes and corrects her, she does not have to accept the assignment. She can give up courting her mother's love by being the repository of her mother's hatred.

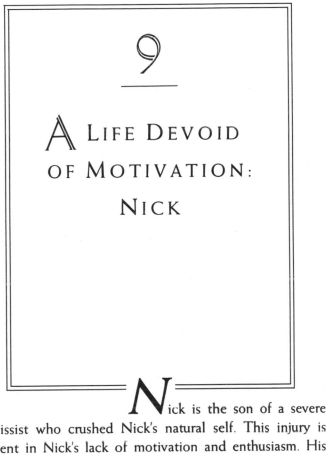

9

A LIFE DEVOID OF MOTIVATION: NICK

Nick is the son of a severe narcissist who crushed Nick's natural self. This injury is evident in Nick's lack of motivation and enthusiasm. His story shows how his father progressively demoralized him and created emotional paralysis. Nick thinks himself unworthy of anything positive. Due to the process of identification with the aggressor, Nick continues to treat himself and others in an abusive way. He continues to exist on the slave level where his father originally placed him.

He is terrified by the extreme destructiveness of his negative inner parent (negative introject) and lives his life partly in bed like a little baby to protect himself and the world from its aggression. He fears that he will be murdered from within if he becomes autonomous and starts living. The model for this murderous introject was his father, himself full of rage. He may actually have sexually assaulted Nick as a very young child, although Nick's memories of the possible event are represented only symbolically by his dreams.

Nick's resentment at having been subjected to his narcissistic father's will is expressed indirectly. He does not even know that it is anger that directs him to the path of negativity. He destroys his career, leaving his father nothing to boast about; he avoids social activities so that his father will be deprived of grandchildren. His lack of funds creates indebtedness, which shows his power over other people, etc. He is ignorant of the rebellious nature of his passivity and so is unable to change it. Nick thinks only that he (Nick) "doesn't care." He needs to develop the ego strength that will allow him to say no directly to the external parent who still attempts to direct him, but most of all to the threatening and punishing inner parent (the negative introject) that would crush him. He needs to declare, "Even if you don't approve, it's my life now."

Nick told me of a dream. He is standing on a rock surrounded by a dark and angry sea. Waves lap at his ankles. He is alone.

In another dream, he is standing on a dilapidated dock surrounded by rotting piers, abandoned boats, and the stumps of fallen-down jetties. He feels like a hobo, at one with the flotsam and jetsam of the sea. He has nowhere to go.

Nick's father has also contributed a dream. In it he was conscripted into military service but didn't want to go because the job could be dangerous and unpleasant. He thought, "I shall send Nick instead." This appears to be a good solution. Nick is expendable while he, the father, is not.

Nick's waking life also has the quality of a dream. He is somewhat detached from reality. Often he does not work but lies in bed watching TV, getting up only to go into the kitchen to make a pot of spaghetti, which is then eaten with the requisite quarter stick of butter. Nick rarely eats anything else. He is overweight.

Nick turns away from commonplace necessities, laughs off monetary problems, and borrows money from his friends. He often forgets to return the money but is so generous with his time and energy that his friends let the debts slide. Nick postpones and delays all decisions. He is procrastinating his way through life. He has no sexual or love relationship and has not had either for a long time. A relationship would take too much effort. Too much would be expected of him.

He leads a life devoid of options. He can see things happening only one way. There are overtones of fatalism and defeat. As long as Nick can lie snuggled in his bed, he is safe. He has the rosy cheeks and wide-open eyes of an infant, one without a care in the world. Nick has never grown up, although he is approaching forty. Adulthood could be too dangerous. He is the irresponsible child who has let the bills accumulate and binges on ice cream and spaghetti drenched in butter. Fortunately, he is a talented architect and when work comes to him— he never looks for it—he will do a fine job. He is not a self-starter, but once the engine is turned on, he can work. He learned to be a compulsive and meticulous worker from his father, who demanded that he give his all. First he repaired his father's boat and car and then began to think about design.

But Nick derives no pleasure from his work nor from life itself. Architecture is what he is doing until he figures out what he "wants to do" with his life. Other people might be overjoyed to have such a skill, but Nick is fully capable of wasting it. He says that talent is not compulsion. "Why should I be compelled to do something that I don't enjoy just because I'm good at it?" Nick's life indicates that he is not committed to anything.

The only thing that Nick respects is friendship. He is a true friend to other people, although not to himself. He will paint his friends' apartments, schlepp their furniture, even offer free architectural advice since "it's not worth anything anyway." He also listens freely to problems and offers sound advice. He gives away much of his time and energy, and when he works he undercharges. He gives little to himself in the way of pleasure, except food. He stymies all his own wishes. If anything interesting is happening in the world outside, something that appeals to his friends, he generally walks away from it.

Nick has always walked out on life. This started in kindergarten when he strolled away from class because "it didn't interest me." Years later, he walked out of his architecture class in the middle of his final year, thereby managing not to get a degree. An architect can function without a degree. People learn of Nick's ability and call on him to work for them. But being without a degree or license has left him handicapped, since others have to sign his work. He is eligible for the licensing exam since architecture is a field where experience can be substituted for classwork. But Nick does not take the exam. He rationalizes self-castration by saying, "The exam and degree are not important," and "I don't know what I want to do," and "I don't care." His most characteristic comment is, "I think I'll stay put." This is given in response to any suggestion that he shift gears, whether to have fun, expand his talent, meet new people, or leave the shelter of his home.

How was such a talented and compassionate man turned into a limpet, a person leading a life without meaning? Let us begin with his father, the narcissist. Nick's father was a self-centered tyrant raised by distant relatives who had no affection for him. Eventually, he became a sea captain, which suited his defensive needs perfectly. A captain can indulge his need for sadistic dominance with lucrative returns while serving a socially useful purpose. Every narcissist was once a rejected child. It was too dangerous for Nick's father to let people become necessary to him in a personal way.

He re-created the same structure within his family as on board his ship. The family were his crew, slaves who jumped to fulfill his whims and endeavored to meet his perfectionistic standards lest they be subjected to his cutting attacks. Nick's father frequently lashed out in verbal rage over trivia. He was obsessed with cleanliness and would pounce on such crimes as a footprint on the deck of his pleasure boat or an object not returned to its proper place. He had something critical to say about most everything. He liked to mock people and would tease his son about his baby fat or the way he walked. Nick was under constant scrutiny and became unbearably self-conscious.

His father attacked Nick's ego. He especially liked to pull practical jokes to humiliate his son.

Nick was about eight years old and attending a private elementary school. On this particular day, he was serving detention as he had done on so many other occasions because he had not done his homework. The other children were out playing in the yard during a free period when his father happened to pass by. Seeing that Nick was not among them, he made inquiries as to what had happened.

That evening there was company. Nick's father started to quiz him in front of the guests, who were a good audience. They were laughing at his father's jokes and not showing a smidgen of feeling for Nick's situation. Such folk are often the friends of narcissists and are sometimes narcissists themselves or children of narcissists, trying to win the narcissist's affection. Nick did not know that he was being set up. He did not think much about his situation. It was too painful. He lived his life in an emotional fog.

"How did school go today?" his father asked. "Fine," Nick answered and he was not even lying. Detention was an unremarkable event. "Did anything happen to you?" "No." And so it went until the story of Nick's detention was drawn out of him, at which point the entire company, led by his father, laughed uproariously. Nick squirmed in humiliation.

A second memory of the progressive extinguishing of his self occurred when Nick's father forced him to betray his feelings. Nick was crying because his father had hit him for doing something wrong. What it was he cannot remember. He was about five years old. His father did not like the sound of Nick's weeping. It might have made him feel guilty over abusing the child. On a deeper level, it probably stirred up a memory of his own hated, abused, and rejected inner child, the weak part of himself that he despised. He needed to cancel out any reminder of that vulnerable part, to attack it sadistically as he, the child, was once perhaps attacked by his foster parents.

He glared at his son and said, "Nick, I want you to stop crying immediately." Nick felt confused. His father's expression was mean. He wanted to please his father to gain his love. His father said, "Nick, I want you to laugh, right now." Nick's inner world spun with the abruptness of the transition. He laughed. He surrendered his sense of self in order to win approval and with that surrender he turned to stone. He felt nothing. He was only going through the motions of human interaction. Some vital inner connection had been broken. It went on like this for an endless series of surrenders. This particular event stands out in Nick's memory because it symbolizes a high degree of self-rejection as well as having been an emotional trauma.

In a final memory, Nick's father's ship had returned to the States after a year in Japan. Nick was standing on the dock eagerly awaiting his father's appearance. At the age of nine, he was excited and filled with expectation. Every little boy loves and needs his father no matter how he has been treated. Nick jumped up and down scanning the people on the deck.

Suddenly he saw his father walking down the gangplank and rushed forward, arms outstretched. When Nick reached his father he was pushed away. His father would not embrace him. It is possible that the man felt shy about showing emotion in front of his crew, but later, in the privacy of their home, he still did not put his arms around his son. Nick felt annihilated. He said, "I felt as if I didn't count. I was a nothing."

What sustains all people is the belief that they are lovable and that they will be loved. If your parent cannot love you, then who will? Nick's father had extinguished that hope.

The child does not blame his parent for not loving him. He cannot let himself see that his parent may lack the ability to love because then he would have nothing to live for. It would destroy hope for the future. Instead, he believes that the fault lies within himself and can still be corrected. Yet in accepting that he is responsible for his parents' rejection of him, he is so devalued that his self is destroyed. If the child is treated as nothing, he must be nothing.

One irony of Nick's situation is that he acquired so many of his father's narcissistic traits. Nick's mixture of attitudes is found in many children of narcissists. He can be submissive, rebellious, or controlling. He fluctuates between his parents' roles: his submissive and victimized mother, his critical and domineering father. These roles coexist with his compassion for people. Neither parent role is acceptable. He victimizes himself by suppressing all activity. He is a crushing tyrant who will not allow his life to progress, cannot have a lover or a wife, cannot enjoy his work, will not seek out adventure. He is unable to shed his baby fat and wallows in self-imposed misery.

He victimizes others by imposing his views upon them. Like his father, he criticizes, demands, and gives unsolicited advice. His friends try to make him understand how he sounds but he cannot hear them. The identification is still too powerful. So they put up with his miserable intrusiveness because they love the generous, compassionate, and self-sacrificing Nick who is one of the last of the really true friends.

Don't overlook that he is doing this to himself and deriving unconscious pleasure from his actions. Behaving sadistically toward himself re-creates the bond with his narcissistic father. Letting go of the sadomasochistic option would mean releasing his father's hand.

All this is being challenged in therapy. Nick is making slow progress, fanning the spark of his original self. He takes two steps forward and one back, punishing himself for every step toward autonomy with depression and despair, since growth represents disloyalty to his hated and loved father. He speaks as if he hates his father, and in many ways he does. Nevertheless, a childish wish for parental love keeps Nick emotionally attached. In therapy Nick feels that he is making no progress at all, but this is not true. It is only that life is going by at such a great pace and his steps are so very small. Still, his overall apathy and numbness have been converted into a recognizable depression. He knows that he lacks and that he needs. The depression will lift when he begins to try to meet these needs.

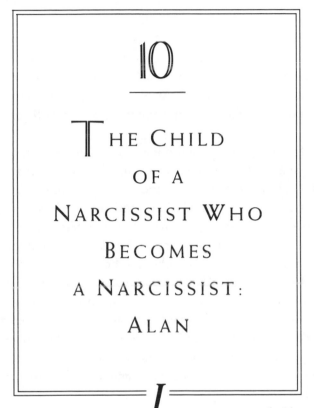

10

THE CHILD
OF A
NARCISSIST WHO
BECOMES
A NARCISSIST:
ALAN

*I*n my meeting with Alan, our narcissistic problems interacted. A child of a narcissist is frequently wed to the notion that he or she must be right and the other wrong. That is how his parents acted, often putting him down and disregarding him. To the extent that he becomes fully narcissistic, he resembles them and they adulate his show of superiority. Fearing their interference, he develops the same defenses as they have, which include being unable to accept views that differ from his own. If someone does not readily defer to him, the child of a narcissist can get quite hot under the collar. When his viewpoint is challenged, it is an enormous blow and insult to his ego.

If, like Alan, he is very intelligent and well read, he buttresses what he says with scholarly references, appearing to be in the know. He has differing views and acts "right" to the other's "wrong." Here it concerned being the child of narcissistic parents, a topic to which this interviewer has given considerable thought. As the child of a narcissist, I am easily raised to ire by contact with a person who acts my superior and will not listen. Alan's treatment plummeted me back into my submissive and inferior position with my father.

This struggle, his and mine, was a combination of arrogance and hurt feelings. Each wanted to be heard and to be thought correct by the other. I was impressed by his endless references and allusions, perhaps overly so since I was raised to worship "gray matter." I am interested in hearing contradictory views as long as the other person does not disregard what I think. Alan chose to be the center of sound, an outpouring of words that brooked no interruption. But I did not want to defer to his need to be boss. I was upset by his attitude of self-important arrogance, having been too often undercut intellectually as a child to be able to observe what he did from a point of neutrality. He clung to his image of superior understanding and I demanded parity. The war was on.

Children of narcissists pick up their share of arrogance. We may not be fully narcissistic or we may. It is to our benefit to track down our narcissism and get rid of it. Without narcissism, we can be closer to other people, learn more, and suffer less.

I arrived for the interview in an artificially buoyed-up mood. My fear argued with the positive experiences I had been having with all the other participants. I clung to the shaky assumption that everything would go fine despite a plethora of evidence to the contrary.

I had known Alan casually for a couple of years and emerged from most of our conversations feeling intellectually inadequate. He induced this with a constant string of scholarly references followed by the question, "Have you read . . . ?" which I hadn't.

Then he would go on and lose me. What was he talking about? His thinking was crammed with information tangential to the point, philosophical and literary asides, name-dropping of specialized social movements. He was a master of quantity and speed. He talked me deaf and dumb, filling the silent spaces I needed to breathe or think. The distribution of talking and listening time was totally inequitable.

He would use the few points I feebly managed to splutter out as a jumping-off point for an ever greater torrent of words. He used words and ideas to hide himself. He would dominate our conversation with his own flow of speech. Quantity, obscurity, tangential thinking, interpolated subthemes, any and every trick to confuse and lose the listener. He didn't want you to get too near him and didn't want to be understood.

This was the man I was coming to interview, hoping by dint of my office as interviewer to maintain control over the situation. Little wonder I felt a degree of trepidation.

Nevertheless, it was not my first interview and I had an idea of what I needed to know, having already found amazingly repetitive patterns in many children of narcissists. These patterns included such problems as paralyzing self-doubt, confusion about one's identity and goals, and oversensitivity to the opinions of others. Most of the participants in the study felt they gained insight from our talking together.

When I came in, Alan and I embraced as near-friends. I was introduced to the baby-sitter, who was about to take his little boy out for the afternoon. The child had large dark eyes and a gentle manner. Noticing my amber necklace, he said, "Mommy has one just like it." Very observant child.

After a brief house tour, Alan invited me to have a bite to eat with him and we peered into an almost empty refrigerator. There was hardly anything to eat, in the interest of controlling his tendency to binge. I found a cold baked potato in tinfoil and he had something congealing unattractively on a plate. With the crumbs and remnants of our im-

poverished lunch before us, we sat down to discuss the topic of narcissism.

But first, he wanted to say something about his son. He spoke in
hushed tones of reverence. "He is extremely bright." Immediately, I felt
a wave of depression. He repeated this several times, giving various
examples of his child's brightness, including fathoming events that he
and his wife were trying to keep hidden. Or at least he thought the
child had. This measure of intelligence was tested by using an indirect
method of questioning, to be met by the child's indirect method of
response. The level of his child's understanding was assessed through
inference. I wondered if the father's interest was in whether they had
protected the child from hurtful information or, more important to
them, whether their child was smart enough to figure it out.

It was not the child's brightness that depressed me. It was Dad's
obsession with it. How he needed his child to be brilliant. I knew this
"intelligence sickness" from my own childhood. In the blindness of
repetition, Alan seemed unaware of spreading the contagion and later
asserted that he had freed himself of his parents' demands to be their
genius. Now, it would appear, the demands came from within and
caused him to lower his child into the same quicksand.

My depression was talking to Alan in my head. It screamed things
like: "Don't pass on the tortured suffering; leave off with expectations
and evaluations. Set no conditions for acceptance and don't hold your
breath every time he opens his mouth, hoping that what emerges will
be exceptional and fearing that it will be ordinary. He senses what you
are feeling. Even the adorable smile on his face may be an attempt to
please." Of course, I said nothing.

I said nothing because I wanted Alan to present himself in a
natural way; I didn't want to undermine the interview before its com-
pletion. There was already sufficient trouble between us. I probably
said little or nothing because he overwhelmed me with his narcissistic
guise of superiority, so similar to that of my father. I knew that if I
commented about his narcissistic treatment of his child it would hurt
him but not get through his blind spot and defenses.

The psychological blind spot is interesting territory. If the blind
spot is yours, you cannot see through it and you cannot see it. You can
deduce your own blind spots through indirect evidence but you have

to be motivated to look for them. Since his disease tells the narcissist that he is perfect, his blind spot is the largest of all.

Alan spoke of his child's artistic talent and how he would draw for hours. I felt his child being weighed for units of specialness. Later, speaking of his own childhood, he said that he was the family artist and "genius" who also "spontaneously" drew for long periods. His parents *kvelled* (Yiddish for burst with pride) and displayed his work. Alan now knows that his narcissistic father needed him to replace the father's dead brother, a man whose paintings covered the walls of Alan's childhood home. It was only later in the interview that I heard Alan's resentment at being used to replace a dead family member. Before he expressed his feelings about being used, Alan had to maintain his assigned role as stand-in artist/genius. Rembrandt was his chosen hero. Alan imagined his own greatness taking a similar vein.

Alan gave further background. His parents came from Europe as "greenhorns." His father needed to resurrect through unconscious implantation the identities of two of his brothers and Alan was the chosen recipient. The first was an artist and the second a man who suffered a great deal and died young. Alan was to develop a talent for suffering.

I know the personal truth of this. Alan is the kind of person you never want to greet with the customary "How are you?" since Alan will tell you. He cannot resist the opportunity to cry on your shoulder, which would be less annoying if he gave equal time to your problems. But then most people would rarely want to speak that long. Alan will hear them out, give a considered response, and then it is his turn.

His ability to resonate with, step up to, and feel universal pain is a benefit he uses in his craft (he is an artist and writer), depicting the terrors and sufferings of other people. He does this in visual art and words. His writing arouses one to tears for world tragedy. He has taken the voices of minorities who never knew they had a history and brought them into our awareness. He has presented the experience of the war-torn. But in his personal life, intense self-involvement undercuts his sensitivity to others. He demands sympathy and interest without awareness of the other's unstated response to him. He wants to see sympathy for him in your eyes and tends not to notice your boredom, exhaustion, desire to speak, your resentment at being turned solely into a listener. His demandingness may allow the unconscious release of hostility stored when his father treated him the same way and made him into an unwilling audience.

By choosing "morally correct" topics to speak about, he can be a wolf in sheep's clothing. "Morally correct" topics show him to be a humanist and sympathizer with the underdog. Alan actually feels this way but the way he speaks also carries the implicit message: I will suffer and you must support my personal value by listening. He runs with the ball of compassion, demanding indulgence to prove what a great person he is for feeling so much.

I returned from such musings to the interview and started to pose a question. Alan cut me off. He had already prepared some material showing his views of narcissism and of his narcissistic parents. He is prone to cutting off the speaker.

He started by telling a dream. I will give it here in an uninterrupted rendition, although the telling was broken up by innumerable digressions, and very nearly did not get told at all by dint of our growing and unmanageable argument over the way he spoke. He was drawing me along confusedly in his wake.

"I was standing in a crowded public square in an Italian town and spotted my mother in the distance. I turned my back and ascended a few steps so that I could get a better view. When she came up to me, she was very upset and accused me of turning my back to hurt her in rejection. I attempted to explain that I didn't mean to hurt her feelings, that I was only trying to get a perspective."

This dream shows Alan grappling with his hypersensitive and intrusive mother. He is attempting to get above her and out of her invasive clutches. This dream explains our interaction with each other. I too am an "invasive mommy" with my questions.

Alan told me about his mother. She was ambitious but educationally deprived, raised in a large and poor family that couldn't afford to keep her in school. She was proud of her son's artistic and academic achievements and wanted him to succeed but she didn't want him to be autonomous. He remembers her envy as he went off to his scholarship classes, while she watched from the window as he left. He felt guilty that he was relieved to be free of her.

It is and was her need to get through to him, to live inside him, that is disturbing. Both parents are sufficiently narcissistic to remain fixed in their defensive demands. He is currently less troubled by his father's narcissistic need to shape his personality. The damage has already been done and Alan is inured. Alan's radar is not set off by his father's distant posturing. His own regal mode keeps the proper distance. His mother's need to get inside him is less easily warded off.

Alan started to explain his parents' narcissism by placing it in a historical context. Jews living in the Polish-Russian shtetls had to learn to live as a symbiotic unit because they were surrounded by hostile anti-Semitic peasants. The pattern of symbiosis entered the Jewish culture and was subsequently exported to America.

Alan experienced this symbiosis in the second generation. He was tied to his family of greenhorns, people who were ashamed of themselves and lived through his achievements. He took his brown-bag lunch to the Ivy League campus where he was attending classes on a scholarship. He took with him as well their feelings of "nonbelonging" and inadequacy.

I felt the need to make a comment, to widen the understanding of narcissism. I was reacting to what sounded like a rationalization, an explanation that covered up individual motivation and responsibility. I said, "Shtetl life is not the only thing that produces narcissism and symbiosis is not its only characteristic." In nature, symbiotes are mutually helpful. Narcissism is closer to parasitism. Symbiosis lets us use each other, as we are two entities with mutually useful needs and wants. We are rather interdependent. Narcissism allows me to use you as if I exist in singular perfection and you are there to serve me. A narcissist feeds on his children but his children do not receive reciprocal benefit.

I said that narcissistic parents wound their children by not loving them and that a lack of love was not culturally ordained by the symbiosis of ghetto life. As an example of nonshtetl narcissism, I spoke of Victoria, also discussed in this book. She is the child of upper-middle-class WASPs, members of the dominant culture. Her narcissistic mother hated her, but not because her mother was fleeing from her own societal enemies.

I was shocked when I received the first wave of Alan's fury. I had contradicted him! I was disputing his knowledge of Jewish history. He started citing sociological texts and asking me if I had read them. He announced that until I did, I was in no position to conduct my study. He was trying to put me out of business.

My mind began to lose its focus, my usual response under such attack, a habitual response to my narcissistic father's invalidation of my thinking. I was no longer clear on what I needed to ask him. The only thing I held on to was my need to have the dream completed. I tried to change the subject by asking him to finish it. I would put the pieces of the puzzle together later.

This set off another tirade. He wasn't about to give me his dream. His tirade wasn't over. I wasn't getting off that easy. He got angry, very angry, the words flying out of his mouth. He went on and on about how I was invalidating *his* knowledge. He had my back to the wall. I held on to my opinion (what else could I do?), although I told him that I would consider his at my leisure. He continued to fire the big guns and I now wonder why he was so threatened.

The back-and-forth between us only led to greater obstinate fury on his part. I feared that the point would be reached where he would refuse to go on unless I apologized for my own opinion and agreed with him one hundred percent. This I could not do. I was experiencing the same feelings of invalidation I had as a small child when my narcissistic father took umbrage over some imagined slight and cancelled me out.

I told him that I felt he was trying to force an agreement from me when we had simply disagreed. He didn't see it like that and now he felt dismissed. I chided him like an exasperated parent, which is how I felt: "Can't we just get on with it?" I was trapped in his child's tantrum. This too annoyed him. *He* needed to call the shots, not I. *He* would tell me when we could proceed. I was getting angrier. Alan was into his pain and he would not let it go. In our interchange, both of us had the rage of a child with rejecting parents. In Alan's adamant historical perspective, he avoided blaming his father's narcissism for undermining his shaky ego.

Frankly, I do not know how we resolved this. The storm just passed, perhaps due to some minor stirring of guilt on his part. From my perspective, his explanation of the shtetl origin of narcissism was important to him because of his pride in his knowledge of Jewish history and his ability to do a historical-psychological analysis, wedded to narcissistic hypersensitivity over any implication that his thinking was not flawless. Additionally, the shtetl explanation, by focusing on symbiosis, lessened his awareness of the destructiveness of his father's narcissism. Having joined his father in like defense, it is safer to leave it alone. Symbiosis was the primary hurtful characteristic of Alan's mother.

Symbiosis does not a narcissist make. The true narcissist lives in grandiose isolation and manipulates rather than experience his dependency on other people, as does Alan's father, as does Alan himself. Symbiosis is an easy target which allows Alan to dodge guilt by association as he walks in his father's footprints.

He had some kind of breakdown as a young man running after his parents' acceptance and afterward vowed "not to need to please anybody through my achievements." He would be content within himself, utterly self-contained and self-satisfied through his artistic output. This is why his mother's attempts to penetrate his shield of grandiosity, to be close to him and share his glory, are unacceptable.

Alan had had some therapy but the surface was barely scratched when his therapist died. Narcissists can be in therapy many years before they change, before they can listen to a contradictory opinion. They may require endless hours of being listened to and of receiving absolute support. The therapist must be perceived as taking their side against an insensitive world. Only after years of building trust will the narcissistic person admit to dependency on the therapist and only then will a conflicting viewpoint be considered.

Nothing I said to Alan was absorbed or accepted. As far as my interviewing techniques were concerned, it was a total rout. My attempts to shape the interview were taken as an attack upon him, his autonomy, thought patterns, the value of his essential being. We both lost our tempers when I tried to force him to answer questions and not to overwhelm me with words.

The clock said it was time to leave, although nothing had been completed. We stood up in disarray and made one more attempt to reach each other but the same subjectivity poisoned our communication. Alan told me with annoyance that he had given up valuable time to see me that he needed for his own work. He said that he had always felt the tension between us and was trying to make it better. I felt guilty but thought, "My time is also valuable and much of it was wasted listening to your defensive perorations."

I saw in him my utterly inaccessible narcissistic father, who is never wrong. And he saw in me his overly sensitive, intrusive mother pursuing him up the steps. My assertiveness and insistence on having my own place in our interview were regarded as intrusive. This is to be expected of a narcissist. As the child of a brains-oriented narcissist, I was hypersensitive to his overtalking and position of superiority and responded very negatively to the mistreatment of not being listened to.

We had run out of time. I had to go. On the way to the door, Alan spoke ruefully, in the tone of suffering sainthood. "What goes wrong between us?" I was annoyed at his tone and still holding on to the illusion that truth could help. I said, "It's because you're too long-winded for me."

Another flare-up. What a fool I was. His eyes were filled with fire, his eyebrows raised in contempt. "People tell me that," he said, "but I am a man of passion." His implication was that they are all wrong. "I am a deeply related person. I care about issues." "Deeply related to your own self," I thought.

I felt totally defeated by myself and by him. Alan went on and on. He had no concept of time. Desperate to end on a conciliatory note, I apologized and said that I was hypersensitive to verbosity because my family had abused my listening. I asked him to consider it as my shortcoming, a sufficiently neutral and self-abnegating statement that he could hear. He said, "Next time, please let me know when I have exceeded your limit." This was a better ending. We were not parting as enemies.

We hugged good-bye sadly outside, standing in front of my car. Truly exhausting.

I emerged from this interview shaken, angry, and confused, guilty about my contribution to the anger between us, my own lack of flexibility, and hypersensitivity. We each had stepped on the other's narcissistic toes. I wondered what the people who knew us would think if they heard our interchange. As for myself, a good deal of time had been spent learning very little. I regarded the meeting as a total loss.

I was so discouraged that I was ready to scrap the whole thing when I realized that the problems of our interaction said a lot about our narcissism.

This was the first person I had interviewed whose narcissism was so great as to require total protection from a foreign idea or voice. His narcissism had been somewhat rearranged and concealed by a facade of therapized rationalization. But it still was classic. Our exaggerated conflicts expressed many narcissistic problems. As Marshall McLuhan said, "The medium is the message."

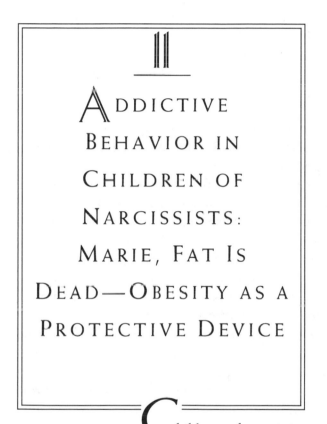

ADDICTIVE BEHAVIOR IN CHILDREN OF NARCISSISTS: MARIE, FAT IS DEAD—OBESITY AS A PROTECTIVE DEVICE

*C*hildren of narcissists are subjected to parental abuse that they come to associate with love. The parent attacks not only what they do but who they are. Hearing not "That is wrong," but "You are stupid" affects their sense of self. As a result, the child needs to hide who he is and develops defenses toward that end.

Fat can serve this purpose. A parent can attack you for being fat, which is glaring and obvious. Behind this defense you can hide your talent, dreams, and wishes, the things that are uniquely you. Your parent is distracted by the fat and doesn't reach for deeper places within you that you want to keep untouched. You also stay fat because you want your parent's love and fear his or her displeasure at your having an indépendent life. Obesity often makes a person unpopular with the opposite sex. Eating is a permissible pleasure that can get out of hand since it comforts you and removes your attention from troubled thoughts. Overeating is a problem for several of the people in this book. For Nick, Marie, Alan, and Victoria, it has led to obesity. Obesity is commonly defined as being about 10 percent above the average weight for your height and build. Obesity is often associated with reduced physical activity, fatigue, and ultimately with damaged health. For Marie, weight change is periodic.

People often speak of dieting without recognizing that fat is but a surface symptom. You can take off the fat but if you leave the problems that fester underneath, it will come back. Or instead of fat you will develop another defense that expresses the same problems and equally covers your interior. If you still need to flee your problems, you may turn to such escapes as drugs or compulsive overwork. If you want to appear bigger than you are and have a child's view of adulthood, you may develop a loud voice and imperious manner. If you want to conceal your sexuality, you may dress in a fashion that declares you neuter, etc.

Of course, some infants are raised to overeat and thereby develop extra fat cells at an early age that later predispose them to being overweight. As adults, they more easily gain weight than other people at the same caloric level. However, with an exercise program and appropriate diet, it is hard to remain overweight.

After years of therapy, Marie still disowns what drives her to eat. She knows she dislikes herself but attributes that to the action of an outside agent. Fatness keeps her single and postpones a sensual life. We must own our self-hatred if we are to deal with it. To love ourselves and seek outside love is a mighty struggle. If we avoid this undertaking, we will have only the limited love of our narcissistic parents.

Marie is a unique being. From the outset, she wanted to help and was open and willing to expose the problems of being the child of a narcissist. On our first call, I was struck by something in her voice, a certain tone. Although her message was hearty, I thought I heard an undercurrent of fear. I wondered if she knew of this and looked forward to our talk.

The woman who greets me is very fat, 212 pounds at 5'1". She is large in every dimension, like a full, ripe fruit, and not unattractive. She laughs easily and is full of energy. Her alert expression radiates intelligence. She tells me that she was not always full of life and raring to go. Therapy is restoring the "happy kid" she was before being caught in the vise of her mother's narcissism.

Marie grew up in Bulgaria, a country racked by insurrection, where her father was a peripatetic engineer who worked in far-off places and was largely absent during her first five years. She and her mother lived in a city far from the sites of insurrection. Mother frequently joined him, leaving Marie in the countryside with her doting maternal grandparents and uncle. She was only eight months old the first time mother dropped her off with her grandparents. The visit was only supposed to last the weekend, but extended into an incredible six months.

Her mother's needs did not center around the infant and her later "weekends" often extended to a second week. A base party to attend, a missed bus, and it was midweek, not worth coming home for a day or two before returning. Marie was happy with her grandparents, who were her caretakers. Later this relationship gave her distance from a mother who wanted total control and would withdraw emotional support to enforce her will. Marie could resist since her support lay elsewhere.

Her grandparents cared for her when her mother could not handle the child's illnesses or did not wish to. Mother was panicked by every city health scare and within hours, Marie was packed and standing at the corner waiting for a taxi to take her to them. She never knew where she would lay her head that night and which school she would attend in the morning. There was little security.

Her grandfather was an Orthodox priest who would come home from a wedding or christening, pockets stuffed with sugared almonds. He would freeze in the doorway and Marie would throw herself on him to search his pockets. She was utterly indulged by him and her uncle, who also loved to play. Her greatest losses were when her uncle left to be married and her grandfather died.

She was so much their favorite that during adolescence, when she and a cousin visited in their miniskirts (Marie was thin at the time), the cousin had to sit with a towel covering her thighs while Marie was accepted as she was. "With them, I could do no wrong." They helped Marie to develop her self but she always feared that what she had could be taken away. An example of this was in her grandparents' encouraging her to sing and dance. At the age of three and a half, she was an uninhibited little performer. When her mother heard her lovely voice, she got Marie booked on the local radio station.

Marie did not know of her right to say no and went to the station in a state of terror. She heard her mother's boastful introduction and then was "on," another lesson in surrendering her will. Lack of control is normal for a three-year-old but this became her attitude for life. She was the property of her mother, a woman who could dispose of her child's mind and body.

And criticize. It started with her body. First she was "too thin" and dosed with cod liver oil, shots, and vitamins to fatten her up. Then she overshot the mark and became "too fat," to be put on an endless series of diets. She was the wrong height and wrong weight. When the body is labeled inadequate, the self feels analogously diminished. Even though Marie is forty-one, her mother still asks her if she has grown taller to offset her rotundity.

She fought back and would not kowtow. The self her grandparents had nurtured was more than her mother had bargained for. It responded even when she was terrified. She challenged her mother's statements. Her mother would call her fat and she would answer cockily, "You're not so slim yourself." Her mother would call her friendless and Marie would ask, "So where are *your* friends?" which was met with a slap in the face. Marie fended off criticisms and believed them, every one. She was fat—and relatively friendless.

The latter problem arose from being three years younger than her classmates. Her ambitious mother entered her into the first grade a year early by changing the year of her birth. Since the month of Marie's birthday fell right before the cut-off date, she was immediately ahead by two years and when she skipped a grade, by three. In the sixth grade, she was nine among twelve-year-olds, mentally precocious but emotionally and physically immature. The other children felt it and cut her out of their social activities. Marie suffered a great deal from loneliness and struck up a friendship with a girl three grades down. This was brought to the attention of the guidance counselor, who was concerned that Marie seemed to be socially retarded and sent for her mother. Not only did her mother not reveal her child's true age, but later bawled her out for playing with a younger child!

Her mother saw no mistake or hardship in forcing Marie to get along with children who were more mature. Narcissists do not make mistakes. There was something wrong with Marie for not being able to do so. Marie had to go along with a denial of her real age and of the propriety of her emotional needs.

Her father reentered the household when she was five. He was puritanical and shunned overt physicality. The only place for embracing was at the airport when saying farewell. If Marie threw herself on him at the wrong time (probably a carryover from her life with her grandparents), he would say, "You're mushy," get up, and leave the room. She would be rewarded by his company if she was a "pure head" and sexless know-it-all. Marie was into endless reading and pursuit of every fact. She was determined to know it all.

Her father took teenage Marie to a movie. When he caught sight of some sex in *The Prime of Miss Jean Brodie*, he walked out and she remained. Later, he told her, "I would have thought better of you." Her interest in sexuality was condemned by him as wrong. This was not what she had felt with her grandparents.

To adapt, she denied her body by getting fatter. Her possum act was "Fat is dead." Strong sensual feelings, condoned by her grandparents and flowing beneath the surface, would not be suspected by her father, who condemned them, or by her mother, who thought her daughter's sexuality competitive. Marie was very much alive and her gross body was a ruse that made her seem maternal, asexual, and safe. She felt superior in her self-abnegation. Her father preferred this brainy daughter to his fleshy, sensual, and emotional wife, who didn't read. Her mother preferred this know-it-all daughter to her demanding younger children. Marie was on a family pedestal as goddess of intellect and substitute mother with younger siblings. As her family's intellectual totem, she was praised as compensation for being suppressed and used. Her feelings rebelled against this and when she looked within, her feelings called her a dismal failure.

Her shape and eating habits were public property. She was not in charge, a common experience for one who becomes obese. Others must control this person's eating because she lacks the strength and will never acquire discipline. Marie said, "my body felt humiliated." Wrongness was painted on by her mother's disgust. Her self watched from a distance, a split reinforced by violence. Mother hit her around the face and head, slapped and beat her. She lived in constant fear of attack. Fat was a lightning rod for her mother's rage. She had "a lot of pain around the heart" which her detached head did not understand.

Shifting back and forth between her grandparents and her mother gave her two different self-images. Her grandparents found her absolutely perfect. They were physically demonstrative, encouraged play, sensual enjoyment, and pleasure. Her mother opposed this. If there was an argument with her mother and her mother's thinking was found to be incorrect, Mother would switch sides and say that Marie's view had been the wrong one. Such "crazy-making" (Marie's expression) pried her loose from reality. It was hard to know who had said what. Crazy-making was there when her mother asked questions without listening to the answers. Marie took this as evidence of her own inadequacy.

Her life was filled with surrender and resistance. She had stopped singing and dancing. "Singing was the most difficult thing for me to do." She was an intellectual who read any book whose title was mentioned, too insecure not to know what another person knew. Her quest for education brought her to graduate school in the United States, and the fatness that concealed her came along. Once here, she started dropping weight at an amazing rate and came down to 132 pounds, size six. Being "large-boned," she was thin. She felt that being thin brought public notice to her sexual availability. She was declaring her womanhood.

But her unconscious mind needed to win her mother's love, so the man she chose to be with was narcissistic. He needed someone to live through and hobble down. As soon as they met, she started losing ground. Her feelings must have been in a state of alarm but the child of a narcissist does not properly read inner signals and an obese person is even less in touch. When he asked for a date, the talking head said, "Why not?" There was no logical reason not to. After they dated for a while, he asked her to live with him. "Why not," she thought and they did. When he said that they should marry, she said, "Why not" and never felt a thing.

Her husband was not only narcissistic but was like her father in that he suppressed erotic expression. At a party, he would allot himself one dance as "enough." Sex happened once a month. Her sensuality was controlled. A year after marriage, she was over three hundred pounds. Eating covered agony. She was back in hiding, again anesthetized and compliant. Her husband did not mind his wife's overweight, which represented the security of her shackles. They had children, and she gave herself to mothering. Her children had enough attention and a decade went by. Marie was established in her career as a teacher and the children were doing well. She got into therapy and saw the importance of her grandparents, who had kept her from madness. It had been easier to forget them and adapt to misery by assuming that everyone's mother was like her own. Her grandparents' love became a standard of light against which she could measure her parents' darkness.

Marie hated being captive to marriage and began to chafe at its constraints. She was ready for divorce despite her husband's unhappiness over the loss of one who had provided for his needs for years. Even her friends had become his. Not wanting to hurt him, she waited until he found a lady friend so that he could let go of her more easily. Then she was alone.

Although she lives a continent away, there is still the telephone and her mother's opinion. Of course her mother called her a failure for divorcing. Marie feels increasingly disconnected from her mother, who is "getting smaller and smaller." She thinks that her mother, who is in her late seventies, is withdrawing in the detachment of age and not needing Marie as much as she used to. She mentions how her sister provides endless caring and is so afraid of Mother's death that she keeps her mother dressed in childish pink. The sister, who is younger than Marie, has no outside sexual love relations. Her life is devoted to the architectural profession in which her mother takes pride, and then to Mother herself.

Mother is not suffering from any particular illness except a general wearing down. Still, I think that Marie's opinion about her mother's lack of need is wrong, although it may not be turned to Marie. Narcissists do not change much with the years except to get depressed if their vanity is not supported. "It looks as if your mother is using your sister the way she once used you."

Marie says that she is not out of the picture. She helps her mother deal with issues that her sister cannot face, information that will make it easier for Mother to die. Her sister dresses their mother in pink and tries to deny the inevitable. I ask if Marie feels that her mother appreciates her efforts. "Oh, no. Mother metabolizes the information and then comes back for more."

She says that she is able to let her mother pass away. But it feels to me as if she is jumping over work that still needs to be done. Obese people often use denial, like eating, to deny inner pain. Marie may be relatively free of her outer mother, but what of the inner?

"Why are you still overweight?" She becomes quiet, then answers, "It is an area of conflict," and "I am still full of self-hate." "Men find me attractive but I am unable to take the message in." She holds on to her mother's view of her body and self, to her father's opinion about not showing sexuality to men, who will think her "too much" in passion, energy, and sensuality. She says she knows that her body has "a certain sweetness about it" but mutes its signal. No sexual signs from her unless the man declares his interest. Fatness is her disguise.

"Why do you hold on to these negative ideas?" I am amazed at the tenacity of suffering. After a pause she says, "Sometimes when I meditate, negative ideas come to me from the outside, as if they had a life of their own." She cites a book by a Cypriot mystic who felt that if you hold on to an introject for a long time, it starts to exist outside of you and to have power. The writer claims to see his introject as a kind of cloud. With this mystical explanation, Marie rejects the necessity for confronting herself. She avoids seeing that she clings to a way of life that shields her from taking responsibility for the attacks of and rejection by her negative inner parent.

I argue against the external existence of this introject with its own power. I say that we are the source of its power and that we can be mired in self-hatred if we don't take responsibility for the contents of our mind. Once Marie anesthetized herself to her emotional pain by acting on the basis of logic alone. Then she thought to diminish further attack by adding the cover of fat. But the negative introject was already in residence.

Although the negative introject feels foreign to all of us, we can eliminate it by admitting to and understanding its presence. To give it a life outside of ourselves is to court madness. Then we feel possessed and in need of exorcism. We do not see our need for control of the attacking thought as an internal fight. I speak of this to Marie and she says that she fears to be her "higher self," and "on my own." "I am ashamed of that." The child of a narcissist is raised to feel guilty for desiring independence. Fat connects her with her mother. Living her mother's recipe for failure makes her mother correct: "You are ungainly, and sexually unpopular." A fat, humiliated person shrinks out of sight. Fat is like an armored car, battened against attack. Fat is like a weight that pulls her down.

Why the tone of fear in her voice? She lives in fear of rejection for being a full person. I believe that Marie will divest herself of the harsh inner parent only by attaining normal weight. I think this because being slim is her statement of freedom. When we live the defensive life, our energy is tied up in defensive structures and we cannot know the self. To know who we are we need to come out from behind the barricade and enter the light.

Therapy can help Marie do this, but she has already been in therapy for years. Intellectual understanding needs to be lived to become a part of our sense of self. As long as she remains obese, she can believe that if she assumes her proper weight it would drive men away as once it did her dad. As it was with Mom, she can believe that all love depends on sacrifice. Weight protects her from having an experience of what life could offer if she were to accept herself.

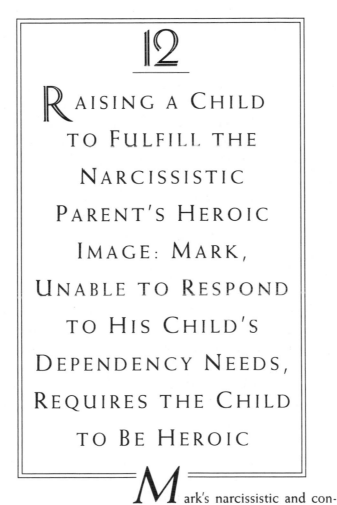

12

RAISING A CHILD TO FULFILL THE NARCISSISTIC PARENT'S HEROIC IMAGE: MARK, UNABLE TO RESPOND TO HIS CHILD'S DEPENDENCY NEEDS, REQUIRES THE CHILD TO BE HEROIC

Mark's narcissistic and controlling mother arrested the development of his psychological strength. He battled but usually ended in submission to her injured state of mind. In their household his mother had her way. She issued the law, which her husband and son followed. Mark's father was distant and submissive, a man who offered a poor model of assertiveness. His hobby was cooking. He hid behind the pots while his wife set the scene.

Mark was distracted by his mother's intrusiveness and accepted her doubtful view of him to the point where his self-esteem was undermined. He wanted to please her and still be free, contradictory motivations that subverted his concentration. His school record was doubtful and he was unsure if there was any possibility of academic success.

Instead of facing his fears and doubts, he adopted the "manly" skills of running, hiking, and camping and became an Eagle Scout. Lanky, tall, and powerful, this man of muscle swam like a fish, went scuba diving, canoed, went camping, and could survive most natural things. However, his mother's narcissistic machinations were not natural.

To quell self-doubt, Mark does things that other people would find extremely difficult, like swimming in an icy lake while others watch; like camping in a snowbound tent in which he stows the ax brought to chop firewood. In his ordinary life he rides a motorcycle through the madness of a city. In all these heroic moments he asserts his worth, and by acting carefree and self-confident he almost convinces himself. If anyone were to ask Mark if he felt sufficiently manly and he gave an honest answer, it would be no. Instead of facing his feelings of inadequacy, he has become physically stronger and functions only partially at developing a career.

He married a woman who would ride behind him on his motorcycle, although in later years she declined. They had a child, in large part because he needed to present a manly image by having an offspring. What particularly affected the child was Mark's need that the child be extremely strong from birth. Mark thought that such a need was delightful fun for his child and could not see his true response. In this relationship, we see how narcissistic problems are passed on.

Mark is a friend of mine from California, a former Eagle Scout who does not pay attention to his young son Bruce's vulnerability. Bruce was in his second year when I visited them and saw Mark let his child move toward an obvious accident in which he fell down part of a flight of stairs. The boy had been standing halfway down the stairs, to which his father paid no attention. He lost his balance and tumbled to a hard landing, where he lay and did not emit a sound.

Mark walked over, picked Bruce up for a quick once-over, and found nothing significantly wrong. He seemed unable to respond emotionally to his child's feelings and to the child's body. His response was as to a machine, a human machine that he hadn't kept from personal injury. He held the child with insufficient affection, as if he were an object. Finding no bruises, he gave Bruce a pat of reassurance, set him on his feet, and walked away.

There was not a word between them. I watched in horror as it happened, noting that the fallen child barely whimpered. This was not a childproof house and he was used to taking bruises in response to his father's need for a two-year-old Eagle Scout. Although a good-natured person, Mark had a narrowness of perception that made him unaware. He is partly narcissistic in that personal ambition shapes his behavior and makes him unable to understand his child. He is filled with compulsive needs that his child must fill, a controlling approach not unlike the way his narcissistic mother treated him. He does not think of his child's feelings when his own important wishes are concerned. Heroic needs rule his perceptions and demands. The child's injuries had but a moment of attention. The child gets little emotional contact, as if he were a hamster running in its cage. It is as if Mark feels there is no way to be at one with his child.

When Bruce was about three, he and his parents visited me. Again he seemed to be in constant danger. This time he nearly fell into a nearby creek. He did not act like an ordinary child, who would have tested before making his move. He was in constant motion, like an outlet for the dynamic energy of a battery that is always on. He was like a wild animal with drugged senses, on the run out of fear and unable to test its surroundings.

Bruce did not heed our calls nor answer to his name. The way he acted made me feel sad and frightened. I thought the child to be seriously unreachable. His mother watched his dangerous perambulations and took me aside to complain that her husband put Bruce into

dangerous situations and took insufficient care. She said that Mark
scolded and disobeyed her when she asked him not to do it. Despite
her anxiety, Mark's need and vision ruled the treatment of their child.
Although she said that she nagged Mark about this, I found her willingness to accept a dangerous situation for her child a peculiar kind of
diffidence. Perhaps a driven man like Mark had done well to marry a
woman who looked at issues from afar. It kept their point of conflict
from generating into open warfare.

That night, the child wandered aimlessly and frenetically from
room to room, unrelated to the grownups who were talking. He was
without rest but his parents did not try to put him to bed. It disturbed
me that we could not reach him. His parents found him difficult but did
not label him as emotionally out of contact. They threatened jokingly
to leave him asleep in his stroller, left parked in my kitchen, so they
could depart on the sly. I believe that his mother had conceived the
baby to please her husband and never fully cottoned to a motherly role.

I could not get Bruce into my lap for a snuggle. One time, I
grabbed him as he went by, held on to find him in a reaction stiff and
distant. What happens to a child's need for contact if his deprivation is
broken into only for a brief hug and then he is returned to Nowhere
Land? What happens if he is disregarded by parents who remain out of
touch and use him to fulfill their fantasies? Rather than having mo-
mentary respite from loneliness, it is better to live like a tank at war.
The pain of feeling on and off again is more horrible than going
without feeling and contact altogether.

He did not respond to physical contact and a friendly voice. As
the night wore on, I eventually coaxed him out of his troubled walking
into a nap on the cushion that lay by my side. I patted it and made
soothing sounds to which he settled in. But he rested without being
touched and kept a frightened distance. This was not a child who
wanted to be held.

Two years later, when the child was five, I saw the three of them
again. Bruce was like a wooden Indian who, at Mark's command, swung
over his father's arm like a top, arms fixed at his side, face and eyes
inexpressive. I barely heard him speak although he later played me-
chanically with the phone. Again, I grabbed him for a hug when he
would not talk and found his body unyielding as a nail. He was without
social contact, raised to be a "superman" by a father who needed to see

his own image reflected in a tough, unfeeling person. One day his child would be an Eagle Scout. But what would be the child's inner life?

A child wants to please his parents. If they are narcissistic and tell him how to feel, he stops knowing his own feelings. A narcissistic parent declares his child's natural feelings wrong if they are in disagreement with his own, if they fall short of the parent's image, are critical of the parent, or express a contrary notion. The narcissistic parent wants to be beyond criticism, to be mirrored as a god. The obedient child surrenders his own awareness.

This child disengages from his rejected feeling self. If his narcissistic parent projects horrifying and unacceptable feelings onto him, these are what he feels. If he is treated as unloving and unlovable but able to show physical heroics, that is what he will be and do. A love-hungry child goes dead inside, an enactment that implies, "I am without love and tough as my parents need me to be." To please them, he is in accord with their need.

Of course, you cannot definitively predict the adult future of a five-year-old. I imagine that he will do many things to show how tough he is. He will enjoy camping, swimming, skiing, the deeds his father likes to share. I think he will not get close to people. Closeness does not naturally develop late. Without help in getting to know himself, probably from psychotherapy, he will go through life at a distance, not wanting to know the horrors of his need for affection, understanding, and the knowledge of an unmet self. If feelings of his unfilled need for love get through to him, he will feel depression and possibly engage in self-destructive activity. Childhood did not teach him that such needs can be met. Psychotherapy would be in order.

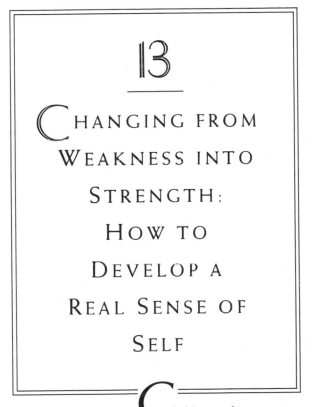

13

CHANGING FROM WEAKNESS INTO STRENGTH: HOW TO DEVELOP A REAL SENSE OF SELF

Children of narcissists can grow from weakness into strength. In order to do so, we must know things inside us that hold us back, and we must change them. The work of change develops strengths that go well beyond the usual. "Usual" means falling in line with the average norms of society. Life with a narcissistic parent always means fitting in with his or her schema. Instead we need to find our unique opinion. We need perseverance to overcome the problem of self-unknowing. In this chapter we look at our specific problems, ways to approach them, and the strengths that we need to develop.

To change, we must know the biases that we hold against our

selves. What did our parents hate and love in us and how much did these judgments define our self-images? We may have learned our parents' values but our history is difficult to fathom since these anti-self attitudes are ancient and appear in everything we do. We are like bonsai plants with prior years of confinements, suppression, and re-shaping. What is our natural shape? It takes years to uncover as we revert by degrees to growing.

Take the following example of a learned error: A narcissistic father had opera lessons in his youth. As a parent, he often broke into sten-torian measures of an opera, his favorite being *"La Donna e mobile"* (Woman is fickle), whose words expressed mistrust of the faithfulness of women everywhere. From her earliest years, he nagged his daughter about being out of tune. He would encourage her to sing a few notes and then would commence with the evaluation. He spoke in tones full of scorn and amazement, sang his correction, and jeeringly provoked her to continue. She stopped singing and retreated into humiliated silence. Had she been out of tune? Probably. Attacked as she was, her incapacity was permanently instilled.

She accepted the diagnosis of being incapable of carrying a tune and lost contact with her voice. She was a stranger to what came out of her mouth. She could hear another person's singing pitch and could tell the difference between notes that were closely spaced, but when she had to sing, she couldn't, not even "Happy birthday to you." Her throat did not respond to her ears. Perhaps she did not hear herself because embarrassment was with her and always ran the show.

Singing in tune came of itself after years of psychotherapy with a therapist who had perfect pitch and could test her. She had not worked on singing, but with better knowledge of what she thought and felt she began to control her singing notes. Without a critical listener to mock what she produced, her attention was less divided. She was not so easily dissuaded from her perceptions and regained her voice as a sign of self-knowledge. Being disunited from self is a problem for the child of a narcissist. I wonder how many cannot sing in tune.

It helps to know how you feel about your life. Although self-blame makes us blind, if we ask ourselves what happened to us in childhood and from this who we really are, images will come. Some of them are

painful but less painful than living an unrecognized image, a fate predicted and thus determined by the parent.

You can listen to your inner self by allowing a fantasy that tells
you what once was. I remember being inducted into a past-life regression by a woman who did such work as I lay on the floor and followed
instructions. I have no belief in past life but had the fantasy of being a
desert slave who slept on a bed of corn husks stacked in a slatted bin.
I was a slave in both sexes for three generations, always sleeping in that
bin and increasingly disgusted till I walked into the starry desert night
to escape. I walked so far that the settlement became a whispering of
lights on the horizon but I found nothing to walk to. Rather than die
out there alone I walked back.

This was not a past life experience. It was a metaphor for my life
experience with narcissistic parents, slaving for the smallest bits of
approval.

Some children of narcissists act as badly as their parents say they
do, and even if they do something well, these children focus on all
evidence that might support their parents' negative view. Although my
secret desire was to become a dancer, I was described by my narcissistic
parent as a klutz and never dared ask for lessons.

Klutz I was when I served ice cream to my narcissistic parent's
girlfriend and to her friend Sabine, a visitor from Michigan. I decided
to balance the dish of ice cream on top of her head and somehow
spilled it on her dress. It was horrible, wiping ice cream off and feeling
utterly clumsy as my father's hateful comments echoed round. My error
proved him right. Better for me to hide.

Did you learn self-hatred? What negatives were laid upon you that
entered into your self-image? Do you have self-condemnatory physical,
mental, spiritual views? Are the views based on something real or were
they told and retold until you believed them? Do you believe things
about yourself that no one has seen, but you cannot be dissuaded? Do
you feel yourself to be in an objectionable state?

Shaped by the forced absorption of our parent's opinion, we are
like hungry frogs whose tongues dart out for the passing fly. Unlike a
frog, we will eat poisonous flies, poisonous comments that make us feel
great or inadequate, distorting messages that reject us as we are. We

feel so unacceptable that if something bad is said about us, we ingest its substance. We do not discard incorrect opinions, especially those put forth by the narcissistic parent. We need to learn to judge information about ourselves and to discard what is wrong.

What experiences verified your parents' negative view of you? I was eleven and at camp. It was a "work camp" attended by creative kids, a place where we could spend the entire day at what we liked without having to compete at such activities as volleyball. We could garden on the farm and watch a cow give birth. Almost everyone went to calf birth. We could dance or play in the orchestra. There were even sports. For me it was painting and sculpture with my counselors, Phoebe and Jack. This was the first time I suspected that there were people like me in the world and felt the possibility of friendship. But burdened with self-hatred, I had far to go before reaching out. I escaped to art and hoped that camp, with its emphasis on being natural, would help me find and accept my self.

The head of the camp was Max, a psychologist from Switzerland. Max would tell us stories 'round the campfire. I was transfixed and listening for the way out of my personal hell. His voice was pleasant and quiet, not like that of my dogmatic and pursuing parents. The story he told was of a woman who thought herself a hopeless loser. Filled with self-hatred, she hid from human contact. I was pierced by this. Wasn't I hiding my inadequate self in painting and sculpture? Didn't my counselors know this? Would Max show me how to end my self-dislike? I was scared and hopeful.

The woman went to a therapist, who tested her. Eventually, there was a report. Her therapist told her that she was inadequate after all. The kids all laughed at hearing this but I was demolished. Another negative nailing. My parents were right in criticizing my every move. The memory of Max's story and my feelings about being in a hopeless state as supported by his story were with me for years. Max, a person I cared for, was insensitive and condemnatory like my narcissistic father.

His story told me not to expect improvement. It showed how inconsiderate people can be when you need them to be kind and understanding. Perhaps Max was narcissistic and criticized others to build himself up. Or he was the child of narcissists who made a joke of the torture he had received from his parents. Either way, the effect of this story made my parents' rating become my fate.

Children of narcissists fear to know themselves, particularly when what they find within is anger. Life with vituperative parents forces them into a compliant posture. When things go wrong they retreat and do not know that much of what they fear from others is a projection of their inner lives. Feelings of their own that are attributed to others make the world a frightening place.

Carol had a narcissistic and attacking mother and was afraid to know how angry this made her since her anger might show and cause further attack. She hated acknowledging anger because this seemed to make her resemble her abhorrent mother. In defense, she had built the facade of a supersoft voice, saccharine smile, and anxious eyes. She found anger in "powerful" people, whom she thought were attacking her. She responded as if they were her narcissistic mother and she their helpless child.

In therapy she walked on eggs, very fearful and too nice. She avoided having a regular session, saying that her schedule was too tight, but always found time to drink in the evening. She cancelled sessions and said she wanted to quit therapy because she thought I was "unfriendly." I discussed her avoiding sessions to conceal her feelings. Instead of looking at her temper she said I was attacking her. She argued against it but then entered a shaky phase of treatment in which she will come to her sessions even if she feels attacked. Anger is omnipresent in her life, a part of herself she has long avoided. Her husband is equally avoidant. He thinks their marriage successful because they don't communicate. Learning how anger rules her thinking lies ahead. Both he and she will have to face their fear of it.

Many children of narcissists are oversensitive, which means that we overreact to what other people say and do, are hurt and confused by the belief that someone intends the worst. We perceive neutral behavior in a negative light. Being hypersensitive is like having skin so badly burned you cannot lie beneath a sheet.

I became oversensitive as continuous criticism rubbed my ego raw. My father criticized my smallest move and I found safety in hiding.

Imagine my panic when I had to learn the slide rule. It was impossible to look long and hard enough to get the proper marks lined up. A correct answer was only possible for bright people and therefore not for me. I felt this way when a friend pushed me to use the slide rule correctly.

He encouraged me and forced me to focus. I said I wasn't sure that I could learn the slide rule, to which he said, "So what!" That he did not think life depended on being free of error was an inebriating thought. Learning for the pleasure of it? Usually I ran from testing myself, called myself inadequate, and avoided finding further evidence of unworthiness. With worry over success and failure stowed, I learned to use the slide rule. I saw from this experience that I exaggerate my flaws. I then resolved to waste less time on worry and more on practicing what I care to do and know.

A common problem for children of narcissists is that we do not know when to stop being mistreated. We do not even know when we are actually being mistreated since we accept suffering as a means to winning favor. The possibility of favor gives pain a pleasurable coloring. I visited my father's narcissistic sister. She had a grand dame aura as if the world revolved around her. She kissed my left cheek after not seeing me for so long, then slapped my right cheek for not having been in touch with her. I entered a stunned fog as she laughed at the vanity of her move. She wasn't bothered in the least by it but I felt embarrassed, angry, and ashamed. She had hit me for not calling her. She was wrong and she was right. Which was it? I always felt punishment an appropriate treatment for me and I shuddered into withdrawal.

I told my therapist about this event. He responded that the next time she slapped me, I was to get her arm in a hammerlock and demand that she explain why she had hit me instead of speaking her displeasure. It was strange to hear him say that I am not to be abused. He has said it over and over since I am psychologically hard of hearing. He was not advising diplomatic retreat but rather that I wean myself of the role of being a punching bag.

Sometimes we feel wounded and do not notice the wound as we are pulled into the need system of the person harming us. For example, at my graduation from college, the narcissistic aunt who had hit me robbed me of my pleasure in this experience. I felt that I was being hurt but could not see the situation handled any other way. In the melee I did not protest against what was being done. I thought it would be selfish to do so since her needs were more important than mine. It was my lot in life to be mistreated and to ignore it.

My aunt had been deprived of adequate schooling in Europe and probably was jealous of my graduation. Her grandiose pride would not permit her to admit such feelings. She arrived at my dorm with other relatives. After visiting a while, she discovered the loss of a necklace of great sentimental value. It had been a gift from someone famous and we devoted ourselves to its recovery. We opened drawers, looked under things, and grilled poor Reenie, the honest and sensitive-to-tears cleaning lady. Reenie's voice quavered as she pleaded that she hadn't robbed my aunt. Of course she hadn't. So terrible for her after years of service and terrible for me to be part of it. I became depressed.

Did I graduate? I remember walking along a path to music, wearing a black robe and hearing my aunt crying for her necklace. When she went home, it was found lying as she had left it on her dresser. Her resentful mourning for its loss had colored everything. No apology to me was forthcoming. No one recognized any damage. Not even I. I was not someone of worth. My graduation wasn't worth much.

In an opposite direction, after being so long mistreated, we can find mistreatment when none is there (although sensitivity may be lacking). Like the day in my childhood my narcissistic father's relatives were visiting. All day, those friendly people whispered and looked at me out of the corners of their eyes. They kept me out of hearing. It was not like them to cut me out so much. I thought they must be saying horrible things about me as my father always did. They had learned the truth after years of erroneous love, which is why no one now included me. No one seemed to care or know how I felt.

This is a narcissistic tribe. Perhaps they didn't notice my depression. Narcissists are involved with themselves. Perhaps they thought that my exclusion filled me with excitement and wonder. Narcissistic people will project onto others the feelings that they want to see created. For a child of a narcissist, the unknown is fraught with danger. I did not feel wanted. What command, criticism, or punishment awaited me? Or perhaps, as children of narcissists, they did know how I felt and were enjoying the power of passing punishment on to one they "loved."

I passed a miserable day that strengthened my belief in my worth-lessness. After dinner, there was a stir in the kitchen and a birthday cake appeared, alight with candles . . . for me. Eight of them. I started to cry with relief. They had been setting up a surprise party and all I had known was rejection. The intended positive had been seen through negative light.

This is an example of looking into corners and seeing only dark-ness. Children of narcissists do not expect the best. We are on familiar ground when all turns out badly. We are flustered, frightened, and sometimes pleased when it goes the other way, if we can see it.

On the other hand, hypersensitivity to how one is treated or to what one fears can have the paradoxical outcome of making us under-sensitive toward others. To safeguard our skin we ferret out and over-react to anticipated mistreatment. We run from it and accuse the person of intending to mistreat us. Our charges are hostile but we call the other person aggressive and charge him or her with having sinister motivation. Our tone is one of trial and punishment. We retaliate in the present for wrongs we have suffered in the past, the sufferings of our narcissistic home.

For example, a woman in my psychotherapy group had always been attacked by narcissistic parents. She showed uncanny accuracy at finding people's weak points. She acted as if they were out to get her, to which her attacking them was an appropriate defense. Nothing could stop her. She hoped that she would one day be close to people but when the group began to point out that she pushed them away, she quit group, saying that no one there could help her. She needed the safety of being shut off. In her self-centered rejection of others, she is close to narcissism.

We have to learn if our reaction to people's errors and shortcom-ings is magnified by the injuries we suffered as a child. Children of narcissists can have bitter views. Hypersensitivity swamps the picture and unless we lower our standards and accept imperfections we will have no close friends. We need to turn our hypersensitivity into sen-sitivity to others' feelings.

Along with hypersensitivity is the fear of harm. Years of invasive mistreatment, of being corrected and ignored by narcissistic parents, make us think that others will be the same. That is what we hear when people speak and act. Our waking world is dark and covered by a blackened sky. Unworthy us and punitive them. Pain is always forthcoming. Our sleep is filled with dreams of punishment. This expectation rules our daily lives, in which we find intended harm. We are hurt no matter what people do. Imagining such intentions is enough to make us feel wounded. If we choose to be with narcissists, they will actively wound us as well. But we can be hurt by anyone. Socializing is our agony.

Addiction is another common response to being the child of a narcissist. We see it in Nick and Victoria in this book. Being over- or underweight is common but anything can be used as an addictive defense. It is easy to fall into a self-destructive lifestyle after being treated as expendable and worthless. Destroyed by our parents' narcissistic blindness and without someone to observe and comfort us, we now destroy ourselves.

Why don't addicts stop? The problem is partly chemical. But more than this, if we ask, am I worth it, the answer from our internalized parent says, "No, you're not." Feeling unworthy, we lack motivation to change our habits and improve our lives. We might as well die by our own drugged hand and have a little pleasure on the way down. We do not know how blind we are to what is going on as drugs cover our hostility and despair. We can be friendly on the surface and secretly bitter.

Pills, booze, sex, chasing after financial success, lovers, you name it. Anything can be used as an addictive distraction that takes us away from what we feel. Because addiction keeps us from dealing with our problems (while creating others), we need progressively more of the drug as unattended problems increase and pull us down. Rather than suffer, we increasingly turn to what makes us feel good and forget. We get further away from the knowledge of self that would set us free.

Often our narcissistic parents were addicts of some kind. They took various kinds of drugs, literal and metaphoric, to shut out the world and we follow them on the same or different substances. Like them, we believe life to be hopeless and take their approach of being out of contact. To become unaddicted and function well, we should know that feeling our pain and seeing reality serves a purpose. The pain only lasts a while and seeing what causes our problems helps us to change in order to appreciate ourselves and our lives.

Procrastination is a common shortcoming of one whose performance has been attacked. Low in self-esteem, many of us think we should put off action until we feel sufficiently confident. It is an error to believe that we must love ourselves before undertaking a difficult project or relationship. We postpone what we think is beyond our grasp, giving ourselves no opportunity to learn from error. Raised to magnify our limitations, inferiority feelings keep us from the world. We fail at school, job, marriage, work, child rearing, and so on. We fulfill our predicted destiny.

We want to strengthen our skills infinitely before going out; we never feel strong enough. One man was afraid of eating most foods and was always readying himself for more extensive eating. He never ate anything but lima beans and "flanken" beef, a Jewish form of cooking in which meat is served boiled or potted. He lived to a ripe old age but always with that sense of putting off the adventure of eating. He hugged a familiar way which he regarded as the safer path.

Our view of self is colored by our narcissistic parents' opinions. If they manipulate us to fit into their schema, which gives them satisfaction, we feel ourselves to be failures. Even if we pass high, we think it failure. I have progressively hoisted myself out of the pit of condemnation and do not know if I am the idiot my narcissistic parent labeled me or reasonably bright. I have gotten all kinds of labels. My concern with this value system shows I am still vulnerable to it to some degree. It is hard to get free of ingrained negative opinion and to use one's abilities fully.

Children of narcissists usually do not know their abilities because the parents' responses interfered with their unfolding. Often the child does not get into something of personal interest. An overachiever may do things important to her parent but not to herself. Many so-called "successful" children of narcissists have weak egos and do little outside of given margins because success is too important to venture into the unknown. If narcissistic pressure forces a child to achieve, her ego may not develop since she gives credit to her parents. To support her parents' vanity she gives away all credit for what she has done. We need to strive for what we truly desire and if we fail to reach our goal, feel stronger for the trying. Self-worth does not depend on the results.

In addition to being hurt we have learned many of our parents' narcissistic habits since they taught us that narcissism is the better way. We do not recognize that we have narcissistic defenses and patterns of perception that make us behave insensitively and feel morally correct. If others complain about us, we cannot understand. Our defenses shield us from their questions, their pained and censuring voices.

We need to know our narcissistic habits, that compote of traits we would be better off without. Our narcissism is like the behavior of prisoners of war surrounded by life-endangering guards. To deny our vulnerability, we manifest the stance of those who threaten us. We acquire the parental traits that caused us the most pain.

Narcissism can be manifested on the inside or the outside. We can be internally narcissistic and externally sacrificing, as when I think myself superior to you for the sacrifices that I make; externally narcissistic when I feel inadequate and act superior to you to hide my feelings. I hide inferior feelings from you and me. Vivian had endless dreams of rejection. No man would want her as his lover, few women would want her as their friend. She avoided rejection by being the first one to reject.

Another common narcissistic habit is to criticize. The child of a narcissist who emulates his parent is always trying to improve the other person. That is what his parents did to him and to everyone else. As an act of identification with his parents, he responds to people's errors with the kind of rage his parents showered on him. He wants to accept people as they are and has been repeatedly told to do so but feels inner pressure to correct. He thinks, "Doesn't he/she want to know that he is doing something wrong?" The other's error causes him pain. Rather than consider the distorting effect of being hypersensitive, he personalizes the other's behavior and takes it as intended to wound. Hurt feelings move him to react with a barrage of criticism.

Another example of parental narcissism appears in the child in a mutated form. Andrea had narcissistic parents who lied to her incessantly. Out of reaction, she became a compulsive truth teller and downright unpleasant. Worshiping the power of the word, Andrea's aggression went into giving unsolicited advice.

People would start getting close to her and then want to get away. She was pained by their departures but could not admit that her truth-telling made them leave. Even when they complained about her "advice," she thought that telling them the truth was for their good. She saw them as afraid of what they needed and had no awareness of her vested interest in a missionary role. If she felt guilty about the pain she caused, she told herself to do it "one more time." Telling the truth did the damage to them that her narcissistic parents did to her by lying. In each instance, the feelings and needs of the other person were not respected. A good example is the time Victoria told me that a man I had known and dated for several years once told her that he wanted to be free of me and asked her for a date, which she refused because he was not up to her level. This is truth-telling with a demeaning and arrogant edge. It is how her narcissistic mother talked to her.

If despite complaints from others our repetition goes on, it shows that we have identified with our narcissistic parent. If we cannot change behavior that we know is causing trouble, look for the gain it brings. Such gain may be subtle and include playing a supporting role to narcissistic parents by resembling them.

Much of the sense of self is in bodily feeling. Often children of narcissists don't know how to read their bodies because their parents did not give the child's emotional and bodily sensations an appropriate label, did not call a spade a spade. The parents were not in tune with the child's emotions and labeled the child's feelings according to their own moods and needs. If we disagreed with them they said we were in error and attempted to change our minds. If we said we were lonely they tried to make us think that people were unimportant. They made us eat when they thought that we were hungry, feeding us portions that they felt suited our needs.

Alienated from the inner self, we do not understand the body's message. Estrangement means that our bodily sensation lacks decipherable meaning. Eastern philosophers say that we are neither body nor mind but that if we had to choose the more essential carrier, it would be the body. By this they mean that we are a vibrating energy system not different from the world at large. But even in the Western approach, bodily feeling is the direct effect of what we think. If we are sad or happy, our body tells us so. The body gives us vital clues to what is going on. Inability to understand the body's messages keeps us from deep understanding of self. The body is the agent of emotion. Thoughts set up bodily feelings although we do not feel the process. If we can't understand our bodily sensations, who or what are we? Only thought? What is the result of having undeciphered emotional messages?

A person who is estranged from the meaning of his feelings is puzzled by an ache in the heart, palpitations in the chest, shortness of breath, a churning in the stomach, etc. He is indifferent to or frightened of them, as if his head were under attack by his body. Mind and body are not one to such a person.

If he gives practical thought to sensation, its meaning may be perceived from afar. Perhaps he heard of similar sensations on TV. Such knowledge is vague—a word, an idea—but not a call to action. Bodily feelings that are disturbing or even symptoms of a serious disorder are dimly perceived. Pain in the body means that something is amiss. Pain is a symptom and sign asking for attention. Pain differs according to the severity and chronicity of the disorder it expresses. Emotions also affect the body. Mind creates a stomach ulcer, upsets digestion and breathing. Often we feel a body ache without understanding its meaning.

Take the way an average person perceives and responds to a headache. A pain in the head signifies something in the body, but what? Most people believe that a headache is an inexplicable occurrence signifying nothing, an occasion that will soon be over. Take an aspirin and forget it. The children of narcissists can be even more extreme in ignoring and dismissing their sensations. Many children of narcissists move in an addictive direction. With their drug of choice, they retreat from body/mind feelings to an unfeeling state. Sensation is removed but its cause remains.

Below is a discussion of some bodily sensations felt by children of narcissists who lacked the ability to understand the relationship to their physical state and what to do about it. There are infinitely more body/mind feelings than these. A person who is alienated from her feelings can misunderstand any sensation of which her body, mind, and spirit dreams. I use the word "spirit" metaphorically here to signify the inner self calling for attention through ideas and feelings that a person can misunderstand or ignore. With such estrangement, children of narcissists may need outside help to understand.

Eric was raised under an onslaught of parental narcissism and was unable to cope. His parents wanted him to be an outstanding scholar, an A-1 achiever compared to everyone else. He was upset by their pressure to succeed and by the stress of competition. Many narcissistic families make their children compete by declaring one the winner and the others the losers. Their children function in response to the parents' need by feeling competitive and imposed upon from without.

Eric was less gifted than his brother, less able to function under stress. He tried but he could not set the record of unalloyed academic brilliance that his parents required. He varied his goals and defensively did not choose a career. In his early twenties, he suffered a kind of nervous breakdown when his kid brother began to show intellectual gifts. When he was unable to ignore his narcissistic parents' comparing him with their other children, his life was undermined by this intrusive system of valuing. He competed for value and felt like a failure.

His parents' wish that he excel and his feeling of inadequacy led to self-destructive eating. He called himself a "genius manqué," a man of undiscovered brilliance who buried himself in food. The child part of him was gratified by such behavioral regression. A focus on eating reinstates a period of life when oral ingestion was central. For the moment, parental requirements are pushed aside. Overeating feels good in the mouth but painful to the body. Accepting such pain supports his parents' view of him as unworthy. He is estranged from his body and does not consider its feelings. There is no self-love if you treat your body with disrespect. Mistreatment of the self is used to quiet the punishing negative introject.

The only thing he paid attention to was intellectual perambulations. His enormous vocabulary did not dispel the mental doubt that ruled him. His posturing and much of what he did was more image than content. He created an impressive image to hide behind, and was out of touch with a body that went downhill. He quoted Shakespeare to hide his sense of nonidentity.

He would appraise his body but did not give it sustained attention. Finding himself too fat, he would grow thin, then fat again. Upset by his appearance, he put himself through periods of overhaul. Diet was allied with intermittent maniacal exercise. He went from no exercise to a program of strenuous endeavor. Out of touch with the meaning of body sensation, he was insensitive to his physical limitations. His narcissistic parents required that he go beyond his abilities, and so even with his body, he disregarded feeling. Perhaps he liked the sense of overwork. One day, while jogging, he died of a heart attack.

There probably were prior sensations of heart difficulty—pain and shortness of breath, exhaustion. His parents' view was directed to outside opinion and unconcerned with the body's messages. Many children of narcissists are so directed. They are unaware of the meaning of what their bodies tell them. They can develop serious and chronic diseases, or can die.

The body speaks about emotional states that the mind cannot understand. Ellen had a severely narcissistic father who aimed to dominate her life. She also had a symbiotic mother who tried to control her by filling all of Ellen's needs. Actually the needs she tried to fill were primarily her own. In symbiotic fashion she thought her own wishes were supposed to be shared by her daughter. Both parents constantly reshaped the child and tried to bring her under their aegis. The child's sense of self was depleted and thin. Her parents dominated her self-perception as two warring negative introjects. These fought in her mind as they did in life. Each wanted a dominant position in her being and further depleted her feelings of self.

From this war, she had the most peculiar body sensations. It was as if each arm were being pulled in an opposite direction and by a different amount of force. This tugging had nothing to do with her desire. She desperately wanted it to stop and felt that she was going mad with this inner sensation unrelated to her feelings. Who was the puller and what was the message? She felt pulled apart but did not know how to read it.

In fact, her body expressed her feelings, which came from the warring parents inside her mind. Each one wanted total control and in trying to achieve this was contradicting the other and crushing her self.

She was emotionally at the end of her tether, even ready to die. She couldn't stand being pushed around from within and entered therapy.

She saw that she was torn by indecision. Did she own her body and mind? Her introject said, "Your parents know what is best for you." This scenario made her confused and increasingly out of touch with her self. It was easier to forget her disagreement with what they said to her than to hold on to conflict. Often she did not remember her ideas, a common confusion for children of narcissists. She tried to think what her parents dictated and didn't recognize that they undermined her thoughts and moved her from her own sensation.

After a considerable stretch of psychotherapy in which she expressed grief and growing conflict with her parents' opinions, the physical feeling of being torn apart disappeared. Although conflict with her parents remained, her self became strong enough to occupy psychological home base.

Sensations vary with their emotional causes. Among the negative sensations are anxiety, fatigue, allergy, feelings from poor diet (like energy highs and lows from sugar, allergic dripping nose and foggy mind from milk), hypersensitivity, etc. Attention to our bodily sensations and our understanding of them can be contaminated by our need for parental approval. A parent-dominated mind says, "Do it," no matter how we feel. It is the parent's ambition that motivates us. Driven to fulfill our parent's wishes, we think that our physical needs represent disloyalty to their personal ambitions. Personality and self are almost unrelated. Personality wants the fame required by the parent while the self wants to laugh and relax. In becoming true to our self, can we stand by its needs if they are not universally popular? Experience of self is the direction we need to take.

Can we develop special strengths from being raised in a narcissistic home and can such strength then lead to weakness?

John in Chapter 5 was demeaned by his father into feeling worthless. Self-hatred and anger caused him to fail at school. Failing was his subconscious way of attacking his father by not supporting the parent's grandiose image. That same failure pleased his father by reifying John's condemned position. After hitting bottom, John fought to recover and tried many solutions. He developed strength from this fight, especially from seeking a view of life that meditation brings.

John lives under stringent financial conditions. Using meditation to observe himself and his life, he is able to accept suffering to the point of mastery. Mastery entails looking at pain without a struggle. With acceptance, pain withdraws to the outer reaches of the mind. Buddhism finds life filled with *dukkha*, a Pali word that means suffering caused by clinging to what feels good and pushing away what feels bad. Dukkha causes people to struggle against what is. Narcissists are especially trapped in a push-pull struggle because they cannot stand their imperfections. Meditation keeps you looking at the contents of your mind until you see that all things change. Then the tendency to cling and resist is lessened.

Meditation is not a good way to solve neurotic problems. It weakens John in his search for his self, since it is an indirect approach to what must change. Many a meditation teacher has told his troubled students to get psychotherapy. This will help them to meditate without distraction. Meditation takes a perpendicular look at what passes by. The mind's eye keeps the fixed position of an observer. Thoughts just drop away. Therapy follows problems horizontally, staying with thoughts to their source. Then you can pull out the problem with its roots. From this you discover the roots of your problems but the observing position is lost.

Because of the weakness of a meditative approach to problems, John has not analyzed what bothers him. He is driven by angry rebellion against unfair beings whose power he desires. He does not know that he is impelled by anger he could not show his dad. Ventilating this anger to his self-centered boss is not worth the consequences. John does not know his anger's roots. Holding anger in would allow him to get certified as a meditation teacher. Expressing anger against his teacher turns him into the failure designated by his father. Children of narcissists have indirect ways of harming themselves to please their parents. The next step John must take is to face the anger he carries from his past.

I asked Delores, John's sister, about the strength she derived from being raised in a narcissistic home. Again there is weakness linked to strength. Strength comes from flexibility. A rigid stance creates problems. Delores spoke of coping with a selfish, violent, and narcissistic dad by a force of concentration that could take her mind away. She could do remarkable things in distracting settings. The miserable atmosphere of her home was obscured for her by her interest in painting and dancing. She created an internal scene that fascinated her regardless of what was going on. Shutting out objectionable events was her strength. As an adult such an ability helped her create a fantasy world in a shop that customers could enter.

Weakness also came from this strength. Used to shutting things out, she automatically focused tightly on what interested her and missed the larger picture. People took advantage of her. Forgetful behavior taught everyone including her daughter not to obey or even remember her requests. She bred personal confusion when she forgot where she wildly tossed her keys and spend vast amounts of time recovering them. There is strength in her concentration, weakness in a lack of control as to where and when she focuses. Being vague may express her need for a parent to take care of her. When Delores met her brother's Zen teacher, he offered her cookies of varied shapes from a tray, and of the one she took he said, "That signifies confusion."

For Delores to grow strong again, she would have to gain control over when she shuts things out through concentration. She needs to feel responsible for the results of her actions and not to accept and act out the poor self-image her father gave her. She must also learn not to inconvenience others with her careless deeds, as her narcissistic father did to her and the rest of the family.

Often, an initial move for independence involves joining a group. Membership in a group represents opposition to the parent. A narcissistic parent wants to determine her child's style and life objectives. Her child wants separation but, fearing to stand alone, joins an all-encompassing group as a halfway move to freedom. He thinks that membership expresses his individuality and cites group laws as buttressing independence from the parent. But such membership often limits his search for a self that needs separation to exist. In order not to be immersed in his parent's narcissistic net he buries himself in a group that operates like a narcissistic family and requires identity with members' goals and ethos. It is a style of life that reinforces personal nonbeing.

Herman joined Jews for Jesus as a young adult to oppose and bug his narcissistic mother, who followed Jewish law. Extremely offended by what he had done, she plagued him with counterarguments and joined a group that kidnapped "joiners" to "straighten them out." She mailed fliers to families that had "lost" their children to such groups and in her unconscious mind every child returned was her son.

Beyond the pleasure of upsetting his mother, how helpful was such membership? Immersion in Jews for Jesus was a step toward independence. Rebellion can trigger growth, but only if it is a jumping-off place to further development. Herman later needed his child to act a certain way to give the image of power, indicating that he did not go on to feel sufficiently strong and autonomous himself.

Eventually Herman left the group since he was tired of fighting his mother this way. Needing to feel manly, he felt it wasn't very masculine to have a group lead him by his nose. To increase strength requires self-knowledge that comes from looking at one's doubts. Herman later foisted a pseudoimage of strength on himself and his child. If a person treats his child as an extension of himself, the child does not feel like a person and the narcissistic problem passes on to the next generation.

My own experience with a group came out of an interest in meditation. Through what happened, I saw how children of narcissists are led by the parent into black-and-white thinking. I was with a meditation teacher in the United States who helped meditators awaken kundalini energy. This is a feeling of vibration that travels a twin spiral path up the spine and is accompanied by meditative experiences. Did such feelings come from the teacher or from my imagination? The teacher seemed to be a catalyst for what happened in meditation but what about the rest of him? Discordant facts came to my awareness and made me wonder if meditative good can come from a person who is far from perfect. Or can any good come at all? I was raised in an "off with his head!" narcissistic environment in which a person was either perfectly good or unacceptable.

I never liked his appearance. Squinting behind dark glasses, he looked like a croupier from Monte Carlo. I didn't like his followers, people who worshiped him and told us to defer. I didn't like his rates, great sums for room, board, and meditation sessions, far more proportionally than is charged in India, where the teaching of meditation is not a business. Where did the money go? The hall in which we met was handsome. I didn't hear much about hospitals or schools being built with our fees.

As a psychologist and the child of a narcissist, I am slow to surrender to the pressure to believe. I want direct experience of the facts. I saw an article in an investigative magazine written by some of his former staff. Not many of the current group would read it but I did. It said that the ashram's money went into a Swiss bank account. It described the meditation teacher as a chaser of moneyed folk and a sexual molester of young girls who were left in his charge. It said that he used the radiance of his position to seduce the young folk and called him a man of temper who had once speared his dresser with a fork. As they say, power corrupts.

This article brought my doubts home. Now I knew why he seemed to have a croupier's face and why I always felt a contrast between how he looked and what he did to help us meditate. His followers described their teacher's wayward behavior as a test of our faith, an explanation that was intended to put one's thought to sleep.

I thought I knew some of his bad side. My sense of what was good about what he could do went with it. I was swamped with negative feelings. How could he teach meditation? I asked others about the facts but could get no answer. How could he or anyone be a combination of bad and good? My narcissistic parents found most people bad and utterly condemned them. Learning this from them, I found bad in my teacher and condemned his good. All or nothing erased the complexity of what is.

It is hard to stop thinking in dichotomies. His followers said he was perfect and the article a lie. They said he did them so much good that they didn't care what was written. Some joined me and called him totally bad. As I matured, I saw that he was a good teacher of a form of meditation that takes potency from its teacher. I also believed that he sexually abused his young followers, overcharged, and took funds for personal use. It was painful to accept him as a two-sided figure, a man of high ability with significant failings, on the basis of which I did not want him as my teacher. Character is more important to me than skill. The knowledge that I developed from this group experience was first, not to believe what others tell me and second, that human good is mixed with bad.

A meditation teacher is like a therapist. The best therapist is one with good character. With such a person we can be ourselves and trust in his or her response. For the child of a narcissist, it is important not to create a false image of self and others in order to please new people. Part of my doubt in this teacher came from a Zen description in which Buddha is quoted as saying, "Slay me if you meet me on the road," which means not to believe in the image of the man but to reach an understanding of the essence of life through self-exploration.

My meditation teacher told his pupils that "leaders come from followers." Too long beneath the narcissistic thumb, I want to test all teachings and not to defer to a demand that I submit. Children of narcissists are raised to be believers. Fighting free of the narcissistic influence, they become overly suspicious. The next step is to develop our own judgment and to change what in our understanding is proved false.

The people in this group had a brainwashed quality. Hypnotized people are happy but not with the happiness of freedom. When I told people at the ashram that I was leaving, his followers said that I would go to hell, which engendered in me a wave of fear. That I could still feel frightened by such threats shows that the child of harsh parents continues to live inside me. The child lives on within the adult but through analysis his power to control gets smaller. The needs of the child are still felt but the adult part of the personality knows that the narcissistic parent cannot meet such needs and directs the self to seek sources of gratification that are more available.

Narcissistic parents used to frighten me by a withdrawal of their love. Despite such pressures I now choose my own path, which is a struggle and a thrill.

14

How to Find and Heal Your Self

We need to counter false images that we have accepted, to break the mold of habits that tie us. From childhood on I thought a sauna utterly embarrassing. My narcissistic father had despised my body as flat-chested and too large in the buttocks. I wouldn't dream of removing my clothes in public. One New Year's week, I visited Vermont with a lover whose friends hauled us into their sauna. I was in a state of dread but there was no way to decline gracefully. I felt so frightened of nudity that I had taken to bed and had to be dragged out to participate. I didn't want to admit my self-dislike to them. I had intense fear of their agreeing with my physical self-rejection.

I won't go into the horrors of undressing. Let it be known that I found a solitary and hopefully somewhat hidden position on the shelf of a former chicken coop turned sauna. It was New Year's Eve and the entire crew, including the children, drank champagne and reclined together. We listened to Caruso on a wind-up record player, laughed, and told stories. Mom was unabashed despite an appendectomy scar. We got so hot that we dashed out into the snow on an incredibly cold night and had a snowball fight. The feel of a snowball on heated skin is like a cool caress. Naked and rolling in the snow, chasing one another with snowballs. What of my nudity? It was the snow that counted. Giving and not getting snow on skin. It was terrific. After this, I stopped caring about being seen naked. Years of subsequent experience made it easy. The sauna was great but I like steam baths better. Nudity, big deal! My body too horrible? Who says? Only one person, my narcissistic father, whose negative opinion hit home.

Look, taste, touch, smell, feel, imagine, try what interests you. Experience confronts what we are taught to believe and what was drilled into our brains. We cling to our notions but, short of insanity, cannot totally disregard the facts.

We can use techniques to become our selves and to develop the self. Techniques are different from the roles our narcissistic parents assume to cover their footprints so that no one can follow and evaluate them. If recognized as they really are, they expect further damage to their egos. Only a perfect image is safe. Roles help them avoid detection but a role will not help the self to grow. Their roles depict greatness but hypersensitivity to the smallest sign of nonappreciation reveals profound and unadmitted doubts.

It is good to experience our selves with a method by which we are transformed but not hidden. A method is different from a role. The self can be itself and use a method to develop. There are many methods. The one you choose should challenge and interest you. Once, I was looking for space to rent from a woman who told me to come to her party that evening and chat. I did not know that it was a casting party. She needed actors and invited me to join the production. After years of therapy, I could not let myself walk away just because I was filled with fear. I told my quaking self, "These are only feelings," and knew better than to succumb to terror. Acting had been one of my greatest fears. I felt that I would die on stage. I had already suffered severe embarrassment in the limited arena of my narcissistic father's critical eyes. Surely I would forget my lines. My maturing self cornered me into saying, "Now is the time to test your fears, to see if you are as inadequate as you believe."

We were into rehearsal when my father visited me and listened with a sharp and critical ear as I spoke lines in the privacy of my room. Although I spoke in modulated tones, his hearing is excellent. Afterward, he mocked me, made fun of my voice and of the necessity of practice. "Is it really so important?" He thought my needing so much practice showed inadequacy. I shrank from his words and felt I should not be acting. For children of narcissists, it is hard to take on any project without parental invasion. The parent cannot allow his child to be an independent being. What if you are doing something of which he disapproves? What if it is something that he cannot do himself? I saw in my parent's treatment the origin of my hypersensitivity and went on rehearsing.

It was a morality play about a man who realizes that living for money and power is useless. At his death he triumphs because he feels his connection with life. The theme touched me deeply, having been so long abrogated by my parent's tongue. I was happy in my role even though I played a hostile and greedy figure. We have all such roles within us.

Rehearsals were a torture because I put the audience above me and was afraid of them. Fear of performing came from seeing them as critical parents. My parents told me to be perfect. Expecting perfection makes your errors wound you. Therapy showed a different way, to see the audience as my friends, to do my best and live with it. It was I who made the audience hard to reach.

The play went on and after initial nervousness I loved the plot's every moment. When the meditative walk offstage to no applause was completed, the audience left contemplating and the play was over. I went out to find my mother hanging on to the stone railing of the bridge that covered the theater's brook. I expected to hear how bad I had been when I asked, "Mother, how was it?" She looked up, eyes filled with tears and a catch in her voice, saying, "It was wonderful." We shared the joy of my courageous impulse. Hypersensitivity grew smaller with each playing. We performed and the audience responded. Initially scared, I grew to enjoy the performance. My exhibitionistic part, suppressed in childhood, came out.

How do we find out what is important for us? It is not enough for children of narcissists to follow the marked trail that others lay before them. Strength develops out of fighting with our handicaps. We evolve from struggling to cope with our difficulties.

My parents made me feel unlovable. My father said that my need for friends was excessive and made me unhappy, that I didn't fit in, lacked what was wanted, so why bother? Thinking this way was a conveyor belt to loneliness. What if my single friend turned against me, was sick, or moved away? Why try to make new friends if the outcome is predetermined? I found relief from such failure in nature. To begin with, my child's mind made me part of a family of pigeons that nested behind the ceramic cornucopia outside my room. Pigeon humming soothed me, that and the love with which the mother pigeon fed her babies. I considered them as backup parents and coaxed them onto my window ledge for crumbs of bread. It was terrible when my grandmother dislodged their "filthy" nest with her broom. I cried out, "What of the babies?" As always, no one listened. Thankfully, the pigeons came back.

Loving pigeons and other animals was the way I bound myself to life. It moved me toward ecology. Each of us must find the thing that talks to our heart. As a child, living part-time in the country, I was very concerned with animals. I was a pantheist then and probably still am, feeling the spirit of living things. One time, my father was driving the final few yards before our bridge when a bird, followed by its mate, flitted in front of the car and was hit. He stopped driving to watch it fall to the ground, with its mate flying over, swooping and circling the body. It was sad, the bird wanting to be rejoined with its partner, who lay quivering on the grass. My father did not know how to help as words and paragraphs tumbled from his mouth. Hard for me to concentrate on his words. Perhaps it was something about the inevitability of death. He did not offer to go for help, to do anything. I was too numb to speak as he talked me back into the car.

We traveled the few hundred light years of yards to our house to find an ongoing cocktail party conducted by his girlfriend. Guests came over as some tears began to flow. Away from my disapproving parent, I could cry. But the tragedy remained and no one did anything about the bird. I felt abandoned along with it.

Years later, I joined an environmental group to keep away a radium dump. Then I helped stave off development of a car wash that would spoil our local well water. I worked with people trying to preserve the local environment from total "development." As I write, I look at my bird feeder and the tiny beasts hanging about. This scene speaks to and from my self.

Sometimes experience is needed to show us what we lack. We feel discomfort and intellectual understanding but do not really know what was wrong in our upbringing until we see that life is led a different way. Experience drives home its point. Travel can do this for us, which is why I am drawn to places far away, even primitive to some. Although initially fearful, I go without an accompanying group to feel myself "there" as much as possible. I learn something of the language and make local friends.

Travel is outstanding, because it teaches about how people can live in nonnarcissistic ways, although much of the growth that prepared me for this occurred by barely perceptible degrees, nourished by psychotherapy. What drew me to Asia had a lot to do with being the child of a narcissist. When I was very young, feeling repressed and inadequate, I read a story that caught my interest. It was about Tibetan monks who constructed box kites in which they stood erect and flew on air currents over vast depths of sky. If flying made them arrogant they would unknowingly shift posture and some would plummet to their deaths. I do not know if any of this really occurred but I was drawn to a people who wanted not to be ego-ridden. I had a secret, almost magical, wish to go and see them.

Years later, in the midst of my training in clinical psychology, I also did physical yoga and was introduced to mystical reading. One book, *Be Here Now*, was by Richard Alpert (Ram Das). Alpert was a former psychology professor who went to India, where he accidentally met and became the student of Nimcaroli Baba, a man with great mystical awareness. Ram Das's writing touched me, not only because it was a fascinating subject but also because he spoke the tongues of psychology and meditation. He described his teacher as a man who transcended the greed of narcissism. I wondered, could there be such people?

I read Maya Baba's *God Speaks,* in which he described a vision of primal intelligence developing upward through all things in order of increasing sensitivity until it reaches divine union with itself. This touched my feeling for nature. It said to me that there is more to life than ownership. I read Alexandra David Neel's writing about walking across Tibet accompanied by a young Tibetan man who was her adopted son and guide. They saw wonders of human ability, like men moving in meditative trances over great distances and at fantastic speeds. They saw men undergoing the mind-controlled test, while in meditative trances, of drying wet sheets that were wrapped around their bodies in the fierce Himalayan cold. It was so fantastic to read this that I experimented with my own mental ability to produce heat. I was able to stand in the cold country air and think myself warm, become chilly, and think myself warm again.

Raised in a narcissistic family that worshiped excessive ego, I felt there was something for me in a people that eschewed it. Asian mystical literature speaks of abandoning the ego-ridden state. I also loved mountains and looked forward to the Himalayas, days of walking foreign paths, hearing nothing but the wind and falling waters. There was the incredible beauty of villages set so high with huge mountains above and below.

And the people! Raised in isolation, it interested me to be with people who regarded friendship as rule number one. I remember reading Buddha's response to Ananda, his slowest disciple. Ananda said, "Friendship seems very important to me. Is it?" Buddha answered, "Friendship is the most important thing." What would it be like to go to a place where at least some people were like that? Would I become free of my fear of rejection?

I was increasingly aware that we barely use our mental powers. It is common to turn off and lead a passive life. But there are many wonders to know and I had too long deferred to narcissistic control to resubmit to it. Darjeeling, in the Indian Himalayas, is near Tibet. The expected journey was a gift I'd give myself when I finished my degree.

When I got my Ph.D. I went to Asia. I remember my first day in Darjeeling, a city of brick and wood whose curved and winding streets crept up the Himalayas. There was a huge round temple with a friendly eye at its brow that regarded all, including monkeys that scampered in its courtyard. In free-standing stalls, there were knitted sweaters of yak hair, hand-woven cotton, Tibetan gems from her inland sea, the coral and turquoise worn by long-haired Tibetan ladies. Appearing from behind the moving mists was a huge and distant mountain, Kanchenjunga, third highest in the world, on the border between Nepal and Sikkim. It was surrounded by so many peaks up there with her.

The people were very calm, some with painted red dots in the middle of their foreheads in celebration of the religious spirit. I passed a boy in his teens who must have had an accident since he walked the street wearing nothing below his shirt. No one fussed or looked at him in an embarrassing way. So much consideration! What kind of city was this? People did not walk about naked. Dress was modest. Clearly his appearance was due to some kind of unavoidable circumstance. There was a fruit and vegetable market in which stood a huge bull, the king of its animals, sedately munching on throwaway rinds and peels. All was alive and strangely soothing.

In late afternoon, I walked past a building from which there came a happy sound. As I stepped back in the street to look up to the second floor, I was spotted by someone near the window. Immediately I was invited to a beautiful dinner given in celebration of the birthday of their dead father. Dinner was served on a banana leaf. I was their father's guest and they became my friends. They were beyond narcissism. In my amazement at what can be, I took them as my teachers, so different were they from the guarded suspicion of my home. My heart opened. How can I repay my friends? With love. By telling others about them.

On a hiking permit, I then went to the mountains with my Sherpa guide, Lagkpa. I was welcomed into villages whose people included me in their nightly singing. I walked with them formally as they pulled me along to receive their monk's gift to us of rice wrapped in leaves, and other holy objects. For each object we made a communal march to where the monk sat. He gave to us and we gave to one another. To people with colds, I gave my vitamin C, to their kids my cray-pas chalks and pad and watched them draw beautiful pictures until all the chalks were gone. I watched a young boy learn to play my newly acquired bamboo flute in a matter of hours. We all sat on the second-floor balcony of a house that rented the open space to hikers. We laughed ourselves silly watching people creep mincingly across a rope bridge that we had just managed to cross. Meanwhile the boy practiced flute nonstop. When he got to quarter notes we sang Hare Krishna to his playing. I had never seen such concentration and sharing. It was impossible to be left out, an overwhelming experience to one who had been raised by distancing narcissistic parents.

Children of narcissists benefit from stepping into the unknown of any type, be it people, reading, growing things, experimenting, playing instruments. It can be a trip to a place so far from parental judgment that it makes you feel beyond your parent's reach, so far that you can try out different ways of being.

Take sexuality. So much controlled by our parents' prohibitive eye, children of narcissists often experience sexual inhibition. In our mind, the parent's eye is on us when we have sex and can't let go. Many discover their sexual selves when far away from the external parent, since their own desire experienced in the absence of the actual parent can lessen the negating power of the parent within.

I was in Puri, India, with my Italian friend Giancarlo, a man I had met in Calcutta, where we both were so terrified of the inquisitive glances and questions from innumerable people that we immediately started traveling together. We were afraid and resentful of their intrusiveness, while at the same time we were fascinated by them. He had come to help the refugees of Bangladesh who had undergone severe flooding. I did not fear Giancarlo the way I feared my narcissistic father. Giancarlo was so open and friendly that I even looked down on him a bit. Children of narcissists must learn to eradicate such narcissistic evaluation. One night after eating a large and special meal prepared for us by Brahmans, who are supposed to be especially clean, I suffered a terrible case of dysentery during which Giancarlo held me for hours over the latrine, which happily was a hole in the floor. A floor-level hole let me weakly crouch there and be supported by Gian-carlo as I went through the throes of dysentery. After that, I had little shame with him.

We were traveling south from Calcutta, each night neatly tucked in under our own separate mosquito nettings. I paraded around half undressed because I never thought of him as a sexual partner. He was too kind to appeal to me that way, not the the child of a rejecting narcissistic father. It went like this until a monsoon cut us off from the world in our cottage on the beach. The utterly black sky brought incredible winds that banged the wooden shutters against the wall. No one was out in rain that poured down in a steady stream, a deluge so strong it could rip your clothing off. I always have been moved by natural things. Perhaps that is what brought me to his bed. That friendly, strong, warm, and generous man and I were eye to eye. Pre-vious experiences of sex had been with narcissistic lovers who closed their eyes and attended to themselves. With Giancarlo, smiling at me open-eyed, I had my first orgasm during intercourse.

I admit that I ran from this relationship. My defenses were falling and I felt that I needed them. I ran away from a repeat of such pleasure since accepting this would mean surrendering, changing into a person who received and trusted. Children of narcissists are afraid to be un-defended. Often it takes years of various kinds of therapy to pry us loose. But I knew a bit more about myself and the people I was choos-ing. I wanted a man who would really make love to me but it took many more years before I would try it again.

For the child of a rejecting narcissist, the route to affection is not direct. The parent sets it up this way, saying in many ways, first I must love you and then the others will. The child finds himself in an infinity of waiting for his parent's loving evaluation. Never having earned this love, he goes on to seek it from other narcissists. It is like a fairy tale in which you assume a golden horseshoe lies in the pile of shit. It's an old fairy tale that symbolizes searching for a valuable item in the most difficult and objectionable of settings. You think the horseshoe is in the shit and so you keep on digging. To give up his search the grown child must acknowledge the love that was offered as insufficient due to his parent's limitations. Knowing this ends the waiting for his parent's love.

Seeing love fully given by another helps dispel the fantasy of his parent's ability to give.

An experience did this for me while I was on the Himalayan slopes. If a mountain is equivalent to a standing person, I was at the height of his knee when Lagkpa, my Sherpa guide, said, "We are there." I was happy to have arrived until he pointed upward to the place of our "thereness," a climb of several thousand feet. A few hours of zigzag trekking and we arrived at a house looking over the world through ancient dark and hand-carved shutters. The house had two stories, with animals on the first. I met the house's lady trailed by a comfortable, naked, and free toddler. I saw him have a bowel movement on the floor which she picked up and washed away. There were no diapers and no fuss.

Later, we all had dinner in the main room, family and friends, Lagkpa and I, our sleeping mats rolled up and stacked against the wall. We sat in a circle near an open-fire clay stove on which baked an enormous number of potatoes. Everyone got a triangular heap of potatoes, which the Himalayans doused with chili and I ate plain. I met the wife's mother and their friends, who came in through the door without the loud greeting of the West. Everybody seemed to fit in naturally.

The next day, I was sitting alone looking out a window at the grandmother threshing grain on the roof of the adjacent shed. She was shaking a straw sieve while her grandson perched in a shawl on her back, open-eyed and looking about. He must have made a noise because there he was sucking on her breast. She also gave him some food from a small straw satchel. After a while he was on her back again. Both of them seemed content as I plunged into a deep depression that lasted days. I did not know what made me sad. Now I know it was seeing a child fully respected and loved. I had never felt that way with my narcissistic parents, who only gave me what they wished.

I was in mourning. Children of narcissists need to mourn the knowledge that such a childhood will never come to us. I saw how things can be and that my narcissistic parents could not give me this. The same can be said of my narcissistic lovers. (This does not include Giancarlo, my traveling companion in the Himalayas, who is not narcissistic.) With them, it will be the same as it has been. My wish and hope of receiving such love from them steals away my energy. I molder in waiting.

Surrendering one's expectation of such a full love from the narcissistic parent or a narcissistic surrogate is childhood's end. There will be a vacuum in response to my need and not the kind that nature fills. I must change the kind of person I choose to love, which means to change myself. I must rethink what I call love. Many children of narcissists have to struggle against what they tend to respond to and what they will ignore. Childhood leaves its scars. Emptiness from the past pushes us into a contemporary arena. I will heal myself by finding love to share.

Meditation can be of use since it brings one to original thought. In the kind of meditation I studied, you watch your breath at the nostril until your mind stops its wandering and remains relatively fixed. Then, with greater power of focus, you can look into the energy of your physical self.

The mind uses meditative watching to empty itself of extraneous contents and get down to its essential substance. It uses our attention to clean house. Everything stored comes to mind, ancient conditioned responses, ballads, memories, and fantasies. As the mental shelves grow empty you see aspects of your self long hidden or discredited.

After hours of looking at endless memories and conversations, rejections and fights, errors committed and jingles from the radio, I felt that I was going mad as my brain poured out these images like discarded garbage. I watched until my thoughts began to quiet into a mental silence that lasted seconds at a time.

In that intermittent silence, I saw a tiny baby beautiful in its innocence and was shocked at what I did not know. It was myself seen from a new perspective. The hatred I had learned had passed. I saw that perfect child was me.

Psychological healing can come in many ways, including caring human interaction, formal psychotherapy, and the creative use of inner vision. It can come from emotional involvement with the natural world. Healing can be an accidental outcome or the result of deliberate intention.

Here are stories of help offered to unhappy children of narcissists. Some felt helped and others went away as miserable as ever. The consequences of their experience were not immediate and clear. A person can be nourished unknowingly. But the child of a narcissist is usually not helped if what is offered is motivated by the other's need to express his grandiosity by giving. Responding favorably to please the giver is deferential behavior that further turns the child into a cipher. Under narcissistic pressure, the flowering of self is slow to appear. Narcissistic parents think that erring is horrible. Their kids must avoid error even at a brand new or difficult activity. The child fears parental judgment and, to avoid failure, is stranded in the "security" of sameness. Errors of omission are preferred.

The child of a narcissist who is fighting for existence will try to resist what wants to take him over. He stays invisible to his parents, whom he wants to please without acceding to their wishes. Children of narcissists need to dare to have their own ideas and goals.

The following story shows how nature can be turned to for help. Wild things can be our healing friends. The story is my own.

Life Among the Savages

There was a little girl who had a little curl right in the middle of her forehead, and when she was good, she was criticized anyway. And criticized and criticized, reshaped by her father the schoolteacher, who, even though they were on summer vacation, never would lay down the ruler. He prodded and shaped and examined her thinking. "Think like a man!" he'd exclaim. (Thinking like a woman was bad? Being female was bad?) He examined her slothful body—"Too broad in the beam; shoulders too narrow, boyish."

Her mother was worse; less intellectual, more basic. She strode about in Dad's torn undershirt, casting further shame on the state of being female. Here, in the summer cabin, she canned and cleaned and worked and hauled, all the while cursing and screaming and brooding about her miserable lot; maligning Dad, who "scribbled," by which she meant that he was attempting to be a writer rather than earning a lot of money by having a second job as many did during the war years. He taught for a living and had no second job. She screamed out her frustration at the little girl, never seeming to notice the great sadness and the endless dribble of tears. Perhaps both parents were like sharks, unable to resist the smell of blood.

The child attempted to help her mother but the mother refused her while cursing the child's helplessness. Once the child forcibly washed the dinner dishes and the mother rewashed them right afterward. The child asked for her own garden patch but was told she'd not do it right. Mother imparted no womanly skills, no skills at all in learning to care for herself or to survive on her own in the world outside. There was no touching in this family, little holding except for her father's formal good-night kiss in the middle of her forehead. Loneliness was as natural as the touch of the sun on her bare skin.

Outside the cabin, the sun shone down and the big stream rushed by close to the house. Frogs croaked and peeped their mating songs and turtles made turtle sandwiches, three and four deep, sunning themselves on the shore. Frogs leaped away at the little girl's approach. She, the little pariah, lived in her senses, hearing, looking, smelling, playing by herself. She felt one with the breezes, the whispering trees, the iridescent darning needle that landed on a twig near the great rock. There were few children to play with and, besides, she was afraid to approach them.

She sat and dreamed and made up stories about the world. The wind talked and sang to her. The birds whistled and she almost understood their message, for she knew there was one. Birds and trees and flowers knew her; they all felt each other. Especially the huge old rock in the middle of the stream was her friend and watched over her. Sometimes she felt scared in the shadows; darker spirits lived there. She'd scurry past to the light. She felt great love for all that trembled and sighed in the wind; the high grasses, the smell of loam.

But still she was haunted by her inability to do anything right. One day she stopped to play in the gravel pit. She found many little flat stones and began to build, not knowing what would emerge. An apartment house of rocks, low flat rooms, with roofs, setbacks, and shadows like Hopi pueblos. There was no plan. It couldn't be judged. It just was. Primitive, crude, monolithic. When finished, it had little terraces, places of sun and shade, somehow mysterious and yet incomplete.

She went to the cabin for lunch. Her mother sullenly pushed extra helpings on her plate which she compliantly ate; her father quizzed her disapprovingly about some scholastic fact. Her mother tugged at the wild, unruly hair escaping from her braids. Each was satisfied at fulfilling their parent role in reshaping the little girl. Then she was allowed to escape to her rock building.

And there it still sat, a little cooler and darker in the late afternoon sun. Apart, stately, and mysterious. Suddenly she heard a little noise. Got down on the ground, her ear to the stones. A shrill, rasping sound, a mournful soprano letting out a little shriek. Then many such sounds, voices singing, alone, together, trailing off and restarting, their own rhythms and harmonies, their own language, swelling and fading—at once a sad and joyful chorus to summer and the setting sun. Her building was inhabited! A cricket orchestra had moved in, finding it to their liking. She was so excited. The little rock houses were liked, filled with the tiny creatures, telling her, thanking her, singing their contentment, sharing her sorrow. She had made something good and useful. The spirit of the crickets sang of sadness, of love, of the goodness of singing together. Now she was separate from her parents and part of the world of spirits. She was whole.

Since I was never appreciated for doing anything right, my ego was corroded and demeaned by doubt. I surrendered to the blackest of moods. At psychological bottom there is no hiding in trivial distractions. Often this opens us to visions that can take us from our agony. The crickets were my children and I gave to fill their needs as my narcissistic parents did not give to me.

When a person plays, the flow of the unconscious is closer to the surface of the mind. Healing increases when unconscious and surface touch in a fiery force that liberates our energy. We need to expose our wounds to the sun. For children of narcissists, open play is difficult since we fear exposure to criticism and the enemy is imagined near. If we are alone, the enemy dwells within our minds and sees our wounded vulnerability. Wounds are defensively left to fester in the dark, un-healed beneath their psychological wraps.

If human company is absent or unacceptable, nature may serve since, with few exceptions, it does not beckon with false love and then attack its lover. Things take their natural place and man can learn to live respectfully with it. The human child, especially of narcissistic parents, in seeing and sharing animal life learns that there is another way.

People always try to heal their wounds but efforts can be limited by self-protective and counterproductive defensive mechanisms of which they are unaware. Most children of narcissists do not perish outright under the onslaught of bad parenting but are slowed down, bound to sticky defenses that limit their ability to change. No matter how difficult, it is better to strive to heal. We may need outside help to free us of constriction. Without help, we often achieve but a small measure of our potential. We may have areas in which we achieve competence while the rest of us is constricted by the lack of confidence our narcissistic parents showed us and we believed was justified.

One terrible defensive outcome is to settle into an emotionally robotic existence in which we feel neither the pain of childhood nor the realization of life's pleasures. Feelingless and neutral, we defer to the parent's prohibition of our becoming a separate person. Neutrality is a compromise that falls between being and nonbeing. Some of us are unable to assume a "protective" robotic niche but cannot walk the narrow path of life. We fall further to become insane, addicted, or suicidal.

Developing a sense of self is a difficult task and we need assistance. How are we to know what we seek if we do not know what help is? Parental narcissism substituted its own needs when responding to our cry, which made our emotional situations worse. Even though we must seek help we may not find it. Then help must find us. Sometimes it does. We are dependent on the generosity of the universe and its chance numbers. Help can come from unexpected sources since a uniform does not a healer make. By uniform I mean a degree that gives a person official status. Some people have innate sensitivity. Many were helped and are inspired to pass it on.

I was about nine when my father and I went on a summer vacation to a lodge that had anti-Semitic patrons. That's what he told me. But why would a Jewish man want to go there with his young child? All of his life he worked at erasing cultural traits that he feared would bring him rejection. He spoke with the voice of a radio announcer, hoping to pass unobserved by hotel guests. His child was to be the same, another who would "fit in." He did not consider me as a separate being with my own needs and feelings.

I had known his anti-Semitic criticism but not the reasons for his receptivity to anti-Jewish characterizations. He made me worry about my "Jewishness" and, living with him, I was constantly scrutinized for such traits. He winced any time caricatured Jewish features were present in anyone: singsong accent, avarice, mother-centeredness. He did not feel bad if a Scot was smacked with his group's stereotype and in fact he enjoyed the person's embarrassment. He lived in the world of bias, secretly enjoying bias against others and fighting off his own.

If someone asked me my religion while at the hotel, I was to say I did not know. Fearful at living in subterfuge and imbued with feelings of inadequacy from constant criticism, I resolved to stay away from people. No questions and no shame. What my dad did during the day excluded me. I didn't think of him as I rowed down the river and saw the beautiful water and riverbank.

There was an elderly man standing near the water's edge. He tended a mesh pen filled with something. I rowed over to look, got out of the boat, and walked over. There they were, rabbits. Big and little, white with pink eyes, babies leaning against their parents. Like rainbows, beautiful and effortless caring. I was drawn to the man with his pleasant smile and no questioning. He was stocky, elderly, and quiet inside. After we said hello, paralyzing embarrassment sent me its message . . . escape. I was silent. Instead of attempting to make me talk as my father would have done, he followed the direction of my gaze and next thing I knew, my arms were filled with a huge friendly rabbit that snuggled into my cuddling. I couldn't do it wrong. No complaints.

Each day I went to him and his bunnies. He would smile, say hello, and fill my arms with rabbits. Moments of quiet, endless contentment. I was happy and didn't think much. Later, my father was too self-involved to ask me what I had been doing, which was good. I continued. The old man accepted me without the painful medium of words. He nourished my need for loving contact and took me exactly as I was. The rabbit man. My rabbit man.

*   *   *

We are raised under our parents' ignoring and scrutinizing gimlet-eyed gaze, hard, divisive, and isolating. The eye ignores what is important to us if that does not coincide with our parents' values. Their eyes are like laser beams, seeking out points of interest in us. They apply concepts of "flaw" and "fame" to what they evaluate. Growing up under such a regime, one feels like a bug beneath a microscope and at the same time a child forgotten in a dusty alley. The glance that ferrets out and focuses on their interest, that applies the label "good" or "bad," pushes us into an emotionally alienated state.

We internalize the quest for our flaws and watch ourselves in an evaluative and rejecting way. Hateful scrutiny stops us in our tracks and turns our spontaneity to paralysis. Exploration ceases along with performance of things we love to do or only do for the hell of it. We constrict ourselves to get away from parental criticism. Scrutiny, criticism, and constriction give existence a lifeless quality.

All children need the beneficial glance of what I call the rounded eye, one that does not focus on and evaluate parts of our being. The rounded eye looks on all unconditionally. It gives us acceptance and heals the damage of our upbringing. Points of light are those situations, animals, people who respond directly and positively to the child. The child may not call it a healing event but something about it sticks. It remains in his memory and is turned to when he feels abject despair or in need of hope. From what happened, his life became more livable. His self-worth was seen and reinforced.

Irwin was scorned by two narcissistic parents who treated him with barbaric sadism. They would humiliate him with the chore of going to the bakery to buy a single, tiny roll. They liked to do this and the salesgirl in the bakery spoke to him with scorn as well. He had to stand aside until her "good" customers had been served. He told his parents about this and they looked forward to sending him again.

They may have been reversing their roles as mistreated German refugees. Or passing on their experience of being callously handled by narcissistic parents. Irwin's large father would slap his son's backside backhand when Irwin walked by and mock him for his complaining. Complaint was Irwin's only outlet for hostility but was truncated by his fear of parental violence. His father had been raised in Nazi Germany as a victim who identified with the aggressor. He used a titrated Nazism on his child, giving him a taste of what he had suffered in his own childhood.

Irwin was self-hating, embarrassed, and angry. He believed that no one could share his pain. There was cynicism in his complaints and he was beyond seeking sympathy. At home, showing weakness caused his parents to mock him, treatment that painted its colors on his world.

Too small and weak to say no, Irwin was en route to the bakery for his father's tiny roll. He fell in the street and lay there sprawling, knees rubbing the pavement, ankle turned. Careless, sloppy, worthy of small knocks and embarrassing falls. In physical discomfort, he was thrashing on the ground when a man came over and helped him up and onto his feet. He dusted off Irwin's hands and patted his shoulders. He wanted to know how Irwin felt and didn't just up and leave.

Irwin heard, "Are you OK?" and was overwhelmed with feeling. He didn't know what to say and mumbled, "Yes." He felt something stir within and wanted to escape before the inevitable harm befell him. What if he cried? He started crying, cried and cried. Crying. Couldn't stop and it wasn't over falling. Was it the back rub and the polite and considerate questions that he couldn't get out of his mind? He had never been treated like this. The man waited for Irwin to feel better, held his shoulder and said soothing words, as if Irwin were a sensitive human being. As if he counted.

A turning point. Irwin talks about it still. He cried to learn that there could be human kindness for him.

Selfhood is created partly out of the inchoate experiences of early interactions between people and animals, and self-creative activities. How do these activities reinforce our sense of being? To improve a self mangled by rejection and improper use we have to experiment with being. We need situations in which to practice the reality of a self, places that reflect our dreams and fantasies, where we can behave in a way that shows who we really are and what we feel. We need responses that support the development of our being.

We are social animals who find recognition within a group. Acceptance of our selves is needed to correct distorted, isolated, and unacceptable self-images. Acceptance draws us back from self-destruction or a solitary and unrelated life. There are various roads to self-acceptance. If we cannot get close to people and are creative, a healing response can come from our imagination. Creative minds produce islands of benefit.

Experiences between humans can be nourishing to the self. A mother's loving attention is usually more nourishing than that of a "stand-in" like the police guard at the school crossing who is kind and considerate to a timid child. To a child with narcissistic parents, however, the importance of "stand-ins" can be crucial. There are rescuers who give more to the child than does his family, who do not see him as a separate person.

A twelve-year-old prepubescent girl, raised by an utterly critical father, is introduced to her mother's boyfriend after her parents have separated. She is immature and needs her sexual self to be noticed by a man that she can trust. Since her father has denied her his approval, she thinks of herself as a reject. The appreciative comments by her mother's boyfriend come as a relief. She is uplifted with glee when he discovers her knees and says, "When you are older, how will we keep the boys away?" He is telling her that she is becoming an attractive woman. Young girls discover their sexual role from the stated reactions of men who care for them but control their sexual impulses.

Another young girl of about six or seven, utterly rejected by her family, is given a spent bullet shell by Roger, the psychotic boy who lives in the building next door. He says that this bullet once took his father's life. Whether any hint of this is true, she feels wonderfully admired. There can be no doubt that Roger loves her, so there must be something about her to love.

A parent's responses are highly valued when given directly but the child can still be moved without immediate contact. It depends on who is doing the expressing and why. A child receives a loving letter from a seaman father who is gone for months. The child is sustained and even happy with his memory.

Destructive human interactions and addiction to technology can alienate us from our creative power. Technology means the hollow throb of television or reams of data on a computer. Technology turns out material that absorbs our attention and distracts us from what we need. Denial of the inner life, its feelings, thoughts, and dreams, separates our awareness from the inner self. If we do not know our creative forces we can become increasingly dependent on our narcissistic parents to give us what needs to come from within. Narcissists enjoy the power of their position although they do not have what we seek. Our self is denied when the parents fail to help us back to it and ultimately we feel that there is no help anywhere.

Self must be found. Although outside reflection is extremely distorted or even missing, there are elements in it that keep us from the most dire of endings. There is the strong biological urge to thrive that walked peasants across continents to gain steerage to America. There is the creative urge to weave the materials of life into a form with which we can function. Creativity takes the destructive threads of life and puts them together with something from within that changes it all into what can sustain a faltering self.

Our creative mind bypasses hackneyed limited thought and shows us who we really are. It uses the raw clay of experience to create meaningful relations that allow us to live within the bounds of sanity. To one who thinks herself worthless, seeing her creativity is a shock. Where did this outpouring come from? Is there a worthwhile self? She escapes into nonentity from this overwhelmingly different image but its spirit calls her back. She realizes that she is a person.

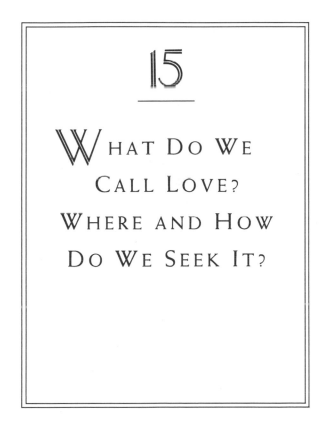

15

WHAT DO WE CALL LOVE? WHERE AND HOW DO WE SEEK IT?

Love for Self, Lovers, Friends,
Employees, and Co-Workers

A huge area of difficulty for children of narcissists, even those who are professionally successful, concerns what we call love. Love is what we search for and give to others. What we call love affects what we look for and what we give.

We left childhood feeling terrible, with some idea of the how but not the why of it. We live in clouds of doubt and confusion. A big step forward is to not take total blame for what we feel. Events occurred with our parents that hurt us even though they said what they did was for our good. We heard that punishment was harder for them to give than us to receive. From all our painful "lessons" and experiences, we should know that our self-hatred is a learned response. This will not make self-hatred go away but does give motivation to change.

Our parents gave us negative responses. They greeted us in temper, saying, "How awful you are." They ignored, threatened, yelled at us, and gave insufficient touch. We echoed their point of view and thought, "I am unworthy of love." We took acceptance of their view a further step and, rather than see them as rejecting, turned their hurtful behavior into love. Scolding, forgetting, demeaning, aggrandizing, demanding—all their destructive ways were labeled love. In an attempt to understand and accept our pain, we think that we have not been good enough to earn sufficient love. We grow up to seek love from similar people.

The adult child of a narcissist does not know his unconscious love-seeking mission as he creates painful relationships. A healthy personality does not seek rejection. The adult wonders why he ends up with abuse. Many complain about the very thing they hold on to and do not admit to the pleasure that it gives them. Delores has a child who will not do what is asked of her, even after she has agreed to do it. That is how Delores raised her and, in spite of grumbling, what she wants.

If a mother wants her child to change, she will refuse to put up with abuse. Delores's child tried on her mother's clothing in rebellion against a stated demand that she not do so. After the trying on, she left the clothing lying on the floor. A mother who is sincere about her wishes would throw her daughter out if she did not stop such misbehavior. If instead, mother pleads with daughter to stop and secretly reinforces the abusive treatment, it goes on. Sometimes, awareness of why we select pain can only be learned through therapy. Otherwise our defenses keep us out of touch and churning in the murk.

When do you think that love was given you and how did you receive it? Do people in your adult life treat you in similar ways? Many children of narcissists blindly repeat patterns of inadequate loving. As adults, our childish minds, which wanted love from the narcissistic parent, choose narcissistic partners with whom we continue to struggle for love. This childish wish undercuts our power of decision to move on. It keeps us on an unrequited search. Our adult minds suspect that love won't come but don't know how to break our patterns of choice. We are out of touch with thoughts and feelings that have their hold on us. We see our habits but not our blind spots. We can be intellectually aware of our interest in narcissistic people but emotionally we are unable to change.

Delores exemplifies this. She does not see how her boyfriend resembles her father. She says, "He is unlike my father except in the shape of his shoulders. They both are short and walk stooped over." She responds to my comment about repetition by asking, "Why would I want to relive my father's love since he had no love to give?" I ask why she stays with her current man and she says that she only likes his intelligence. Sex is horrible since he will not learn to do what she likes, including touching her breasts. Sex is only for him and infrequent as possible but she enjoys sleeping curled together like two bears.

She doesn't see the picture overall, that father and boyfriend were critical, argumentative, violent, withholding, and financially on the take. I ask her to look more closely at her feelings for her boyfriend and she explodes with, "I can't stand him." This is said of the man she calls darling as she perpetually wards off his verbal attack. She tells me that she does not like any of the men she has loved. I ask her if she misses good sex with the current boyfriend and she says work is the only thing that counts. Unless pushed, she stays away from her feelings by leading a peripatetic existence like the one her mother led with her dad.

Like many children of narcissists, Delores gets pleasure from misery, a process that is sadomasochistic. With her boyfriend as a stand-in, she works for and awaits her father's unavailable love. She walks an emotionally spiked path out of childhood. Children of narcissists are miserable but hang on by taking pleasure in such misery to make life bearable. The child enjoys her parent's scolding, forgetfulness, demands, and intrusions. Such pleasure continues to have allure.

Here is another example of selecting a partner with whom each episode is pleasurable torture accepted with the hope of change. Since his self was rejected by narcissistic parents, the child of a narcissist turns away from his self and finds its need for love unfamiliar. The area of love is taboo and frightening. He is so hurt that he avoids dating until emotional needs mount to the point where resistance is overcome. Then he turns toward a narcissist who cannot give. He takes the pain of deprivation as love or at least the path to love.

A woman had an affair with a narcissistic man. He was very sexual. He even grabbed her breast in a joking way when the subway car took a darkened curve. She found love in the sexual crumbs of their relationship. After an agreeable bout of sex, she was lying beside him feeling spent and happy when the phone rang and he answered. It turned into a lengthy long-distance phone call with a woman she later found out he thought he still loved. The woman had rejected him and the hook of desire remained. Perhaps it was baited with the worm of rejection. A narcissist wants to be the one who deigns to leave.

The child of a narcissist lay beside him as he talked. She couldn't believe the call and tried to deny it. The call would soon end. It was impolite and. . . . Time went by and talk went on as she rose, put on her clothing, and departed. He did not notice her leaving as he talked to his "chosen one." He had enjoyed their sex but now did not have a flicker of awareness about her feelings or whereabouts. His attention was on the phone call.

She read love in their passion, clung to him, and hoped for change but he did not say a word about permanence. In his sexual orientation he was like her father, who valued female beauty and wanted it on call. Her father handled his Oedipal attraction to her when she was a child, along with his need for superiority, by denying that she was attractive. He called her body unworthy, which kept desire out of his mind. She believed what he said and thought herself ugly, though early photographs show a pretty, wide-eyed girl. He did not easily kiss her but held her head firmly between two hands for a mid-forehead buss. It was like the three-way holding machine on the head of an animal about to undergo surgery. From her parent's touch she got the notion, who would want to touch me?

She was used to being ignored and submerged in her dad's self-centeredness. Although she hated being criticized, she associated it with love. Sometimes she felt loved when nothing was given. Children of narcissists manufacture this feeling from whatever comes their way.

She developed distorted notions of loving. It was a familiar situation if her lover was not there when she needed him. As an adult, she became pregnant by her boyfriend and wanted to have their child. After arguing with her to have an abortion, he totally disappeared. Although she intended to have the child, the pregnancy ended in miscarriage.

We find ourselves confused and hurt by what we call love and think it a thing to be avoided. This is often the result of having at an early age loved something that was deliberately taken from us. It is worth remembering experiences in which our love was nipped, when the thing we loved was removed, lost, destroyed, or turned against us. This memory shows us that it is untrue that we have never loved at all.

Regardless of what our narcissistic parents say, we learn to love by loving. Narcissistic parents often frown on their child's love for an animal. They think he will never will love a human being, as if the capacity for love were limited as a pie. The narcissistic parent thinks in simple equations. If you love this, then you cannot love that. Rather than recognize the limited capacity as his own, the parent projects it onto his child. If his child loves lower down the animal scale he cannot love higher up. Loving a cat means he will only care for cats. Parental judgment is communicated to the child, who responds by limiting the loving he feels and filling his mind with doubt.

I remember at age eight how my kitten set it off by running up the curtains. Also there was Smoky, my fox terrier–type dog, and Uncle Al, the alligator who stretched out on my hand for a belly rub and scared my grandmother with its carpet runs. I was told that all my adorable pets must go. I defended against total loss by holding on to Smoky, my dog friend since I was five. We were barricaded in my room with my dresser to the door and my shoulder to the dresser, pressing against the screaming and pushing from the hall. Smoky barked by my side. It was a desperate situation.

Later I emerged to see no kitten and no alligator, and no one would discuss my loss. It was later said that Uncle Al was "somewhere in school." I was bereft, but at least I had my dog. I couldn't share what I felt. They were right. Love is risky. My parents said that loving animals kept me from loving humans. Now I was fearful of loving animals and humans. They probably saw in my fear the justification for what they had done.

It is painful to lose what you have loved. The desire to love is flanked by the fear of loss. My parents blamed this feeling on my pets. Would I want another pet? The inner parent criticizes my need. Does loving an animal cause lack of love for people? I need to test the hypothesis that love for one stands in the way of love for another. I think that love breeds love. The narcissist's love pie is limited since he is preoccupied with self-concern. I do not subscribe to the pie theory.

I learned from current examination of my love for animals that the more things I love the more I can love. I see that my parents constantly criticized the things I loved and that my fearful holding back was learned.

We need to stay open to new information in the face of learned negative judgments against the self. Pauline was on vacation. She had been persuaded to go to a certain hotel that bordered on a state park and had beautiful walks. She dreaded meeting the people with whom she was to socialize. Versed in self-hatred, she entered the hotel lobby and heard laughter. She thought, "They're laughing at me," and wanted to leave right away. She thought, I can walk right out this door with my suitcase in my hand.

Previous therapeutic work on self-hatred came to her mind. She remembered that she tended to personalize unrelated behaviors and decided to stay a bit longer, signed in, dragged herself to her room, deposited her luggage, washed her face, and went downstairs filled with fear at having to meet the laughers, who turned out to be friendly. She saw her error in thinking that people would instinctively reject her. Her rejectable self-image dissolved a bit more. Just a bit. All of such experiences add together until it is impossible to assume the worst.

We need to allow people to get close regardless of how poorly we regard ourselves. We can learn from social errors. Victoria is sitting on the dating fence again and speaking of how hard it is to change. If she shows interest in a man, she thinks she will be rejected. Her narcissistic mother raised her to fear men, to feel incompetent and ugly, although she is beautiful. Victoria says, "You know that I was toilet-trained far too early and later was a soiler and wetter. I walked around with shitty pants and still feel that way." I laugh and respond with my own remembered physical failings. "When I was young and upset or even pleasantly excited, I always had a nosebleed. I had nosebleeds when the person I depended on left my side, like the night I discovered that my mother had gone away for the weekend. She had left me without explanation in the care of a narcissistic aunt who criticized me until I worked myself into an asthmatic fit with tears. Oh yes, I had asthma in those days. No breathing when I was upset. My nose would bleed and pour blood all over everyone. Like the time my girlfriend Barbara was visiting. She shared my bed. That morning we woke up in a pool of my blood. It turned out that I had my period and my nose was also bleeding. I gave Barbara the full treatment. Of course, I thought that every mishap including nosebleeds cast me in a miserable light.

"Also, I almost forgot that when I was younger, I would vomit in the automobile. Also on the trolley car. We would have to get off the trolley before our stop. Once, on a car trip, I complained so much about needing to vomit that my friend Alice lost control and without saying a word vomited on me. I didn't vomit that time."

Victoria was laughing. My nosebleeds and vomiting matched her shitty pants and even with such an image, I was dating! Hot on the topic of feeling objectionable, I reminded her of how we children of narcissists are raised to think in terms of black or white. My father was perfect and my mother horrible. I was a genius or an inadequate idiot, good or bad with nothing in between. I was perfect or unacceptable. I accepted these standards in order to see myself as a failure and so did she. Men have to make it to the upper rung to count with us. I said, "Those who don't meet our values are worthless. You with your bed-wetting and me with my nosebleeds are defensive stinkers. Who would want to know us?" Victoria laughed again as I added, "We get rid of them first. If I meet a man I fall upon his imperfections."

From Victoria came, "It is horrible that we follow such habits. We know ourselves and do it anyway. We're stuck." To this remark I counter, "We call ourselves stuck to avoid taking chances. If we're stuck we're safe. One of the most healing things ever said to me was, 'Go out and make a mistake.' You say no men are interested in you but they are looking for a sign of interest. If no one comes over, you are not sending the signal. Was your mother right when she said no man could like you?" I challenge Victoria to go out.

Victoria agrees and adds, "All people are good and bad. Can I accept a human being with his errors? Can I accept myself that way? I see myself as an ugly child with shit in my pants." I tell her, "Go out as ugly as you feel. Me stupid with a bleeding nose, and you with shit in the pants and insecure." She says, "Yup. At least I no longer have to cover myself with makeup." Victoria had always worn a ton of makeup. Before any of the other girls, she was made up by her mother, who found that she had ugly "fish eyes." The idea of ugliness went very deep. Clearly a disguise was needed.

16

PEOPLE IN STAGES OF SELF-DEVELOPMENT

We become ourselves by emerging from surrender to our parents' need for us to be a certain way. We need to develop a point of view independent of the one held by the parents whose love we need, even if they take our independence as a personal rejection. In the material that follows, we see the development of inner strength from less to more, the problems, shortcomings, and weaknesses commonly encountered. Also, we see the unusual abilities that develop out of becoming a unique person. Although the best judge of what you need is you, if you cannot hear your inner voice, it might be good to seek outside help. In this light, some kinds of therapy are discussed.

*   *   *

The people next depicted—Mary, Lorrie, Nick, Tillie, Alice, Doryan, and I—are children of narcissists in progressive states of breaking loose from the abdication of our selves. Mary has surrendered so much that her life is directionless and miserable. Lorrie's surrender is less destructive in that it moves her to develop skills that make her happy because they help others. She enjoys and lives through their pleasure. Nick hates containment by his parent's need but movement toward independence is stuck in a negative and rebellious stand. Tillie also rebels but in a way that is useful to others by being compulsively "helpful." Alice gives personal effort to vocational goals in which she retains control, but does not get close to people. Doryan has mastered his craft and gets pleasure from a love relationship whose closeness he limits to a degree that he can stand. The acceptable level of closeness for him is well below average. Then there is my story, still growing and unwilling to accept neurotic limitations as permanent.

Mary

Mary is a San Francisco girl whose defensive nonexistence excludes regular work. At twenty-one, her life lacks commitment to long-range goals. Nothing gets the attention that it needs. Even her vow to be thin is an up-and-down affair whose frequent falls are torture. Having chaotic objectives makes her miserable but she also laughs at her constant changing as if it were a joke. She basically remains the same, so there is psychological gain in what she clings to. Otherwise, why would she choose to live on a low income, without a career, with no material way to enhance her sense of self-worth?

She wanders between uncompleted objectives, impulsively seizing and dropping goals, some of which her mother likes. Other activities are simply done for cash, like waiting on tables or baby-sitting. Menial jobs have replaced spotty attendance in college. In so many ways, she is paralleling her mother's career. Her mother was an academic star in high school who avoided college and had inadequate income in her early years.

Mary's mother had a narcissistic, critical mother and an extremely narcissistic father who demanded service and obedience. He deplored, hit, and eventually abandoned his family. Abandonment became his daughter's dread event, which led her to seek dependent lovers and to raise Mary as a clinging child. Mother's unstated needs run counter to her stated expectation. She is concerned about her daughter's future but does not require her to have a vocation. (A lack of maternal financial support would force the issue.) Does she want an independent daughter or a child who will never settle down?

Mary's grandmother's husbands were alcoholic and her mother's were into alcohol and pot. Daughter Mary followed suit with a boy-friend who drank and was financially dependent on her, which made him indirectly dependent on her mother. A child ordinarily walks the parent's footsteps. If the parent has a narcissistic bent the pressure to copy is strong.

Mary's mother is angry at her daughter for not doing what she tells her but this is only surface grumbling. Unconsciously she enjoys her child's dependency and disregard for feelings. Criticism flows from daughter to mother since Mary is angry at her mother for having problems she must copy to please.

Mother was raised to be beautiful, popular, and a good student, but she was also full of resentment at the pressure of parental demands without the reward of adequate love. She never found out how much attention was enough to give or get and now her child suffers from the same confusion. Mary gives too little attention to others and to herself. She also expects too much. Here are three generations of women raised by narcissistic parents to be abused, abusive, and narcissistic.

Mother does not know her proper rights. She puts up with mistreatment and doles it out. Her daughter was raised to worship Mother's idealized image but one of her mother's primary traits is not needing or respecting limits. A trait that smacks of power can be idealized, even or especially one that made you suffer. Here is an example of the truth that you cannot give what you have not received or developed. Daughter respects no one's needs, including her mother's. Raised in confusion, she passes it on.

Extremes of caring come up all the time. Mother's inattentiveness is bracketed by "spoiling." Mary hates being ignored and behaves badly to get attention, caring little for what others need and deserve. The main thing is to get her needs met.

Mary is endlessly on the dole, taking advantage of people, misusing her mother's charge card, which was only supposed to be used in emergency, overwriting checks, running up bills, acting like a spoiled rich girl on a spree who will always be bailed out. Mother is working hard and financially only up and coming. Her daughter's spending sprees make great holes in her budget and bring hardship around the bend. Mother rationalizes what she does, saying that what she gives Mary is an "investment," but in what? Daughter says she will repay her mother but gives so little back that it is but a token against the mounting hoard of things received. Mother fills her child's endless requests, soothing her as she once soothed her narcissistic father by filling his materialistic needs. Copying of the self-attentive narcissistic attitude occurs and the child becomes like its parent. Narcissism passes on.

Last night I had a dream about the two of them. Mother and daughter gave a party to which I came. I took off my shoes, which they took, and soon forgot where they left them. Mother brought out several pair of pumps, attractive, purple suede shoes which she held up for me to see. It was unstated if I was to wear them, but I saw that these would not fit. In bringing me such shoes, she may have been showing off what she possessed and offering me what was inappropriate. In the same way, Mary was trained to be endlessly on the take from Mother and not to earn her way.

I then realized in the dream that Mary had taken my handbag to a neighbor's house and it was missing. Mary and her mother searched for my things but were not much concerned. There was a likelihood that I'd have to leave without my shoes and possessions. A missing pocketbook indicates that I was financially abused. They acted gracious but did not seem to care. This dream shows the self-centered vanity of narcissism. My suffering at their hands was not understood or appreciated.

As a narcissistic duo, Mary's tirades express her mother's rage. Mary's beauty and charm express her mother's desired image for Mary and for herself. Mary complains about confusion and works beneath capacity at what she takes as an experimental lark to be dropped when its novelty wears off. She doesn't recognize that people make commitments after years of work. She hopes that the star of truth will one day fill her sky and until then, she will lead an undirected life that ties her to her mother.

But there is progress in that Mary has come to know that she is miserable and has entered therapy, where the question of who she is and what she wants to be is constantly asked. To this end, to achieve a career she has reentered college. To change, Mary will need to stay in therapy. Her mother has become a little aware of her ambivalence over this but without therapy of her own still needs her daughter to be a dependent child.

Lorrie

In contrast to the unhappy and withholding state that connects Mary with her mother, Lorrie, discussed here, and Tillie, in a coming description, are agreeable people who focus on helping other people. Lorrie's childhood was shaped by a narcissistic and extremely insecure mother who demanded that Lorrie greet people with eyes opened wide and a generous smile. She was to feel their pain and react with sympathy, to show interest in their problems and, before that, to care about her mother's self-dislike and misery. She was not to consider her mother's self-centered demandingness unfair. As her mother needed her, she was to be a "giver."

Giving was to rule supreme. Lorrie thinks of giving as her natural state. She takes feelings of inner emptiness as a sign of personal lack from which she is to turn away and give. The more she gives, the less she knows herself. It is satisfying to see another's joy but this does not answer the question, "Aside from satisfying them, what do I want?"

She did not have sufficient access to the force of early childhood, as, for example, a two-year-old's statement, "I won't do that!" Identity grows out of self-assertive events. Instead, Lorrie was pushed into saying yes, to which she complied with forced acceptance that sent a self into hiding. There is strength in her ability to understand others but no increase in personal power. Children of narcissists serve their parents and if the parents are pleased, find satisfaction in self-abnegation. They feel rewarded by the response to the degree that their selves do not count. Without a sense of personal value, they do not recognize the misery that submissive fealty brings.

Lorrie feels the other's plight and negates self-interest. She does not try to know that self and thinks it not worth the trouble. Self is felt to be distant, vague, and fearfully rumbling. As Sam's wife, she supports his narcissistic needs, listens to his problems, and applauds his feats. She ignores or demeans her own.

She became very sensitive to people's feelings because her mother was so easily hurt. Mother always demeaned herself and needed redeeming praise. She saw personal evaluation in all that her kids said. They had to have the "right feeling" toward her and her causes. Since she required them to tell the truth, it was protective for them not to know what they felt. She would beg them for comment, to which they acted neutral, pleasant, and unknowable.

As with her own self-regard, Mother's remarks to her kids were full of contradiction. She was demanding and critical, full of adulation and disappointment. She swung up and down, from awe to jealousy and back. Her compliments were unreliable as she called her children good but not good enough. She even talked to me that way about myself. "You are brilliant" she said and then asked me about an embarrassing cyst. "What is that red mark beneath your eyebrow?" She called Lorrie beautiful and then pulled at her hair, saying, "Why do you let your bangs hang that way? They look terrible." I heard that Lorrie's aunts found her "mature" at an early age. She had to be mature since she was her mother's advisor.

The sense of self for Lorrie and her brother was demolished by the way their mother fed them. She thought that feeding them made her a good mother and tried to make them eat. At the same time, she revered thinness, so their not eating also pleased her. Perhaps not eating pleased Mother more because that is what they did. They resisted and complied at the same, sealing their lips against food and becoming so thin that in the movies, she had to hold down their seats while they were sitting in them. Luckily, she was not so forceful that they were driven to assert themselves by bringing noneating to a suicidal end.

Saying no to controlled eating could have been a step toward independence, of which there were too few. But it was as much compliance as assertiveness that turned Lorrie toward the rejection of all things nourishing unless it gave another person satisfaction. Lorrie could not overcome the guilt she felt for her mother's reactive pain at her independence. Lorrie's sacrificial response became a conditioned habit. Like Nick, she said no to self but unlike him, said yes to others. She found acceptance in supporting their plans and pleasures.

Lorrie's child shows the next generation reacting to parental narcissism and sacrifice. Her young son remembers what people say, notes their needs, and makes sacrifices to help. Like Mom, he eats little and is thin. Like Mom, he asks for little and is appreciated for that. Remembering unusual facts shows his intelligence, a value that his dad respects. It is the brilliance of which his grandmother always speaks. He draws with crayons, which his dad favors. Brilliance wins his father's approval. Brilliant is what his grandma calls him. When sacrificial and unbrilliant, he vanishes into a supportive haze . . . like Mom. Overall, he features intellect, talent, few needs, much sacrifice, and a smile.

Lorrie became a psychotherapist who would not take credit for her work. She denies therapeutic ability, showing modesty that keeps her in line with her mother's feelings of inadequacy. Mother was too jealous and paralyzed to accept a child who appreciated herself. Lorrie puts herself down and the other person up. I asked Lorrie why she did not continue her schooling. Therapists need a lot of it. She responded, "I am no scholar," and added, "My papers were only 'copied.' " Weren't all our papers derived from other sources? She does not think of that and speaks this way to justify ending her education.

There is a lack in her work if she tells a patient to expose himself but she cannot take the risk herself. Lorrie speaks of her failures, which she exaggerates. She thinks herself a beggar who is generous with another's money and does not know the money is her own. She needs to know who she is when not serving another's need.

She has talent for living in a submissive position and is used to taking second place. She does not like doing psychotherapy with a prison population although she may be good at it, but does not seek the necessary training to move on. Her lifestyle has extra limits that are self-imposed. She may be unconsciously angry at having to focus on others, which shows in low-level grumbling about petty details. But her philosophy pushed her to sacrifice. A change in modesty would break the role she has lived so long and might endanger her marriage to a narcissist. All these forces come together in keeping her the same.

Thus, Lorrie's need for self-assertion is unexpressed. She may need psychotherapy to define its risks and to help her decide if these are worth taking. But going for therapy itself means breaking the self-sacrificing mold. Till then, she goes on saying yes.

Nick

A position of strength can turn into weakness if it grows rigid and fixed. This issue haunts Tillie, to be discussed later, and Nick. Ordinarily, when behavior that once served us is outgrown, it is discarded. Steps toward independence follow one another. As a first step Nick said no to his controlling, frightening, and narcissistic father. Instead of growing out of saying no, it metastasized against all desire. He became a withholding person to self and others.

This is the opposite of Lorrie's compliant yes to everything that pleases the other person. Nick's no deprived them and himself but was an act of hatred whose pleasure he did not see. Being out of contact with the deeper meaning of our actions makes us believe incomplete or incorrect interpretations of them. Lack of self-knowledge keeps destructiveness alive. Nick lacked proper understanding and saw no reason for his lunacy. He called it lunacy to be unwilling to do pleasurable and beneficial things like sending out bills for services rendered.

Saying no began in childhood to parents who were utterly self-centered and demanded he always be on hand to help. If he failed them in any way, they were furious. If he served them well, another demand would follow. His father was the captain of a ship. At home and on his pleasure boat, he would run his white-gloved hand on shelves to see if they were clean. Nick cleaned the kitchen to pass inspection, repaired and drove his father's car, did endless household chores, and was demolished by his father's cruelty and humor.

His parents gave him little and expected a lot. They wanted to bask in his school achievements but gave him no desk to work on. He used the dining table when it was free. Few of Nick's needs were attended to. His father's needs always came first. Father had a boat of his own to play with but could not afford a bedroom for his son, who camped out in the living room. Nick was like a serf to his father, who had been raised like a serf by his own distant relatives.

Nick started to withdraw and withhold. He played hookey in the lower grades and didn't finish his final term in architecture school. He strolled away with a nearly A average and can offer no explanation except, "I didn't feel like it." Possessing considerable intelligence and talent, he alternately accepted and rejected his father's quest for greatness. Nick's work was very good, when he worked. Probably hatred for his parents caused him to drop out. In later years, they boasted to guests about their "architect son," for which he embarrassed them by demurring. "I am not an architect."

Nick is so much tied to dislike and resentment that he cannot see what he would like to do. All he knows is hatred. When he went to see a therapist, he could not speak about what bothered him. Raised by a vain and violent father, Nick's jaws were psychologically glued shut and he did not learn to open them. Feelings of spite were expressed by not speaking.

He treated his therapist as a parent figure. The fearful child within him thought he could not speak but did not know why. Nick also did not pay for all of his therapy bill. He said that he did not earn enough to pay but spent money for entertainment. Hostility to his father came out toward the therapist. Being broke allowed him to express his need to be financially carried, which would not happen with his demanding and narcissistic parents. Nick did not see the pleasure he derived from his pain.

After a while, the therapist called a halt to unpaid treatment. He had not been able to analyze Nick's negative reaction, if indeed he saw it as such. Negative reaction is an analytic phrase used to describe enjoyment of the imagined result of one's failure. Some people kill or attempt to kill themselves for such pleasure, reveling in the fantasy of their relatives weeping with guilt. In therapy, a negative reaction keeps you from getting better. You do not want to give the therapist your improvement so that he or she can feel good about his work. Your narcissistic parent would have boasted about what you accomplished with his great genes and under his care. Your need to see the parent crushed is repeated with the therapist as his stand-in. Your therapeutic failure brings down the parent (or therapist as a parent substitute).

Nick undermines himself but labors for his friends. He paints their apartments and redesigns their kitchens. He listens to their problems and drives a friend to the hospital when she has a miscarriage. He shops for people, deriving the infantile pleasure of pretending that he has endless funds. He helps them keep their ships afloat as long as doing this does not interfere with letting his own ship sink. If his friends want to do what he does not, he will not comply. His definition of love involves a lot of sacrifice and little fun.

A person devoted to not achieving is in trouble. Nick's self-deprivation has a tantrum quality. Living to say no and withholding what he has to give show how closely he is tied to his parents. Far better not to assign them so much power that their opinion shakes him to the bone. Let them speak their minds and let him do what he wants, whether it pleases them or not.

In imagination if not in fact, he strikes at them by surrendering his ambition. He cannot see that what he does is voluntary. He complains, feels sad, depressed, and miserable, but does not admit that he chooses to exist like this. If offered a way out, he does not take it. If his life had more pleasure, he could note the difference. With little pleasure and knowing the satisfaction of rejecting his parents' needs, he does not assess the magnitude of what he does to himself. Chronically depressed, he goes from pain to pain in the excitement of disappointing his parents. Their emotional state occupies so much of his inner world that he does not feel anything else. Parental pressures are everywhere and his self is nowhere.

If you ask Nick what he wants, he does not know. If you ask him if he likes architectural design, in which a licensed architect must sign his drawings, he says no. Abundant in talent and experience, he says, "Why should I do a thing because I'm good at it?" Life is cornered by the word *no*. He undercuts his parents' ambition but rebellion ties him to them. He upsets them by refusing what they want. He makes promises he will not keep and no one can control him. He is lonely but does not see that he can be closer to his friends. He calls himself out of control.

A life determined by rejection means living on the rebound. Better to express anger in a different way and be there for himself. Nick is arrested at the stage of saying no. Pleasure in withholding keeps him in neurotic stasis. If he were more honest with himself, he could not go on this way. Therapy with a new therapist, also soon discarded, brought him to a greater love of life. He sensed his anger at his father and the role anger played in his nonfunctioning. He has found a woman who loves him and now has married. He has grown more aggravated at not operating for his vocational good. He has started exercising. As he becomes more active, he is confronted by the need to stop holding back. Although he denies the value of psychotherapy, his treatment of therapists shows how much rage he has and needs to deal with.

Tillie

In contrast to Nick's self-denying negativism is Tillie's self-denying helpfulness. She takes a stand that runs counter to her mother's self-centered hatefulness. To not resemble Mother, she focuses on others' needs. Phone calls, visits, most of her work contacts are treated as friends. They believe this and subsequently act on it, leaving her barely a moment for herself. Feeling overwhelmed by this, she wants to control people, which brings her closer to her narcissistic mother's behavior. Growth beyond this is arrested because compulsive acceptance does not develop into action that discriminates between people. There is no room for needs unrelated to giving. Tillie is controlled by the desire to be unlike her mother.

Compare Tillie and Lorrie. They are helpful for opposite reasons. One became helpful to please herself and one to please others. Lorrie was required to become helpful by a narcissistic mother who revered a helper image. Tillie became helpful to be unlike her suspicious and withholding narcissistic mother. Tillie's understanding of another's misery is different from Lorrie's. Tillie is less trained in sacrifice and not as accepting of their weaknesses since it reminds her of the state in which her mother tried to raise her. Since both are therapists, which one is more helpful to a patient? It depends upon the patient's need. Most of all, a patient needs a therapist to be free of blind spots, the compulsion to be and do. To the extent the therapist does not know if she is trapped, the patient will suffer. Both Tillie and Lorrie have significant blind spots about themselves and in similar ways will be blind to their patients.

Compare how Tillie and Nick oppose their narcissistic parents.

Tillie's opposition takes a positive approach and Nick's a negative. To foil his narcissistic parents, Nick says no to all desire. Tillie fights the control of her narcissistic and paranoid mother by compulsively saying yes.

Tillie's mom thought she could see right through people. She looked for evil and found it. Tillie found her mother utterly self-centered, someone who used people to her advantage. When Mother's picture is taken she shows her knees. Not that she is sexual. Sex is used to snare and hold a man. She superstitiously made preteen Tillie sit bare-breasted in the sun to develop breasts so that she could later catch a man. Mother had many odd illusions, which she imposed on her children. Tillie's older brother told his mother everything about himself, which later ended in her attacking him. Brother's tears alerted Tillie against such sharing. In this family, Mother suffers and the child takes the blame.

When Tillie moved out, Mother saw rape lurking everywhere and would call to see if she had survived. Mother tried to keep control and thought her judgment best. She panicked if her child was not home by a certain time. Tillie saw her mother's negative slant and decided to be utterly unlike her. She would accept and trust all. If someone needed help she gave it. If people behaved suspiciously, she saw them as worthy. Once she found a wallet lying on the street and asked the person standing next to her if he owned it. "Of course," he said and took it from her hand. Tillie's power of judgment was suspended by her need for innocence. Her mother was close to no one, including a seventy-year-old husband, and saved money for the time that he would leave her. Tillie was close to all, attracting them with smile and wit. She encouraged their demands and lived in a state of exhausted sainthood.

By not looking at her needs and disappointments, mistreatment of self continued. Her boyfriend promised a trip that never arrived. He described a dreamy future on foreign shores but did not work for it. His brilliance was in the puffery of speech. Nothing materialized to support his schemes. She was not supposed to criticize him and didn't. He promised her great sunsets but wanted her to show him love by living in his bedraggled mess, which she could ignore or clean. For him, showing negative behavior tested her love. For her, loving him without limit disproved her mother's hatred of men.

Tillie's new strength of acceptance turned into weakness since her positive comments were not tied to awareness of what she felt and knew. She was unrealistically positive, a Santa Claus figure. One day, we were eating in a restaurant when a woman came over whom Tillie hugged and complimented. Later she told me that she could not remember who the woman was. This idea made me anxious. I want to be loved by her as a friend because I am known. It upsets me to see her so free with her hugs. She once told me that she thought me cold until she read some of my writing. I do not trust her profligate intimacy. She gives in an undiscriminating way. She is popular, but what does it mean if she says that she cares for me? Compulsive acceptance evades true intimacy. Intimacy is a matter of choice. Her mother avoided intimacy through suspicion and she avoids it by being all-embracing.

She was locked into "doing good" when a new profession started to shake her loose. It was psychotherapy with "clean" addicts and their families. Being able to tell them the truth has to start with the self. Looking at her Pollyannaish approach birthed a new and fragile phase in which she tries to know and care for herself and worries whether this is narcissism. Counseling addicts keeps the pressure on. She needs to be free to make decisions if she is to help codependent mates break free of the compulsion to please their addicted mates.

Living to please another is codependent, even if it is undertaken by your own choice so as not to resemble someone else. Tillie cannot help an addict to leave a self-destructive path if she destroys herself with indiscriminate giving. She has to struggle with this since even a preference for one thing over another causes her alarm. If all is not equally good, has she become a rejecting person? Is she like her mother if she does not live to please?

It was a sign of her growth when she felt conflicted about a guest who stayed for the weekend. A sloppy and angry person, he left his unwashed dishes in the sink. Tillie washed them and later said to me that doing this was not good for his independence. She thought of the damage done to him but not of its cost to her. The prospect of not being self-sacrificial is contaminated by the memory of her mother's selfishness. It is hard for her to put herself first and to think it acceptable.

In terms of development, she has her toe on the next level, where she can allow herself to be a real person with likes and dislikes, choices and preferences. At our last meeting, she spoke of the self-destructive behavior of her boyfriend. She no longer feels responsible for his fate but finds it hard to watch him destroy himself by inches. Harder still to stay in an exclusive relationship with one so destructive that she finds him physically unattractive and does not want him to fill her sexual needs. It would be good to remain his friend, perhaps to speak of her concern for him, but at the same time to find an appealing boyfriend who is not dependent, a man whom she wants to give her sexual pleasure.

Alice

Alice buries herself in her work and generally has a nonexistent social life. She may date on vacation but otherwise has "no time or energy" for it. She once dated a weak-willed man who liked her to be in command. Although she did not enjoy his personality, his weakness did not threaten her. It was years before she tired of knowing him, when feelings of boredom led her to end the relationship. She feels safer practicing social distance. She would rather dominate a man and be bored than accept her mother's fate of being overwhelmed and controlled by a narcissistic husband. Like many children of narcissists, she sees no other option than those practiced by her parents.

Between boyfriends and for long periods of time, Alice stays alone. Social avoidance comes from an estranged childhood in many countries, since her father constantly changed jobs. Both parents were critical of any problem in their children and did not support Alice through the anxiety of meeting new schoolmates and teachers. Contact was doubtful with a distant father who acted her superior. Mother was a frightened, hysterical woman who complained a lot and found her children's needs a burden. Alice avoided both parents' disapproval by focusing on schoolwork.

One time, in a Catholic school assembly, she was pushed around by a nun who bore down on her for an unknown crime. When she told her parents about this, they did not take her side. From such treatment, she came to expect disloyalty and to mistrust love. As a grownup she is often silent while others converse, which drives them away or causes them to chat without addressing her. She fears that her speech will turn people against her and in fact often has a confronting tone like that of her father. This resemblance shows awe of his authority as well as years of repressed fury that by identification with him turned her submission into a bossy commanding facade. Isolation is the safest way to go. The only person with whom she feels safe is her sister, a person who she thinks understands her without speaking.

In her first psychotherapy, she said little and departed in a year or so, almost as unknown as when she entered. This therapist respected her defensive constriction. In a more recent psychotherapy, when lacking an external problem to discuss, she is at a loss for words. If her therapist tries to discuss her closed-off state he is met by misunderstanding. She feels attacked by his questions and responds with rationalizations, arguments, and tears. She cannot be objective about her silence because it offers her protection. Years of defensiveness have brought her to the defense of denying her inner life. She is not committed to marking a path to where she hides, let alone to changing her route to safety.

Alice needs to become acquainted with her inner self. She has too long shut it out in fear of social censure. She needs to know her anger, of which she has an abundance. She also has to know her need for love. Living with so much anger and fear, she is not much troubled by social needs and stays away from thoughts that would reveal them to her. Much of her affection goes to animals and to her sister. That Alice was expert at attacking her parents to get them to support her siblings is no reason to think herself hopelessly unlovable. Personal change will mean knowing her fears and then what she desires. As with most children of narcissistic parents, she has the undertaking of finding out what holds her back.

Doryan

If you become a slave to refusal, you are glued to rebellion and unable to find out what your self needs. The people described thus far live mostly for or against another person. Let us look at one whose growth went further and turned him toward his self. Doryan broke free of the narcissistic mold to follow his own mind. When I asked him, "What special strength came out of freeing yourself from your narcissistic home?" he said, "To find out for myself. Never to accept anyone's word on an issue. To break through to my own understanding."

More than most people with narcissistic roots, he makes it on his own. He serves many but needs few. His strength goes out to public issues. His weakness is hidden in his private life. He is very strong in his public actions and somewhat limited and weak in private. In all he does, he is an individual. He is ruled by the need not to submit to outside pressure.

He was raised in Europe by narcissistic parents who told him what to do. First there were parents, then governesses and tutors, then parents again. He shrank from all, looking through the eyes of his camera. He wrote plays and studied lizards and bugs. Developing an inner world was necessary for one who was subjected to what his parents thought of as "the best."

One summer, when he was about fourteen, Doryan visited an aunt and uncle who were vacationing at a northern European lake resort. There were too many people for his pleasure so he climbed into a canoe and paddled off. The more he paddled the quieter the shore and the more beautiful the scene. This trip brought him joy and launched him on a search for wilderness. His family did not much protest his move since he had a mountaineering uncle who explored. Uncle modeled activities that his parents did not find altogether strange.

In his teens, his area of expertise was acrobatics, at which he worked to overcome a small and slim stature. He was one for trying to win any contest, although competitiveness did not mean that much to him. It was a way of existing. Still, disappointment came from receiving unfair treatment. Like being first in a language course and seeing the reward given to a lesser student who was older and therefore thought more appropriate for the prize of a trip. Or when his mother promised him a spendable sum for an excellent report card. He studied hard and got A's, except for singing. She held back the prize because of his grade in voice. He felt cheated by this and his studying ceased. When he found treatment unfair, he would stop his activities. He was able to withdraw, a good defense against the invasion of narcissistic parents. All this led him to be on his own.

His parents talked Doryan out of studying biology so he entered engineering. Due to family pressure, he was in his junior year at high school and engineering school at the same time. Aside from this, he resisted. He knew he had to make a living and the rest was up to him. He paid for boat rentals out of limited earnings and was a student between exploratory jaunts. At age eighteen he emigrated to the United States. Education went on. So did voyaging. His trips went farther north until he traded canoe for kayak, a covered boat for bad weather and blustery water. He made voyages down rivers never mapped and became an expert on survival. He catalogued the Arctic life, its flora and fauna, the religious shrines and bones of those who were left behind. He rested his eyes on wild things in the natural state, like butterflies with hairy wings in the Arctic summer.

He tried not to disturb animal life and carried no weapon except for a wasp spray, thinking that a gun gives too much superiority. A wasp spray had not been used against the polar bears but he assumed that they'd take notice if he sprayed their sensitive noses. A bear once stalked him while he was sitting on a rock waiting for his plane. Since the trip was over, he had put his gear away, including the wasp spray. The plane arrived shortly before the bear, which the people on board had seen but he had not. They were wild with excitement as they pulled him into the plane.

Wanting to be the animals' witness and guest, Doryan would fit in as he never could in his parents' narcissistic home. He did what he could without mechanical help and was sad at being physically small, which led to further development of strength and special skills. He did as much as anyone, if not more. It was his mind, not the facts, that called him too small. The child of a narcissist is always too small for them. Doryan went where only rare beings can go and survive. He developed hardiness and scholarliness with a keen mind that harked to the simplest of elements. What he did with his energy is helpful to the world of exploration and preservation.

Doryan leads small groups by kayak to the rare beauty of that desert we call the Arctic. He gives lectures about exploration and lowers his voice when he walks with people in the wild. He gives lessons on how to fit in, looking at stems and roots to see how things grow through time, witnessing the cracking of stones under ages of freezing and melting. He has the gift of being in nature that comes to one raised in submission to the throne of a narcissistic family.

He is a man of strong mind who tries to understand and will not be led. He does engineering for a living but nature is his love. He has amazing biological knowledge and his thought is penetrating about natural things. It changes when you get to his topic of fear, the emotional why of human relations. He is uncomfortable and puzzled when I ask him why he does something interpersonal. In nature he sees a multiplicity of causes, things meshing and progressing out of one another. In viewing his self he avoids the emotional determinant. He is socially undeveloped, avoiding the intimacy where others try, fail, learn from their mistakes, and try again. He says that his parental home and his marriage, which was painfully unsuccessful, were too upsetting to want another "experiment." Instead, he focuses on his interests and keeps his distance, even from his kids, hoping that he will be loved as he is, deeply loved but not seen too often.

He says he does not suffer emotional consequences from his physical mishaps. He only asks what he can do in response to such crises as a freezing spill into an Arctic river. Like the Möbius strip, one of his favorite forms, his thought has no top and no bottom, no beginning and no end. Möbius is a twisted figure, like the symbol of eternity. Like a Möbius strip, Doryan must be taken as he is.

Does he miss his lover when they are apart? He told me that he does in the protective pain of his heart's isolation. He feels empty without her but if he thinks about what is missing, his mind is too divided and frightened to change. He will not test closeness, seeing if he is as weak as he fears, as weak as he was with his narcissistic parents. He sticks to his freedom and must be alone. He gets together with his girlfriend as a break in his "important affairs." Then he goes away and there is little sign for her of an ongoing tie. She feels very cut off when they are apart. He does not hesitate to have many women friends and some casual lovers. All are a means of reducing intimacy with the woman he loves.

Constant breaks are his protection. In therapy he became able to say no to his widowed narcissistic mother, who had a stranglehold on his emotional life. He moved out of her apartment and left therapy with the closeness issue unresolved. The therapist offered intellectual information to him but they formed no emotional tie. He says that the therapist admired Doryan's ability to live through any difficulty and stand it alone. I think he has always stood alone. What Doryan did not hear was the weakness side of this equation.

What he gave to his children and now his girlfriend is his emotional "max." He is afraid to delve into self-knowledge more deeply. He lacks motivation to change and calls himself too old. He now has reached seventy but has the resiliency of an arctic explorer. What if they get together and "the experiment fails," which then will leave him without his friends. He talks as if an eligible man is ever without company. He has many excuses that are constantly changing . . . too something . . . young-old-poor-busy to try getting close. He fears the extremes of closeness and distance. His fear of closeness with people verges on the phobic. What if his lover or friend gets a narcissistic hold on him? Freedom is his primary concern. When asked who his friends are, he says that he has few, but mainly associates. His closest friend is his girlfriend.

This child of a narcissist gained strength from freeing his physical self from narcissistic parents but still has troubling connections with them. He fears that the power his parents had to run his life will reappear in the one he loves and she will take him over. His intellectual life has so much interest and value that he wants to live with his deficiencies and not to change himself further. He is afraid of getting close to a woman because what if he grows old in the relationship and then finds himself alone again. This is partly a rationalization. A man can usually find new girlfriends. The associations which Doryan enjoys do not have the pains and pleasures of an intimate love affair.

In closeness, this intrepid explorer is ruled by fear. One cannot see his future. Currently there is insufficient motivation to change, perhaps because his fear is too great. Let us hope that something will nurture his roots and cause him to grow, that motivation will come. Overall, he is a man of rare achievement and strength grown out of the struggle to separate from constricting, narcissistic parents.

Elan

An idea about changing the self is slow in rooting. Not being narcissistic does not mean that one should be a slave. For the narcissist there is only self. For the normal person, there is self and other. If we were

not born only to serve or take, how much care or self-care is reasonable and how much do we need? Strength comes from considering you and me. Weakness consists of being trapped in caring for
only one or none.

The struggle we take to achieve identity is an interesting one.
After childhood with narcissistic parents we need to follow our in-
stincts. These lead us to our selves and teach us that it/I exists. Mun-
dane approaches imply following other people's rules, a practice of
which we have had enough. Wanting to develop, our struggle often
takes us down unusual paths.

Self-development is difficult if the sense of self is undermined.
Where and what is that devalued self? If we are overly discouraged we
lose the desire to look and try, fall to a low level of despair, or hang out
in neutral and are unknown. We go to extremes of conformity with or
rebellion against another's opinion. As a youth, I was too confused to
do anything but conform, but lacked a clear image of what to conform
to. My narcissistic parents were rebels and attacked anyone else's
thoughts and ideas, including each other's. For example, one said cut
your hair, the other said grow it. One said I read too little, the other
said too much. When I complained about loneliness, my father said I
cared too much for people, etc. They did what they thought was right
regardless of majority opinion and often were in mutual opposition,
which made my position even more confusing.

They said, "Resemble me," but opposed each other and neither
gave a clear image to follow. My father wanted to be the more om-
nipotent one, the chief, but his image was vague. My mother was so
unique and clear that I lacked the courage to be like her even if I felt
that she was right, which I did not, having been taught to disapprove
by my dad.

I did not know what I was supposed to become. My appearance
was generally "wrong," but what was right? I begged for a fuschia
satin jacket like the one worn by other kids but my father was opposed. He said that I was not supposed to resemble "them." What
should I look like? When my mother opposed him and bought the
jacket, I already felt so different that it was more like a disguise than
an outfit that joined me with the others. At a time when adolescents
try to look alike and hang out together, I felt and looked the oddball

and hung out alone. When the girls stayed together, I accompanied the boys and vice versa.

Kids want friends but my father insisted that one friend was enough. I accepted this since I found making friends so difficult and had been raised to feel the outsider. I entered college feeling hopeless, especially in the face of so much company. Adding to my shock, the college looked upon my supposedly low ability with favor, which made my depression worse. What if they were only fooled and later saw the real and inadequate me?

Success drove me to therapy, especially being made editor of the school magazine. I could not live with the inconsistency between their image of me and mine and dropped out of editing. I graduated and, after floundering for a while, went to graduate school in clinical psychology. While this went on, another part of me was developing while I studied about and traveled in Asia, which I describe in Chapter 14.

In the part of Asia where I resided, every woman wore a skirt that covered her legs. I hiked in trousers, but when living in a village wore a calf-length blue cotton jumper with a long-sleeved white blouse. It was commonly worn, distinctly Tibetan, and handmade. When I returned to the States, having been away so long, I wore it still. I felt at home in my Tibetan dress, having grown accustomed to it in a place where I was more accepted than anywhere else, a mountain home where I could leave my wallet unmolested on the trail.

Asia is good for a person inquiring into who she is. Asia has more to do with manifesting the inner self than does the outer-directed and self-conscious West. Outside Darjeeling, I lived in a house shared by people who were studying Tibetan meditation. My mountain friends included Tibetans who had sat through three years, three months, and three days of isolated meditation. They had wonderful humor. I remember their laughing over difficulties that would have made me cry, like the time we gave them an increase in beans to improve their protein intake and they stood on line all night waiting for the latrine.

After Asia, I had to learn how to fit into society without abandoning my emerging sense of self. I had to determine what was important and figure out how to preserve it. I returned to the West in my classical Tibetan robes and was told that I looked like a Chinese aristocrat of the fifteenth century. To me I looked nice. After years of passive acquiescence, I had entered a stage of self-assertion. Looking unusual did not make me want to change my dress. I looked like everyone in the part of the world from which I had just come. My outfit was a step into independence.

I took the assertiveness of dress further. Between the times I wore my Tibetan dress and mood, I began to wear miniskirts with fishnet stockings. I hated my job, which required I learn computer programming and insurance math for a stodgy insurance company. The complaints I received about my stockings barely registered above my anxiety and annoyance with computer math. Flow charts were used to delineate my weekend. On them appeared office tasks as given by my boss "Alphonse Cohen." I gave him the name "Cohenballmaus," my way of showing his quest for power and underlying timidity. This timidity did not stop him from firing me because I still wore my fishnets. They knew from my dress that I would not fit in. I knew from my math that it was so. Still, I learned from this that one does not need to dress to proclaim originality. I also learned not to work at what I hate.

Strategy was a new concept for me. I had been raised to believe that my father could read my thoughts and that nothing I could think or do would change his mind. After much discussion in therapy of my dress, I recognized when I fit in and when I stuck out. From the way people treated me, I saw that I could be more outspoken if I dressed in inoffensive mufti. I was beginning to stand for what I believed in, but not to be compelled to cause unnecessary trouble.

Years later, I seek the original because it pleases me. I don't feel compelled to be different but prefer it. I have some of the strength that was nourished by my struggle to be free of the dominance of narcissistic parents.

The next step in psychological growth has to do with knowing what can be changed and how to ask for it. It has to do with not staying with what does not satisfy. The child of a narcissist is often hungry and waiting. We need to break our identification with the parent and not attempt to change what cannot be changed. If what is offered is insufficient and unchangeable, move on. Life is a classroom. We are left back until we understand the lesson. There is always a more difficult lesson ahead.

Helpful Approaches to Change

A sense of self develops from interaction with people and from deeds that set you on the road. A person trips over his feet and laughs to discover the error of his ways. Do you know what you need and what you have to offer, what you can and cannot do? Are there people who rely on "inadequate" you and seem to enjoy it? We can feel hopelessly confused, wonderfully good and horribly bad at the same time since the parent put our ideal image on a pedestal and our ordinary self in a ditch. If we throw caution to the winds and do the best we can, we find trying to live up to the narcissist image of being a perfect person to be a waste of time.

All this has to do with knowing our buried selves, so far out of range that sometimes we feel nonexistent at the core and strangely empty. Are we centerless and different from other people? Can something unfelt exist? Can a self grow out of emptiness?

Psychotherapy can be very helpful, but what we call therapy can come from ordinary people who see, hear, and feel us. It comes from friends and relatives, from fortunate encounters with strangers like the Rabbit Man and the man who helped Irwin to his feet. When we are afraid of doing something lest we fail, we meet someone who loves the doing and shares it. To have such experience we must take the risk of doing or at least of being around a doer. We think that our families' ways are the only ways and then we meet people with entirely different values. Like a Korean family of acupuncturists that has so much joy in helping others and an outrageous sense of humor. From the happiness in their voices and the pleasure in their eyes, you know their way is good.

You think that you are odd, for example, in your sexual preferences or in what you call love. Your parents always treated you that way. Then you attend an art show that features what you think of as horrible and a host of self-accepting practitioners are represented. You realize that you have overreacted and misjudged yourself and that staying in isolation brings misunderstanding. The greatest source of hatred for yourself, regardless of what others say, comes from you.

You think that you are without value and are driven to write it down. It turns into a story that you read in a writing group. People talk to you about it and your writing. You begin to see that there is a valuable life inside.

Formal Psychotherapy

Since the reflecting mirror of our mind is stained with our parents' views, how can we see ourselves? Where and how can we see ourselves at all? We need a reliable mirror in which to look, to be accepted as we are to achieve a sense of being. For many, the therapist is the one with whom we first can be ourselves. The therapist should be a reasonable person free of pressure for us to achieve his wishes and fulfill his values. He should be one with whom we can disagree.

Group therapy is often useful. In group we show ourselves to others and learn how we affect them. Out of our terror, we learn to speak our minds. We start to feel our temper. Always having heard our parents' distorted opinions, foreign perspective is helpful. We learn that we can differ and go on.

After hearing their responses to us, group members seek our wisdom in return. We find that we have identities of our own. We recognize that not everything we do, especially what we have learned from our parents, is socially useful. Our notion of narcissistic perfection crumbles. With growing awareness, we can offer useful comments and feelings. We learn that there is someone inside us.

At times, we may think that the therapist is mistreating us in narcissistic ways. If this is our transference, it shows the experiences that a grown child carries from her past. Transference means experiencing and having feelings about a current person in the same way that we did about an important person in our early childhood. Although the resemblance is illusory, transference causes us to relive ancient expectations, wishes, feelings, and attitudes and offers the opportunity to examine them and to change them if needed. Of course, it is only transference if the therapist is not narcissistic. Narcissistic parents say that we should be perfect, and that they are entitled to a form of worship. Such concepts paralyze us. What if I do something and do it poorly. Is the therapist criticizing me? Or is it me thinking that it is in his mind? I remember my personal hell of tennis lessons, agony to be a beginner. I imposed my feelings about the situation onto myself, confusing the "it" of my practice with the value of my being.

Self is not the product of a propaganda machine. It has its own needs and identity. If never felt, self's arrival can give a shocking jolt. For years of therapy, I wept over all the things that I was missing. The world would never accept me with my "small" brain and breasts. My narcissistic parents had declared me unable to love so I saw my cause as hopeless. Psychotherapy helped me look at the facts as well as my dreams and fantasies. In my current problems I had been reliving the issues of early life. I began to see my neurotic expectations and to stagger over blind spots. Therapy opened my eyes so that I could look another way.

I looked into my memory of the past. Had there been any freedom to be myself? Inside my head, I hear my father attacking my need for independence and hating the therapist for presumably being against him. My memories offer more to me than this—many of them are sad, some of them are hopeful. They show me what I care for. A narcissistic parent often applies restraint before his child is capable of understanding. It is hard to distinguish what was introduced into an atmosphere that always existed. You tend to think that is the "way it is."

Many think they should deliberately replace the parent's views with a new, untested image but this is covering self with another false identity. To avoid false identity we should not bury our emptiness under rocks of nonbeing. How are we to know the self long buried, so far out of range that we feel nonexistent? Can a self unfelt exist?

For me a great jolt came after years of expressing unhappiness in therapy. I was talking about something when emotion welled up inside me. My therapist interrupted what I was saying to ask me what I felt. I spoke of it with confusion. I did not know what it was until he called it love. Imagine my joy. If I could feel love then I was lovable. Years of declaring myself emotionally void were at an end.

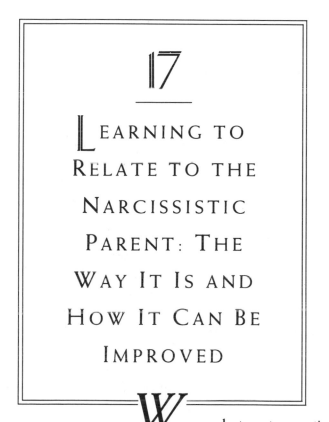

17

LEARNING TO RELATE TO THE NARCISSISTIC PARENT: THE WAY IT IS AND HOW IT CAN BE IMPROVED

We need to stop acting like sponges to our parents' negative opinions. They will try to push us in narcissistic ways but what they tell us need not determine how we feel. We are demolished by such comments if we accept them as valid and take our errors as signs of inner worthlessness. We feel guilty for rejecting their view of us if we think loving them means to believe all they say. We need to see ourselves as we are and not the picture that our parents paint of us. If in some ways we fit their negative descriptions, that behavior can be changed.

If we want to be treated in a different way, the change in treatment must start with how we present ourselves to them. This problem was present in full glory during a weekend country visit by my father and his wife. I again experienced what narcissism can make me feel. Not having seen each other for months, he greeted me with his standard opening, a negative aesthetic evaluation. This approach was one that filled my childhood, an approach in which body and mind were on trial.

Stepping over the threshold, he went into his act, holding me at arm's length for a physical reading that was characteristically negative. He frowned at me and said, "Your eyes are swollen. You look tired." Already a double dose of what my doubtful self-image didn't want to hear. I responded with, "I stroked a cat and probably rubbed my eyes. I'm allergic to cats." This offered him a new beachhead to conquer. "You should have known better than to do a thing like that." His tone and words implied that I was stupid, weak, and thoughtless. To some extent I took it. It is hard to be sensitive around a parent who always rubs in your problems.

I defensively changed the topic to my strength. I was responding to his judgment as if it carried great importance and was indirectly fighting back. "I am going on a three-mile run. Will you join me?" To this his guns took a new position. "At your age, make it a mile and a half." Did this cautionary note apply to him or me? Narcissists often confuse identities with their children. "Can you run three miles?" I asked again and he returned to, "At your age . . ."

Having to announce the distance of my run shows that his comments hurt me. It would have been healthier to have run and let him have his opinion. Being oversensitive to critical comments is the frequent weakness of children of narcissists. We can work on our hypersensitivity by seeing who does the judging and by knowing that everyone has shortcomings.

I don't like being treated as a puny child and can't stand negative opinions because I haven't sufficiently separated my self-evaluation from the critic's. In this context, my analyst told me a story about Charlie Parker. His band expected him to come and play but he was too drugged to get out of bed. Finally they went to get him and dragged him to rehearsal. He sat there in silence while the band played through many of his choruses. Finally, he lifted his saxophone and played a single note. A narcissist would have disregarded that note—

"Worthless without . . ."—but a famous musician who was present said, "What a note that was."

I see how I was overly defended because I did not know the proper response to their demeaning comments. My father's wife felt too weak to assist with the luggage so I went out to help carry things from the car. I had his typewriter in one hand and a bag of vegetables in the other, to which he said, "Give me that. It's too heavy for you." I held on and moved away, half inviting him to wrestle. I walked off, feeling more the weight of his judgment than his luggage. He followed me with acerbic comments. "You're as crazy as my ninety-year-old father was." Grandpa was big, a man known for religious pressure but very kind to me. I would join him at prayer in a tongue I did not know. On the harvest holiday, we would shake a lemon and a sheaf of wheat. He was Russian and always kissed me hello on the lips. This man I loved.

Linking me with a man both ancient and decrepit is supposed to make me weak. But does his putting me in his father's image make me weak? Dad is feeling old and passing on the trait. Then comes the narcissism of his wife. I enter the house with their luggage, change into my sweat pants, and am ready to run. His wife is sitting on the couch and looking at me hard. She seems to have become more like him when she says, "You aren't skinny anymore." She is alluding to the great amount of weight I lost while recovering from a concussion. Her tone is not complimentary. Weight is a point about which I am vulnerable since I used to eat compulsively when I felt self-hatred or depression. Once you are fat, you always feel fat regardless of your size.

The sequence of events during this weekend shows me why I overeat. "I wear a size eight. Do you think I'm fat?" She says no and retreats from an argumentative scene. In the back of my mind, I know that she has a problem with weight. Her daughter is very skinny, as are her daughter's children. The family seems to share a need to be thin. She has focused even more on weight since her recent gain of thirty pounds. Trying to get her to take it off, my father verbally attacks her for every extra pound. He clings to a controlling and judgmental position.

I tell him, "I'm ready to run. Would you like to join me?" He holds us back, embarking on a lengthy search for the right kind of shirt. Then he joins me for his walk-run, which I accompany, kicking high in the back to make up for our slow pace. He talks and I see more deeply into why he speaks to me in a demeaning way. "Can you imagine an eighty-three-, almost eighty-four-year-old running like this?" It is narcissistic to change his evaluation of aging to suit himself. His father was crazy to act strong at ninety but he is terrific for running at eighty-four. Praise to him and blame to me. He is more critical of me because his self-esteem is low. Aging is hard for the narcissist. Some of my annoyance dissipates. But annoyance is not the entire story. The criticism that was given stays with me and has its effect. When he slows down to a walk and turns around, I take the rest of the distance in a solitary run.

When I get back, I invite my father to go for a swim, to which he responds, "Invite a man of your own to swim." I answer, "Sorry I invited you," but should have said, "I shall have one as soon as I am ready." My father increased my feelings of loneliness in an unresolved situation with a boyfriend who needs a lot of separation. Father's lack of sym- pathy arouses my pain and embarrassment. Later he adds, "That man treats you as his concubine. He sleeps with you but will not take you anywhere." I have been very unhappy about his keeping me from the doings of his active life. But then again, he sees his kids and grandchild rarely and has no close friends. He fills his life with acquaintances and socially useful work. Still, my father's words sink in and misery replaces the memory I have of many happy hours my boyfriend and I have spent together. I forget that he often says he loves me, and it is true.

Later that week, there is a telephone argument with my mother in which I tell her that something she has done resembles what my dad would do. Being compared to the man she has divorced and hates drives her into a temper. She writes me a letter in which she says that he never paid a cent of the agreed-upon child support and that she was too proud to ask him for it. She says that he was demanding and inattentive to her sexually, far more concerned with his own satisfac- tion than with her pleasure. She only found real satisfaction years later with a boyfriend. She summed up with, "Your father treated me like a concubine."

There is that word again and it was independently introduced. I see that my father attributes to my boyfriend his own view of women. They are hollow, tubes for him to invade with his organ and his words.

No wonder he used to say that the best woman was a Japanese geisha. A geisha is a beautiful and delicate woman who serves men while walking lightly in paper slippers.

I saw the effect of his criticism of my appearance in my behavior the following day. I was overeating to damage the beauty that they denied me, enacting the inadequate image that both of them projected. Overeating had troubled me in previous years. Now I saw some of the reason for its being. I overate to show respect for their criticism of my weight. If I want to help myself, I can refuse to please them by becoming what is not good for me.

I also was troubled by my father's evaluation of my boyfriend and brought the issue to therapy. My therapist said, "Your boyfriend loves you as much as he is able but not enough for you." The therapist is not implying that my needs are too great in general, but only for this man. I hear his words and understand, but as soon as the session is over it starts again, my feeling of despair at not being loved.

Like many children of narcissists, I automatically gravitate toward the negative. Long demeaned by our parents, we feel hideously unworthy if there is no one who loves us and in whose love we believe. Without love to contradict the parents' message, their opinions and treatment rule how we feel. I told my therapist that his pointing out how unloved I felt made me feel hopeless about my ability to benefit from therapy, to which he responded by further showing me how I caused myself pain. Belief in my parents' view makes me feel unworthy of love. In support of this belief, I take my boyfriend's limitation as evidence of my unlovability. I act as if he could give more love to another woman and twist unrelated information to use against myself. My father's words are used like an emotional knife that I thrust into my heart.

If I accept my parent's vision of me as unworthy, I will have trouble getting along with him. On this weekend with Father and spouse, criticism is adding up to a heap that infuriates. When his wife says that she cannot stand this country place because there are no people to do things with, I respond to her in a narcissistic way, an error that adds fire to fire. I criticize her inability to spend time with herself. Acting narcissistic is a common failing for children of narcissists. The parent's desire to control me brings me to try to control them in the same way. I say, "Why don't you use the time to paint? You always say that is what you want to do." She angrily responds, "I need a teacher to help me do it," and I come back with, "Why must there always be another person in everything you do?" In sharing their critical technique I make the habit stronger since my doing it means that this approach is OK.

I remind myself that what they say is only an opinion. Children of narcissists are surprised to see that their parents do not fit the image of a superman or superwoman who won't repeat an error (or make one in the first place). Belief in the parents' "perfection" makes it hard to generalize from known limitations. It is better to know our parents' fallibility. Then their negative words do not sink so deep. My parents talk of happily married people and advise me to follow suit. Divorces and unhappy marriages come to mind so that I can think, What is wrong with living the life that I think suits me?

If I want them to talk to me in a nonnarcissistic way, I will have to do the same to them. I could have responded to his wife's complaints about loneliness with, "When I return from the city, I would like to see one of your paintings." This is a request and not a command. A proper approach has no accusation. It supports a voluntary spirit. If she paints, it is for her pleasure.

My therapist told a story that exemplified not being swept into a competing ego trip. In a band all but one of the musicians were playing very loudly. To "achieve balance," they wanted the soft one to raise his volume. He didn't like it loud and lowered his volume instead. The band grew angry but could not make him get louder. Instead, they had to lower their sound to achieve balance.

We need to learn how to get out from under parental pressure without declaring war. After years of criticism from a narcissistic family, children accept what they hear and are plagued by low self-esteem. We grow older and develop independent ideas, but still fall prey to doing what our parents like. Then we get stronger still and are sad, mad, and no longer willing to tolerate manipulation. When they tell us who we are and what to do, we fly into tantrums and counteraccuse. Although we rebel against what they say, this reaction shows that we are not autonomous.

I had many angry moments on my parents' visit, which showed

that in some way I believed their opinions. When his wife asked if she could hold a family party in my house, she was pleasing my father while bringing inconvenience to me. Knowing of my emotional distance from these narcissistic relatives, she was going to get us all together and pour on the glue. Because her party would interfere with my work, I said an angry no. Later, I realized that if I had felt less threatened, I could have said, "Do what you like," joined the party for a while, gone for a run, and retired to my room with my ears plugged against sound to work.

How do I feel about my response to them? Overall, too sensitive. I see how I learned to hate my face and figure and that it is hard for me to treat demeaning remarks as comments to be evaluated. Trained to feel inadequate, objectivity is a hurdle I will have to practice jumping. My father is as fallible as any. When I am hurt by what he says, I must have forgotten this.

How to react to unacceptable comments and suggestions? If you are inured to inherent attack, say in a friendly tone, "Interesting opinion; I shall consider it." Consider it in your own time and when you are ready. If your parent demands agreement now, say that you need time to think it over. Do not be bullied into agreeing in order to still his or her insecurity. Do not defer to critical manipulation by projecting a state of awe. An attacked child cringes, cries, argues, and feels inferior. Outgrow this and treat criticism as a suggestion you will consider.

Give what is said the respect you reserve for any kind of comment. Do this even if you are hypersensitive. If you want to agree or disagree, say what you will and let your comments rest. Avoid combat no matter how unruly or insulting the response. Your life does not depend on other people's opinion of you. Children of narcissists are so much criticized that they accept criticism everywhere and train new people to speak to them that way. But criticism should be stopped as early as possible. Destructive criticism is not a pattern to encourage. If an older child or adult cannot accomplish this in his family home, he needs to move out as soon as possible.

Practice noncombative firmness. Do not support a critical approach by falling on your knees. If you hear remarks that cause you to worry, seek outside evaluation. You may need to change something but don't want to feed the critical method a meal of grandeur. A narcissistic man criticized everyone because his approach was never stopped. He was told fifty thousand times not to criticize but criticism remained his calling. If reprimanded, he would say, "I'm sorry you took it that way." Nothing stayed his tongue.

An effective way to deal with compulsive criticism is to ignore what is said. Do not fuss about its put-down quality. The compulsive critic relies on your attention to feed his ego. If you remonstrate, argue, deny, feel hurt, you show that his comments hit home. Such a reaction to one who needs attention keeps his technique alive. When we train an animal, it repeats behavior that it thinks will bring reward. If there is no response to what it does, positive reinforcement is removed and the behavior stops. In the same way, bland indifference takes the weapon from a critic's hand.

Sometimes the attack is too much to ignore. In families of narcissists where criticism is favored, there are unspoken tenets of behavior, like: "He who wields the knife is powerful. If I tell you what to do, I know more. Smarter is better" and "I raise myself by putting you down." I was raised under such an onslaught and was too often hurt to shrug it off. Children of narcissists can develop emotional soft spots from parental pounding. We are like tenderized veal. Criticism keeps hitting home because we believe what is said. Children of narcissists have been pounded into belief. Our parents know our sore points because they originally created them.

If what is said is objectionable, goes too far, or is said too often, we may need a more active approach to eliminate this critical behavior. Humor is one of the most effective and harmless ways of teaching. Humor does not have to be of the ho-ho-ho kind. It can be an event that stops the attacker cold, like showing by gentle comment and question that he is ill-informed about something you know quite well.

Take your parent's insistence on publicly criticizing you. You feel humiliated and unable to stop her, which may call for "heroic" tactics. This can be humor of the outrageous kind that takes courage to effect. One who succumbs to his parent's tongue does better if the humorous scene is rehearsed. You are going to make it impossible for the parent to continue without self-humiliation. She will see you as a person not to mess with, one who can interfere with her manipulations and tricks.

A father plagued his thirty-five-year old daughter for not marrying. He disapproved of her lifestyle, which he thought reflected badly on him. He had just married a social climber whose sons were engaged to "model" females with page-boy hairdos, polished nails, up-to-the-minute clothing. They had the look that was "in" at the time for upwardly mobile yuppies. This made him insecure, ashamed, and determined to reform her by rubbing her nose in her "embarrassing" condition. His way of life was devoted to reforming people. He began discussing her unmarried state while driving a car full of people, including his wife and two stepsons, on an elevated driveway near the water.

His daughter was waiting. He raised the topic like a sledge hammer, pounding nails into the plank of her being. She had asked her analyst how to get out of victimization, being grilled, embarrassed, and wrong. He told her to do what she would never have dared without his advice. It was a piece of theater that used her parent's values. Her shrink was a respected man who had helped her before. His script would offer her father a lesson.

Her father was launched on her marital condition. Why was she not married and at her age? What of her loneliness, etc.? He regarded his point of view as the one and only way to be. Her stepbrothers looked at her reaction. She did not think it then, but they too put up with plenty of criticism from him. She felt surrounded by criticizing enemies, drew a deep breath, and pictured the vulnerable position she would soon be in. In her mind, her shrink said, "Do it," and she did.

"Dad, there's something I've been meaning to tell you for a long time." "What?" he said, with mounting sadism in his tone. "I'm gay and I shall not marry." Her father didn't know the truth, but was thrown by her lack of propriety. The car swerved a little. She had been heard by the class of people he wanted to impress. He would have unabashedly pinned her for living alone but gay was something else. Gay lost him points with his audience and a narcissist is always trying to score on image.

He snorted and swerved the car, too anxious to ask more. "You can't be," he sputtered into his collar, to which she said nothing. He dared not pursue it. I am not using this story to demean homosexuality. It is only an example of how to use an atypical point of view or one of the parent's weak spots to lay the narcissistic attack to rest. Her tone was friendly and then she was silent. It was his decision whether to continue discussing marriage.

The narcissist did not admit that what she said hit home. That would entail a loss of face. Deep inside, what she said pertained to him. It is difficult for a narcissist to give a sign of change. If you are looking for change writ large, you should go to someone else. A small but significant change not directly stated was that he did not again discuss her unmarried life in front of other people. Perhaps, as was said to me, this was a big victory after all.

Narcissism is a tale of codependency. The codependent person cares for the person who abuses some kind of drug. The codependent has her arms wrapped round a person who has his arms wrapped round his drug, be it alcohol, cocaine, fame, power over people, money, etc. If the abuser is narcissistic, his arms are wrapped around his image. From his defensive isolation, the narcissist demands that his codependent child get vicarious satisfaction from the parent's pleasure in self. The child hears what is wrong with herself or about her and her parent's "greatness." Otherwise the child is ignored and must be happy that her parent can have an admirable and independent image. In the parent's philosophy, his child cannot say no.

Insensitivity was shown by a narcissistic father who, despite his ex-wife's death two weeks before, sent his daughter a Xerox copy of the letter he had mailed to the local newspaper without its being published. It concerned our nation's unnecessary expenditure on items of war to shield us from "Red" enemies while vital services in the country fell apart. Disappointed by the newspaper's lack of response, he asked her for a reaction. Not a word was said about the loss of her mother. She did not answer his letter, for which he undoubtedly blamed her.

Children of narcissists are confused about what is fair to self and parent. They need to develop such judgment, but how are they to do it? It helps to talk to friends and to observe relations between non-narcissistic people. Psychotherapy may be necessary to get the stuck engine of self turning. A grownup's desire to lean too heavily on his child, while pitiful, is not fair. The narcissistic parent is needy, which makes his child feel guilty for withholding. But the child should not surrender to pressure that he go beyond his means and reason.

I remember wondering who and what should be the recipient of my care. My analyst set me to thinking about it with a mythic tale. He spoke this way because he knew that I would overlook the truth of direct comment. Children of narcissists are trained to ignore reality and to stick to their parents' rationalizations. The analyst wanted to circumvent this by entering my spirit through imagination and the unexpected. His tale was tough to swallow. It lingered in my mind for months and years. It is with me now.

A mother bird was able to fly only one of her four babies at a time across the ocean. She put a fledgling on her wing and said, "When I am old, will you fly across the water with me on your wing?" "Oh yes, Mother," said the birdie out of love. Mother took this baby out over the ocean and dropped it in. She went back for her second and asked the same question. "Mother, I love you so much that I will save you then." The second birdie followed the first into the drink. Mother dropped the third one to drown for the very same response and approached her fourth. Asked what this birdie would one day do when it was grown and she was old, it answered, "Oh Mother, forgive me. I love you so much but when I am your age I shall have my own young to carry across the sea."

This baby was carried to the farther shore. It is natural to support first ourselves and then our young. It is not our wish to turn our parents down. We want them always with us but should not sacrifice ourselves and the next generation to save our parents' lives. It is our obligation to look ahead.

This biological perspective contradicts the narcissist's demand for primary position with everyone. He stars in a psychic play with only one character, who is looking in the mirror. His child does not have the time or energy to supply what the parent's deficient system needs. The child's energy must go to his or her own future, which includes the lives of his children. Like all grownups, the parent must fix himself. Narcissism is a sickness and a weakness. You, his child, can be angry at the lack of love received from him and can bypass rage to feel compassion and regret. But his problems require expert help.

We get along better with the narcissistic parent if we stop living by his opinions and his rules. As a child, I backed down from what I thought important, to please him and avoid attack. I did not want to be associated with something he thought wrong and undermined myself to win approval. For example, my father kept saying that the math I couldn't understand was easy. It made the matter worse that every lesson with him was filled with pejorative comments.

Rather than investigate my difficulty with numbers, my trouble with one and two, I was told, "You are stupid," and "Math is easy." Accordingly, I acted stupid and got the lowest marks in the class. How stupid I must be if it really was so easy. I remember receiving a 15 on one test. I always thought that I would fail but sometimes concentration surged forward out of fear and my work improved dramatically. It was strange to get a near-to-top grade on a test like the New York State Regents exams, which kept me from failing in class. Afterward, I would sink back into obscurity with a teacher who would scratch her head and wonder who I copied from. According to my narcissistic parent, except for math I did well in school because I somehow faked intelligence and bought my teachers off. Actually, I loved to read. Aside from this I backed down and kowtowed to him in the deepest way, acting out what he thought of me.

Seeing him as correct, I was dragged into the lowest of moods by his assessment, which considered my problems disastrous, inevitable, to be cured only if I followed his advice. Years went by and his negative pressure started to get me mad. But anger is not a final step. It shows that my expectations of him were unrealistic. A narcissistic father phoned his child to say that he read one of her newspaper articles and it was not good enough. At the same time, he said that she underestimated the magnificence of his contributions to the world and to her. Such comments were familiar intellectual pap for her to eat. When they stopped talking on the phone, she exploded into well-chosen epithets.

Her response showed a combination of strength and weakness. It was a strength that she didn't feel too constricted to admit her anger and didn't need to try and back him down. It was a weakness that she expected something different from the critical/superior message she always got from him. She thought about how to handle future situations in which he would want to evaluate her work, since his comments undermined her. She lacked sufficient perspective to disregard them.

Her analyst suggested that she let him read her work but ask him to make comments only on paper. She was to tell him that she would not attend to any criticism of her work that was verbally communicated. When his notes would appear, she privately knew that she could file them in the garbage. Of course she would have to enforce her rule with him, and narcissistic parents will often try to slip one in. They are power-hungry and self-righteous about their "giving" you what you "need"—the image of superior judgment that makes them speak. Also it is hard for a child not to read a parent's notes since she is always waiting and looking for his positive response. She has not yet decided to deprive him of reading her work but does know that telling him to stop criticizing her will not meet with success. He has already been told this innumerable times by many people.

What do we do with our anger toward them? Anger has a healthy side if it puts us on the road to change. Tillie was raised to smile and conceal her anger. Negative emotions were treated as undesirable by a mother who ruled and was obeyed by everyone. After years of analysis, Tillie feels good about expressing mild anger at her mother's provocation. Such expression makes her feel free and she enjoys its heat. Anger expressed is better than being a Goody Two-Shoes.

Sometimes, though, we hate ourselves for getting mad. We think that we should be beyond such response. Nick was angered by his parent's self-centered drive and attacked himself for feeling angry. This demand showed he has narcissistic values that can't accept his imperfections.

Unrealistic expectations and consequent disappointments keep us unhappy with our parents. If we understand that parental egocentricity is based on feelings of inferiority, narcissistic outpourings can be heard as notes upon the wind. If our narcissistic parent repeatedly disappoints us by claiming to possess more value than he has, anger comes until we understand. A therapist spoke with humor of their posture when he said, "How reassuring it is to know that in our changing world, the narcissist remains the same."

Review your understanding of narcissism until it automatically appears in response to your parent's controlling words and gestures. Once you can disregard such behavior, you may get in touch with your feelings of affection. Where does this love come from? In early childhood your parent felt some love for you. You walked and talked together. He tickled you and shared the butterflies interposed with criticism and intermittent unavailability. Little things mean a lot. From such moments grew love that lives on despite the clamoring of your anger and your need.

As you grow more realistic and see your parent's blocks to loving, look for fuller loving from a nonnarcissistic person. Raised with the narcissistic version of love, it can be a lengthy process before you know the kind of love you need. It is difficult for many children of narcissists to expand their definition of love to meet their deficit.

Perhaps you have changed and want to get together with your parent. The issue of your change comes up. In the past, you always did what he wanted but now your own interests are precious. You do not want to return to your formerly empty state by subscribing to the parent's call for replication as if you lacked identity of your own.

You want to spend time together doing something pleasing to both of you. Since you once shared an early life, it is unlikely that you have no interests in common. State what you would like to do and hear her response. If what interests you is unacceptable to her and what she suggests does not appeal to you, try a second idea and a third. Keep proposing until you find something that appeals to you both. Compromise means finding what suits you although it may not be on the top of either list. If she likes history and you like museums, go to a museum that shows historic events. Each loses and gains a bit.

Giving in is different from compromise. Giving in has the spirit of surrender in which you please the other by disregarding your self. The narcissistic person stages a scene of temper or grief. Feeling frightened, guilty, or oppressed, you give the squalling person what she wants. You give, but do not want to do so, in order to get the relief of her calming down. Such pacification is not compromise since the profits go a single way. Trying to create a bargaining table with the narcissist can lead to strife since listening to you as if your needs counted is new for her. Fighting takes two people. In your new way of being, a self can be firm without a fight.

The child of a narcissist who is used to pacifying his parent feels the hopeless longing that addicts and codependents label love. Addiction is a longing that is never satisfied. Becoming real by self-expression brings the possibility of receiving a different kind of love. You will be loved for who you really are. The narcissist hopes that others subscribe to her view even in their silence. Hearing your viewpoint and giving it weight makes her feel demolished. This is the narcissistic illness and why she must be lonely. Arriving at a mutual decision will not be easy for her. She must learn that sharing the power of decision will not objectively vanquish either one of you.

Once you arrive at a mutually acceptable choice of activity and are on your way, there will be less pain, although the narcissist will still feel some. Her own parent disregarded her real self, which is why she allows no one to get close. Now you, the child whose love she needs, introduce the necessity of there being two people and viewpoints again. She fears to be discarded but you cannot fully solve her problem since it needs psychoanalysis. Your goal must be limited to finding an activity that is pleasurable for you both. If none is found today, look for one another time.

In getting together, it is good to know the limits of your relating. If you want to improve how you get along, do not underestimate its difficulty. Rather than revert to a submissive state, and knowing how hard it is to change, be progressive in your demands. Go from easy to hard. What are the expected problems? Each family is different. In my tribe there are compulsive talkers, know-it-alls who parade knowledge and leave no room for you to speak. You are supposed to fade away and look interested. If you enter their monologues and disagree with them, their speech will cut you down.

If your parent is a talker, establish ground rules that stop interruption. He is not to interrupt you and you are not to interrupt him. Interrupting is a psychological way of killing the speaker. When you are interrupted, let him speak until finished and then pick up exactly where you left off until your thought is completed. Eliminate interruption until you both can converse in relative freedom.

If he wants you to share an activity that only he enjoys, and a narcissist commonly believes his choice to be the best and only desirable one, the child part in you will want to win his praise by acceding. You cannot regularly do this and be thought of as an autonomous person. Instead you need to gently indicate disinterest in the activity and to underreact to hurt feelings he expresses in response. Sympathy for his feelings is not surrender. Explain what you would like to do and keep looking for what you can share.

The child of a narcissist can fool himself into expecting a different parent and then be driven to distraction by what occurs. Do not fall into such fantasy. If what he wants to do or discusses is of little interest to you, change the topic to what interests you both. Such change is not as destructive as phony talk in which you secretly die of boredom. If the narcissist is a compulsive talker and you do not like such verbiage, avoid a meeting that allows for endless talking. You do not want to battle against his need for an ear.

Don't be shocked by continued narcissistic arrogance. Appreciate what you can but don't lie. It is possible to point to his strengths without treating the narcissist as a god. If he puts you down, jokingly put yourself lower. I don't always put myself down, but sometimes doing it exposes the competition behind the criticism and thereby disempowers the parent. Don't complain about his acting powerful. My analyst gave the example of trying to make yourself bigger by getting on another's back in a deep swimming pool. The person beneath goes down but the person on top is no higher.

Limit your time together to how much you enjoy. Set time for nonconversational activities, a play or concert, a walk in the woods. Your parent may also need to remove herself from your talk and demands. Do not overrun established boundaries. She has not often respected your personhood. It will be hard for you to state your limits and for her to follow. If your needs clash and your boundaries are overrun, go with the limit of the person who can take less. It is like Jewish law about a window. If the one who needs it closed is weaker than the one who wants it open, the window is closed. You do not want to injure the weaker person. Defer to the one who suffers. It is easier to meet again than to generate frustration, and it takes a lot of knowledge and discipline to keep it kind.

How much time together is pleasurable? This can change with time and become less or more. You learn by observation. What do you do about the lack of positive response? Many say that we should not expect a damned thing from the narcissist, but this is not possible or necessary for one who is her child. There is love for both of you. You learn to love by separating the wheat from the chaff. Love appreciated means not asking for the kind of love that the parent cannot give. And vice versa.

You will have a kinder relationship if you do not have to defer to and buy into each other's images. This gives you the freedom to develop compassion. Set it up so that what you do together offers opportunity to feel. You may be surprised at how little love there is. Or how much. The more you support her faltering self, the more you will know the love she brings. I know a parent who led a self-centered life. In his eighty-fourth year, he told his daughter, "You are the center of my life," and it was true. By seeing the parent's limitations and fears, we can allow ourselves to feel the love we have for him.

18

Sending Home the Negative Introject

How do you confront the negative inner parent when it attacks you? How do you get rid of it, refute its hateful message, and make its influence less destructive?

It is as hard to end this book as it is to acquire self-appreciation. Children of narcissists need to learn to discriminate, not to absorb every negative opinion and directive that comes our way. Once we were too open. Then we reacted by moving toward total closure in defense. Closure leads to boredom and deadness. We need to find a middle ground where things can enter consciousness and be subject to evaluation before they are accepted as a part of our being. We need not absorb what we don't find valid.

It is difficult for us to find the middle ground. We were raised in extremes and do not know the middle. When life is easy, the middle is easier to establish. When life is difficult we need to work to find it. It is the struggle toward this objective with which I end this book.

The negative introject is partly the voice of your attacking and restrictive narcissistic parent whose thinking took up residence in your mind. It is not rightly a part of your self but a hostile foreigner that watches you with a critical eye. Little escapes its quest for control. It criticizes you with such comments as "You're a failure" and "Why try?" Your feelings of depression strengthen its force. It makes you discard appreciation and distrust affection. Its punitive demands and paralyzing arguments stop you from trying to change.

We want to please this uninvited judge that sounds so much like our narcissistic parents. We succumb to its messages, the thoughts that we hate and almost believe. We want to reject such miserable input but lack the foggiest notion of how to do so. We resentfully accept its presence as a fact of life.

My negative introject entered the scene a few hours after a phone call from my esteemed agent to tell me this book was sold. Up I went in mood and spirit. Hours later I arrived home and my feelings started shifting strangely. Soon I was depressed. It was as if the depression had come from the sky but actually it came from the attitude of my negative introject. I was anxious and despondent as I questioned my ability to do the work. It was as if the person who wrote the first half of the book was a million miles away.

My negative introject said, "You'll never finish the writing and will be humiliated, marked as a failure, a tragedy, a landmark of shame." I felt pummeled by this. It seemed to make sense. My hopeless mood was evidence of my worthlessness. With a note of triumph, my introject said, "That is you." Later, while brushing my teeth, despondency drew me to memories of childhood. I felt asthmatic shortness of breath and wheezing, something I had not suffered since that era at times when I was emotionally abandoned, stressed, and pressured. Being unable to breathe was the physical aspect of my emotional horror. It was amazing to have an attack on the day I heard about selling my book about children of narcissists.

The negative introject squashed my feelings of success and raised fears of humiliation. Achieving and then losing again can be more painful than not achieving at all, which is why many children of narcissists do so little. Barely functioning defends us from loss. We were taught to feel responsible for fate rather than to do what we can and let results fall as they may.

Don't be discouraged by this tale. It was not a total loss but showed the response of my introject to achievement that took me above my expected level. At that time and totally discouraged, I could not laugh. After a period of emotional hassle, I laughingly resisted the introject's attack on my commitment and returned to work. When we measure the achievement of a person, we need to know her past, the place from where she has come.

I heard my introject's call to failure. It said that I would not be paid for my work, which part of me believed while the rest of me pushed on. I heard my healthy side saying, "The gods can have their way after you have finished." I am happy to have written this. It represents the triumph of my self.

A house divided, children of narcissists must struggle to exist. They fight with their negative introjects and feel trounced on and wearied by its endless attempts to suppress their efforts. They receive its directives as punishment or correction and are led into hopelessness. If undermined, they accept messages that read like poison. The power they give to their introject makes it hard to eradicate.

I increasingly identified with my goals. A measure of health is the state of your self. Self and health are one. Strength came from sharing insights with other children of narcissists. Working on the book directly involved loyalty to my self. Could I do it justice when continually undercut by my negative introject and by narcissistic outsiders who focused on potential negative reactions? My worried self still drove me to think, feel, and write. Never had my personality and self been so close. My operations and feelings were as one. Wonderful to feel myself being.

In repeatedly silencing my introject I learned more about the struggle. Eradication takes deliberate thought and effort. You need to identify the introject as foreign to your self. As long as we think of it as ours, we are at a disadvantage. If we see it as a non-self, an identification that drives us to unacceptable roles, feelings, and behaviors, we

can work on it. Labeling it as non-self is difficult because we unconsciously see the introject as an aspect of our narcissistic parent. What
do we do when loyalty to the parent opposes loyalty to ourselves? We
have been trained never to put self first. The narcissistic parent would
call us selfish.

Sometimes we think the introject a part of us and sometimes not.
The introject feels strong, then weak, then strong again. Outside circumstances affect it, as does therapeutic examination. Group membership and individual therapy help. Logic attenuates its form and negative
circumstances bring it back. The battle can last a lifetime. But it needn't.

This attacking and foreign agent first enters our realm when we
are babies and need our parents' love. If they are critical and narcissistic, their disapproving eye and angry mouth start hurting us from
within. As we grow, the negative introject imposes states of limitation
with which our self disagrees but is trounced by it and imprisoned. The
introject wants to be top dog and, unlike a conscience that leads to
reasonable comfort, it removes security from the self. Despite its negative effect, a childish idea that this can lead to love glues us together.
Parent love was slow in coming but we knew no other way to get it.

An adult is sickened by his introject and thinks it harmful. He
wants to set himself free but finds it hard to do. He may be unaware
that his child portion clings to childish ways and ignores the consequences of such attitudes. Childish expectation can be hidden in the
unconscious and only detected by inference, for example in the content
of our dreams.

You are bemused and anxious about what you do. An extra portion of cake, the important job undone, choosing an unloving lover.
People dominated by negative introjects blame it on the stars. They
treat their introject's pressure as a joke and ask, "Why am I doing this?"
They follow its instructions to fail, surrender responsibility, and admit
that their child self is in charge. "You know me when I . . ." They speak
as if they are inhabited by an external control. They suffer from repetition but do not mark their behavior as addictive, which would ob-
ligate them to try to change. Since their problem is addictive, they
indulge in childhood needs and pleasures while their adult lives fall
apart. They say "somehow" and "maybe" of their intentions while stav-
ing off adult needs, responsibilities, and expectations.

They indulge in childish behavior stemming from the unstated wish that this will cause the narcissistic parent to love them. All people have childish wishes. To realize our potential, however, we must stand alone and face the fact that the narcissistic parent cannot now adequately meet our childhood needs any more than he or she could when we were growing up. If we stick to childish behavior, we will continue to inhabit a dreamland of wishes and illusory expectations, addicted to the unrealizable desire for the narcissistic parent to meet our needs.

The introject uses our parent's values. If he or she is narcissistic, such values cannot lead the child to happiness. We do not know that we were propagandized into many of our beliefs, which makes them hard for us to know and surrender. It takes more than introspection to see them. We need the input of friends, therapist, therapy group, people who share similar battles but who are not bound by identical constraints. These others are also puzzled by the working of their unconscious. All work at depleting the negative introject's power.

Therapy groups are usually not exclusively formed for children of narcissistic parents. But most groups help in multiple ways. In group, you find out that you are not the only one with a hideous self-image that was put in place by endless parental demands for change. The narcissistic habits that you manifest will be responded to as objectionable in no uncertain terms. Group therapy bypasses the social inhibition against expressing displeasure. Some group members would flare up at me when I took an all-knowing and commanding position toward their behavior. Inwardly insecure, I had no idea that I sounded like my parent in speaking as I did.

Then there were friends. One was Hal, a Viennese gentleman who also attended graduate school in psychology. He was a lover who reminded me of my physical beauty. Of my small breasts he would say, "More than a mouthful is wasted." He helped me with my fear of statistics and when his ministrations were over, this child of a narcissistic got the higher grade.

He had an outrageous sense of humor that appeared in a series of photographs he took of me in my despair. In one photo, we were on vacation in Provincetown and I was lying on a rock jetty, pummeled into hopelessness by my introject. He lovingly called it, "Golomb gives up."

He would cry with me from sadness—his, mine, and ours together. His had to do with being a refugee from Nazi Germany and losing his family, especially his beloved cousin who had set out for Israel never to be seen again. At times Hal would act like a robot, a mechanical creature that walked with a jerk and increasingly lost control, which thrilled and scared me as it woodenly followed me around mumbling inanities. He was acting the role of a person who had completely lost his ability to feel, a common defense for people who have gone through the horrors of war. In actual fact, he had many feelings, some so strong they scared him.

Together we adopted Effie, a dog that became my friend for life. Effie was the name taken from my own and given to the doll I most loved. By six or so, I had washed the doll, which stilled its voice, but I loved it just as much. My parents intended to buy me a "better" one. No one asked me if I wanted to hold on to Effie, that extension of my self. One day I came home from school to find that Effie was gone. A new doll with Toni hair did not still my grief. It was one of the many moves they performed which said you have nothing and no place to call your own.

Hal helped return to me the spirit of what I had once loved and missed. He took joy in the dog's personality. We both had so much fun living without having to prove or be something different. He shielded me from my parent's narcissistic opinion. When things appeared dire, he never gave up hope. For the first time, I was with a man by whom I felt accepted.

Do negative thoughts lurk at the back of your mind like uninvited guests? Such ideas can be so habitual that you do not think them strange. In freeing yourself, it helps to be funny. "You here again?" Humor cuts the power of oppressive ideas. Laughing, you can see that you don't believe in everything you think. It is good to tell your self-demolishing messages to those who have similar problems or who can enjoy a good joke.

Sometimes you listen too long before acting. The introject gets hold of your mood and outwits your common sense and humor. If you can't politely back off, continue on your way despite inner criticism. Reason and will can keep you going till you get support.

A time of need can open you to the negative introject. My negative introject had been quiet for a while when a catastrophe brought it back. At age forty-seven, I had gone for a bike ride that led to an accident in which I injured my head. Local hospital X rays showed two concussions and a small fracture of the skull. This hospital would not treat head injuries and told my parents to send me to another hospital. Instead of my parents explaining to me what was happening, I found myself strapped to a stretcher and against my will was carried away in an ambulance. I was terrified, resistant, and they knew it. I have a long history in natural healing and wanted to see my Chinese herbal physician. But my parents were too scared by the doctor's story to tell me what was happening and acted in a typically narcissistic way.

In fear and over my protest, I was taken to the second hospital, where I received the medication I did not want. The right to make decisions was taken from me and given to my parents. They allowed the doctors full control of treatment and ignored my endless requests to be removed because the doctors had implanted fear of my demise.

I would have done it otherwise but had lost control over my medical treatment. I call it "medical" but in fact the only medicine I received was tranquilizers. I wanted to leave but was literally tied down and drugged. I was always kept tied, since the hospital knew I intended to leave. I was tied neck, wrists, midriff, and ankles, except for the few hours that my mother visited and would untie me against hospital disapproval. She never could believe that I was otherwise kept tied and chose to think it occurred five minutes before she arrived. However, my unhappiness, anxiety, displeasure, and sickness were slowly sinking into her awareness.

The hospital concealed the fact that I was continuously injected into a state of confusion and stupor with a tranquilizer used for psychotics who are difficult to control. My relatives were told that I was on no medication, although from it I suffered depression, anxiety, confusion. My speech was slightly stilted from the head injury but mainly from drugging. These and my constant demand for departure were used as evidence by the staff that I needed to stay a minimum of six months. Such treatment was not for the concussion for which they had nothing but to make me renounce and forget my intention to leave. They persuaded my narcissistic father and his narcissistic family, who held conference in the corner of my room without any input from me.

I was desperate to leave and becoming sicker by the day. I constantly demanded, begged, and pleaded with my relatives for release to my treatment of choice, but no one would listen, which was a paradigm of the usual situation for the child of narcissistic parents. Sickened and helpless as I was, it could not have been more horrible.

My mother would feel terrible and say, "You'll leave tomorrow." But lying was her way and she was too scared to follow through. That I expected to leave was put on my hospital record as a sign of my living in delusion.

I became my child self in search of a loving parent. I wanted a hand to reach for mine with no strings attached. I needed understanding and support for what I judged important. This a narcissist cannot give. Denial of my need set my negative introject in motion.

I was not without ideas of my own, a little unintelligible due to the drugging, but desperately trying to communicate. I never had imagined that I, a well-trained clinical psychologist with twenty years of experience in mental health care, would not be listened to. It was too frightening to contemplate. On the edge of consciousness, I toyed with the idea that the hospital was killing me with nontreatment and drugging. I gave up on receiving help and was sinking into thoughts of suicide and murder. I fell into the severe anxiety and hopelessness of a stress disorder that lasted well after I left the hospital. It had everything to do with the care I received and little with my response to concussion.

Narcissistic torture feeds the introject. To visitors who would not heed me, I was an "it." Not knowing that I was drugged, they ignored my requests as fantasy. My narcissistic uncle later told me that I begged him to get me out, up to the point of flirtation. It was horribly sad to hear him speak. My mother untied me each day for our four hours of visitation but would not let herself believe that I was tied down all the rest of the time. Everyone avoided awareness of the painful facts of what I tried to tell them. The doctors knew best. My mother, less narcissistic than the others, saw that I was not getting better and heard my mounting anxiety and depression. Each day she promised to remove me, then fell into fear and paralysis.

On my ninth and final day in the hospital, she found me wrapped in restraints from neck to shins and arm to arm. Before this event, I had managed to untie myself and had gone to the desk to demand release.

They refused and it turned into a fight with eight in staff to pin me down. My horrified mother arrived and asked, "What is this, an asylum? My daughter is here for concussion." As always, I begged to leave.

She saw my fury, hating her for what they did with her permission. It was too much for her. "She is leaving." Staff was up in arms. "She'll be ruined on the outside, will fall on her head, and take to bed forever." I left A.M.A. (Against Medical Advice), feeling how few people can understand your needs. Friends had been instructed by the staff to dismiss my words as babble. They forgot me as a person because I was trauma-short on vocabulary. Now that time has gone by and the facts have come out, they are shaken.

This tragedy was in keeping with the predictive voice of my negative introject—a split skull and a major battle against the forces of institutionalization before I could get on with healing myself through natural methods and the writing of this book. My struggle echoed the introject's words: "You will be killed for trying."

I don't bob as much for my narcissistic parent's praise. Before, desire kept me wide-eyed in hope of approval. Now I do not trust his word and intention. One does not care so much to win the flattering words of people you do not think are on your side. What is that praise worth and who is the one they are praising? When I am falsely flattered like this, I no longer feel like the original me. I am looking on.

I had forgotten my passivity as a child of narcissistic parents but this accident brought it back. My concussion caused dependency that was used by my narcissistic parent to attack and push me further down. He considered a "healing" institution when I was asking for release. The narcissist always knows what is best for you no matter what you say. Now I look before I react and events are not coming at me so expectedly. I am better able to judge what is going on in other people.

I feel the subtle sensation of change. I do not feel and think the same way. When conducting a therapy session, I have visual imagery of patients that they later confirm, which shows that I am picking up even minimal cues. I am more aware of lying, that people say what they think you want to hear but which they don't intend; that some people are reliable and others are not. I am more sensitive to subtleties. Sometimes I ask myself if I am growing paranoid, but from the amount of love I feel, I would say that I am growing up.

Without personal analysis, children of narcissists suffer worse consequences. Using the writing of this book as a metaphor for any plan you choose, it is a struggle to carry it out. If completed, your book will not leave the drawer. If a publisher is found, will you perish in a hospital? It is interesting that the biking accident happened to me on the day following the sale of my book.

The introject is ruthless. At varying times, you will have to battle its self-suppressive force. The introject will activate to knock you back and down. Your assigned position is what the narcissistic parent wants.

Being in a crisis with greater expectations makes you more accessible to your negative introject. If you have narcissistic parents, relatives, and friends, your hopes are often disappointed. You rarely get what you ask for even on your birthday. What is it like when your needs are stated and the parents still go their own way? A parent teaches her child to blame himself for parental shortcomings and later for all bad events. In a crisis, you will see yourself as at fault. The negative introject is fed with anti-self material and gives you messages of self-hatred in return.

Even in an extreme situation, it is wrong to think the narcissist will be ready to meet your everyday hopes and needs, much less extreme ones. Do not attack yourself for wanting this. You are a pupil of self-punishment. Your introject will turn against you when there is insufficient consideration and love. Needing nurturance from those who lack it to give is no cause to attack yourself.

Your introject babbles about your lovelessness in explanation. This learned distortion can be undercut by relating to a person or creature by whom you feel loved. On my post-accident "vacation," I was in love with a Vermont puppy, a huge black Labrador that followed me around, even onto my couch, where it deposited its tiny 100 pounds on my chest, nibbling wildly at my fingers and face. It was so full of outrageous life that it made me laugh and got me going. It was so friendly and assertive that I could not remain in a bleak mood.

Find people who can love you and vice versa. Bring them into your life. Are you affixed to narcissists? Do you need to learn to recognize a different type of person who will support you in happy times and emergency? If nurturance is available, the fingers of your negative introject will not clutch at your throat.

Although we may not be aware of it, we spend our lives separating from our parents. When we are in emotional need, our need for parent love becomes strong again. We think the appearance of this need should make us unhappy since our narcissistic mind is vain. It says that childish needs are eternally childish. But people *are* eternally childish and eternally growing. It is resistance to the process that makes for problems. Maturing never ends. It is immaturity that declares us finished. The narcissist arrests his pattern of growth with a stance of perfection and does not mature. Denying parts of self that need work means hiding in a limited state.

Children of narcissists must fight for independence from the narcissistic parents who would live through them. Such parents treat their children as imperfect and rejected or perfect and connected to the parent. Such a concatenation of self and value is not the road to development. Narcissistic parents do not grant adulthood to their offspring as people on their own. The parent cannot conceive of such a relationship.

We are always becoming autonomous and separating from our negative introject. It fights to hold on and we struggle to let it go. It is self versus introject and each thought system claims to be the real you. There is a guilty conflict between love of self and love of parent. Can we live untrammeled by our parents' word as expressed through the introject? We would not have introjects like these if our parents hadn't rejected our basic human parts out of their own irrational pressures. Holding on to a negative view of self keeps the introject alive. We need to believe in our intrinsic value and right to err if we want to be introject-free.

Our narcissistic parents see us as a rehabilitation project. We express negative introjects inherited from their own rejecting parents. Such introjects kept them from humane responsiveness to us, a nightmare passed from generation to generation. With knowledge, we will try to stop the transfer. We will not carry on its decisions even toward ourselves. It is a battle. For life.

If you want to change your thinking to feel less pain but run from the pain introduced by the negative introject, your pain will increase. It is like a helpless child's response to an attacking parent. "I must get away from this. It is too horrible to bear." Pain grows in proportion to the magnitude of your fear.

Instead note, "I am giving myself hurtful messages but I know my tendency to think the worst and shall first assess the difficulty." Objectivity reduces your introject's power. If you find a problem in your behavior, it is not equivalent to the worth of your self. A narcissist confuses his behavior and self, which renders him defensively incapable of seeing his difficulties.

Your negative introject can haunt you with tragic fantasies about yourself. To heal, say, "Tell me all and let me see it in a clear light." Fears grow in the shadows. Phobic people are haunted by fear. The more they avoid what they fear, the worse the phobia. Phobia spreads to new objects that are connected with the old. Contamination spreads through flight. Avoidance is a poor response.

Approach the thing you fear and do it till your fear runs out. If what you fear is the punitive voice of your negative introject, do not run away, argue, or cry over its attack. Fearful adulation gives it power. You wept to arouse your parents' pity. It is the awe of insecurity that attested to their greatness. They were flattered by their power over you.

In our culture, women often cry instead of showing anger. Tears announce their inferior position. The child of a narcissist is in a similar position. He cannot be openly angry with his parents and later defers to their representative in the negative introject. He needs to stop groveling beneath his introject's heel and sniveling at its words. He needs to remove the negative introject from its pedestal.

If instead you support the introject by letting its pejorative comments hit home, you are trading punishment for the hope of love. If you put off the quest for freedom, you always will lack love. Back and forth you go but once you surrender your quest for love from a narcissist, you will feel emptiness, which hurts and makes you wonder why you live. This is a time to mourn for what you will never have. In mourning you accept that the narcissistic parent will never give as much love as you need. No more chance to win the love that was absent. After suffering this loss, you will move on. A loss that is known eventually can be healed.

Coming from a childhood of frequent pain, minimal touching, and little understanding, you can barely tolerate your feelings. You falter at the crossroads and return to the destructive mouthings of your introject or choose a narcissistic partner. Finally you prepare yourself for the pain of knowing what you lack. This is like an empty dock at which you can tie a different boat. The boat of a person who loves you.

Children of narcissists are raised with the belief that they have traits that make them special and unlovable. The narcissist focuses on his child's flaws as reason for his own incapacity to give. The child later is hurt by her introject's criticism because she believes her parent's words. Exaggerating her own flaws keeps her in character.

Nonnarcissistic people see a different image. They love one another with flaws perceived like smoke rising from a fire. The fire is what counts. A narcissist projects his unacceptable and secret flaws into his child and feels a lack of love for one so ruined. His child feels alarm and depression when things go wrong. Her flaws justify a troubled life. She doesn't know that she lives an image handed down.

You need to develop a neutral and inquisitive attitude. How can you be friendly with the negative introject that attacks you? A bully is strengthened by his victim's fear but is thrown by neutrality. If you are attentive to your introject without undue anxiety, you will achieve a degree of separation.

Listen to negative thoughts without automatically accepting them as true. A nondefensive approach is good with the critical parent as well. Objectivity achieves more than fighting. If you fight, you are dismissed as infantile. When your conduct is neutral, your views are more likely to be reckoned with. Listen and decide what is true and to what degree. You may need consultation. If you are new to self-evaluation and readily demolished, bring the comment to another person or group whose opinion you trust.

Creativity can help you heal. When I had the notion of examining my introject, I was feeling weak and fearful of the undertaking. I was in a macrobiotic center in California for my summer vacation. This was a Japanese-style dwelling surrounded by mountains. It was built in a hot valley where every possible fruit and vegetable was raised. It gave cooking classes and helped us analyze our physical weaknesses. We learned how to change our way of living in order to feel better and walked on the damp grass of early morning to get our energy moving. It had many minor healing workshops, including yoga and meditation.

At that time, I felt that I didn't need more negative thoughts than

I already had. I was in a personally discouraged mood when I went to a workshop on healing imagery. After the guidance of a slow entry into inner calm, one envisioned living in a favorite spot. For me, it was the wilderness.

I hoped to find some strength and was skeptical, while wondering in what form it would come. Into my mind came a moose, a beautiful, large, and quiet creature, sticking its antlered head into my primitive, next-to-nature abode. My place was blessed. The moose stayed a while, just was there and then left. I felt inspired by its presence and sought its meaning in words but none would come. It simply was, like the self, the song of connection with the earth, a spirit without words. It was love of, to, and by the self.

What does this meditative vision and practice mean? Children of narcissists distrust and devalue their inner selves as if nothing of value could come from inside. This is wrong. Listen to your intuitive part and look with awe at what it produces. Outpourings can take any form or meaning. It is your own symbolism. Creativity does not come out of a can or TV. Children are creative but grow up to be average adults who are pulled away from creativity. They think themselves without creativity but have learned their impoverishment. Narcissistic parents undermine your creativity with, "Is it good enough?" Good enough for what? People talk about my writing and painting. "But you're creative." We are all creative in our way. Talent, imagery, strength from the unconscious is human. Your vision is different from mine but it is there.

By creativity I mean allowing your wishes and visions to inspire you. If you are moved by what comes to your mind, something will emerge to express your inner state. You may find the solution to a problem, write a song or story, a poem that captures deep meaning. You impulsively take a walk in the woods and feel its life around you. Suddenly a recipe comes to your mind for the curious remains in the icebox. You remember the pleasure of an ancient friendship, and so on.

Some therapists have said that creative people avoid knowing their neuroses by turning their problems into art. But this can be quite untrue. A creative person hears his crying self and can't avoid what he thinks and feels. He may use creative powers for healing and seek imaginary or real solutions. The narcissistic parent often teaches her child that there is only perfection or failure. If you open yourself to creativity, there is an infinity of visions. Look at your dreams, the tales you love to hear or tell, and things you find beautiful. You will see a young self waiting to develop. We are always young and always old.

Children of narcissists are trained not to trust their unconscious. Everything they do must meet an external standard. Despite these blinders, our inner lives wait to nourish us. Creativity comes if we are open and receptive. There is more to our self than a learned opinion.

Narcissistic parents taught us to overvalue what we received from them and to undervalue our self and its byproducts. Good was to be like them and bad came from following our own ideas. From their condemnatory reaction, we learned to be afraid of filling our personal desires. We live in familiar hell and call new behaviors negative before the results are in.

You need to live according to experience and differ according to insight as you go. Your values can be your own and not compulsively tied to external measures, such as those of your narcissistic parent, which might include money, fame, beauty, smartness, power. We can stop leading lives to impress the narcissistic community.

We give ourselves a lower rating than others do. Like all people, we make mistakes. These do not merit condemnations to wear upon our breasts but are to learn from. Humor and courage make good partners. Seeing your difficulties and your tendency to exaggerate blame, humor makes it easier to change.

One time I was meditating in a large group. It was dark and the woman in front of me was restless, continually moving her body. Meditators are supposed to sit quietly. In my highmindedness, I hated her for her noise and spent a lot of my attention calling her selfish and a thousand other names. It was all hatred and resentment at her ruining "my" meditation. She was to blame for my mood until the lights went on and I took a look at my "enemy." She was crippled and found it hard to sit.

Children of narcissists are much hurt by narcissistic parents and become prone to thinking themselves attacked. We believe people are out to harm us, an error that is hard to eradicate since we are always adding new examples to our list. Such thinking is eradicated when we see nonenemies in their stead. It was so hard for her to sit. I was amazed and sorry about what I felt. I learned about my tendency to misperceive actions as intended to hurt. I misread facts based on limited information and my predilection for feeling mistreated. A great teaching. As I try to stop personalizing events, my life is becoming easier.

How are we to get over this tendency, called personalizing? A meditation teacher once told a story about this very problem. An Oriental man was rowing on a foggy lake. Unexpectedly, his boat was crashed into by another. He cursed that careless rower and was beside himself with anger at the other's intolerable nerve. Then the boat that hit his floated by and he found it empty. Bent on seeing himself beset, he had created the plot of deliberation that gave him pain.

If you want to get rid of the personalizing tendency to think that people are against you, start with your experience of growing up with narcissistic parents. Your life with them has shaped your vision. They were destructive in their need to see things their way. Was their aggressive and invasive ignorance meant to harm you or merely a mirror view of their own inner world? I think the latter, since there was nothing and no one outside their selves. There was no intention to do you harm as they tried to fulfill their wishes and responsibilities. You were felt to be an extension of them, with your own needs barely heeded. They were drowning people clinging to a spar of wood. So desperate was their situation that they could not see your position. If you broke through their protective reverie it triggered a horrible mood.

Then they would become intent on giving injury or being mean. Their child was fighting their influence and trying to stand apart from or against them. In narcissistic thinking, good is to be identical. Infallibility is contradicted if their child takes another path. They would attack you because in their desperate self-centeredness, they misunderstood your motives.

Emerging from this imbroglio, you perceive an undesired response from them as deliberate. Your parents were sarcastic and enraged and much that they did turned into an attack. This is how you saw them. To expect harm and to see attack gets your running legs going, which sets you up for less disappointment. You grow and still react to people as hurtful. Freedom comes from not seeing malicious intention where none is intended.

Hold back on concluding the presence of malicious intent. Doubt your supposition and, before you draw a conclusion, find out the facts of motivation. Use outside information and underplay your predilection for injury.

We are afraid of change and repeat behaviors that wreck our lives. Sameness to sameness. If we try to change, we do so at a snail's pace that never arrives or move so hurriedly that little change occurs. Lightning speed protects us from being snared, cornered, and hurt. We are afraid to hear the cry of what was left behind, an expectation from our hypersensitive parents who overreacted to our changes. We learn from this that all we do is hurtful, even a new hairdo or a way of speaking. We worry more if we are changing a known habit. Will we lose our friends? We look for and find responses of pain. We hurry past our feelings, so fraught with anxiety, guilt, and grief.

In change, there is losing and gaining. We need to mourn our losses and to grow from the rotting wood of renounced ways. The additional pain we feel is what we inflict on ourselves in anticipation of the critical reactions from our parent stand-in.

A woman wants to change but says she can't. She claims to like what she is doing, eating and smoking herself to the grave. She thinks that her self-destructive behavior started as rebellion against her narcissistic and controlling mother. She had to do it her own way. Her mother lectured in scorn to those who could not learn. It seemed like a giving but was really a taking. Daughter's self-destructiveness gives Mother a project to work on. She served her mother as an untoward kid and does so now in gorging food and cigarettes. Her belly hurts from overeating and her obesity hangs down. Does she know when her stomach is full? She never listens to her feelings.

With controlling parents who need to be right and in charge, we do not learn what we need. Whether to stay or go, to change or to stay put. We leave home as frightened fugitives, beset by our negative introjects. We need to hear from our selves. That is the moose, the beast that entered my vision and showed me a form of down-to-earth being. That moose is an image of my inner self. It is my truth for me.

Do not be surprised if stress activates the voice of your negative introject. The child of a narcissist falsely attaches her sense of self-worth to outcome, which creates desperate worry. If your introject says worry, send it packing with questions like, "What's the big deal?" "Are you personalizing the outcome?" "Are you measuring yourself with dollar bills?" Money does not imply value. Do not apply external measurement to your self.

Do not leap through externally designated hoops. A scientist had to make A's for his punitive and narcissistic mother. Anything less led to a beating. As an adult, he suffers from severe depressions and cannot work. In his mind his mother is at his buttocks with a whip. He needs to remind himself that he likes to work and need not seek outside approval for doing it. Put the introject in mothballs.

We need to know when therapy would be a good approach. Many people who suffer from an overwhelming and intrusive negative introject are told, "It's impossible to like yourself better." They have to live in misery as if it were the only way. Their introject says "Follow me" to repetitive misery.

A narcissistic falsehood is to believe that one should appear perfect and need no help. Narcissistic parents said that you should be able to master all problems, while finding you incapable of adaptation. This attitude overlooks the fact that useful efforts are stymied by aspects of your personality.

You may see only your best and call it perfect, or see only your worst and feel hopeless. You have been parent-trained to look this way to please them. You may be unreachable to contradictory comment. How are you to find your blind spots and errors if your introject makes it too miserable to approach your self and your personality disregards you self's comments as a problem.

Given such obstacles, reasonable input is called for. Solitude is not efficient in getting the job accomplished. Some of the most original people, scientists, artists, etc., have asked for help. They questioned knowledge and openly showed their confusion and error. They had little shame about blind spots and shortcomings since they already respected their selves. By exposing weakness they got more strength. They learned what they wanted to know. We do not advance by focusing on our image. We want to change from a self-hater who refuses help and exposure to a self-lover who accepts errors and openly works on difficulties.

How do you know if you need outside help? Are many people saying the same thing to you about you? Is their tone exasperated and do their comments show that they think you are not getting their message? Do you think that you are treated differently from others? Is something wrong with your interactions but you cannot say what? Outside help is in the offing.

Childhood with narcissistic parents means being overly subjected to criticism, which sensitized you to your shortcomings. Are your faults as bad as your parents called them? What should you do with outside criticism? A nonnarcissistic attitude is appropriate. You can benefit from a group that works together on what is happening and what is perceived.

We were raised to think that narcissistic people like our parents were the best people and that nonnarcissists didn't count for much. Getting to know nonnarcissists shows that this is wrong. Children of narcissists can share their stories and speak about their negative introjects. They share their troubles and move on.

We need to investigate opinions and hunches. Do not accept ideas at face value. Your narcissistic parents raised you to swallow the family line. Mom/Dad was "correct" in viewpoint and "perfect" in parenting. Now you are easily misled by forceful sellers. Focus on your habit of acceptance. Know that you will bend under pressure. Inquire about the facts and take the time you need before making a decision. Do not renounce what you want just to please another. In searching for friends, give up codependency. Wait for one that you like and hunt for one that you trust, a person who accepts you as you are.

EPILOGUE

*B*ecause children of narcissists are raised to follow parental dictates, to believe that what the parent thinks is right and to defer to authority, it is important for these individuals to break the habit of allowing other people to set their path.

For this reason, it is inappropriate for me to recommend a course of action. This book has presented many kinds of examples and methods to get you closer to your true identity. There are various techniques of meditation and a large variety of therapy workshops or individual therapies in which you can work to change yourself. If you do not know which one to choose, attend various workshops and test them out. Read books on the subject. Speak to people and hear what they think about the method they follow.

As with all of life's experience, you must be the judge of its worth. What someone else values and what you hold dear may differ. The main thing is to accept what you have tested and personally found true. Membership in a group can be comforting but not as comforting as learning to stand alone.

INDEX

abandonment, 57, 60–61, 73, 75, 76
  fear of, 49, 83, 92, 199
  feelings of, 46, 101
abuse, 56, 63–64, 104–105, 152, 190
  "accidental," 77
  by fathers, 50, 51, 59–60, 73, 74, 77,
    112, 115, 185
  love equated with, 59–60, 74, 131
  by mothers, 50, 87, 134, 136, 258
  by narcissistic mates, 74, 75, 77, 83, 84,
    87–88, 89
  sexual, 112
  verbal, 77, 114, 191
acting, 170–172
acting out, sexual, 30
addiction, 74, 78, 88, 106, 183, 209, 236,
  244

alcoholism, 62, 87, 106, 199
  drug use in, 52, 62, 75, 86, 87, 99, 107,
    155, 225, 232
  to food, see eating; obesity
  overcoming, 155–156, 159
admiration, need for, 12, 20, 32
adult children, 12–15, 25–33, 51, 147–168,
  171, 218
  anger of, 14, 43, 69, 126, 151, 162, 163,
    203, 206, 207, 211, 228–229, 233,
    234, 235
  anti-self attitudes of, 147–148
  belief vs. suspicion in, 167
  biological perspective needed by, 233
  blind spots of, 33, 122–123, 191, 207,
    221, 258
  codependency of, 232, 236, 259

adult children (*cont.*)
  common problem of, 28
  critical attitude in, 100–101, 108–110,
    154, 157, 176, 195, 199, 227–228
  criticism believed by, 29, 134, 228, 229,
    230, 233–234, 241
  dead family member replaced by, 123
  dichotomous thinking of, 165–167, 195
  discouraged by real-life difficulties, 46
  emotional numbness in, 51, 94–95, 115,
    117, 143–145, 183
  functional constriction in, 111–117, 185,
    203, 204–208, 243
  gullibility of, 30–31, 259
  harm feared by, 136, 154–155, 255–257
  hypersensitivity of, 30, 32, 121, 128,
    151–152, 153–154, 157, 162, 171,
    172, 224, 229
  insensitivity to others in, 123–124, 154,
    157
  intrusiveness in, 116–117
  learned errors of, 148
  maladaptive behavior of, 29–30, 31, 53
  mourning for childhood needed by, 128,
    252, 257
  narcissistic character traits in, 32, 116
  narcissistic habits acquired by, 116–117,
    143, 157–158, 227–228, 245
  negative expectations of, 153–155, 227
  open play difficult for, 182
  as overachievers, 156
  paranoid tendencies of, 30, 102, 255–
    256
  parental perfection accepted by, 228
  performance problems of, 29–30, 46, 48,
    67, 107–108, 153, 156–157
  procrastination by, 113, 156
  projections of, 151
  psychological helping professions en-
    tered by, 107–108, 203, 207
  roles played by, 12, 14, 33, 61, 81, 94,
    116, 203
  self-presentation of, 223–229
  separation feared by, 81–83
  sexual inhibition of, 99, 176
  shared repetitive patterns of, 121
  social isolation of, 59, 66, 94, 174, 181,
    184, 194, 198, 210–211, 214–215,
    216, 219, 226; *see also* friendships
  solitude feared by, 82–83
  spouses of, 48–49, 53, 56–57, 75–76,
    136–137, 142, 143–144, 151, 214
  strength linked to weakness in, 162–164,
    204, 215, 216, 234
  submissive conformity of, 13, 30, 35–44,
    83, 89, 92, 101, 115–116, 120,
    135–136, 151, 201, 202, 203, 216,
    228, 236, 237

  talent for suffering in, 123–124
  transference by, 31
  unknown feared by, 153, 176
  unrecognized abilities of, 156–157
  see also children; healing
aging, 53–54, 137–138, 225, 226
agreement, demands for, 35–44, 119–120,
    125–126, 158, 229, 236–237
Alan (intellectual superiority), 119–129,
    132
alcoholism, 62, 87, 106, 199
Alice (social isolation), 198, 210–211
Alpert, Richard (Ram Das), 173–174
anger, 14, 43, 69, 126, 162, 163, 203, 206,
    207, 211, 228–229, 233, 234, 235
  acknowledging, 151
  crying vs., 252
  see also rage
animals, 184, 193–194, 211, 213, 246, 250
Anne (negative introject), 45–54, 97
anti-Semitism, 183–184
anxiety, 20, 46, 49, 73, 82, 93, 162, 248,
    253
  separation, 81–82
  signal, 98
approval, parental, 19–20, 79, 80, 81, 103,
    115, 122, 127, 142, 149, 152, 162,
    180, 233–234, 235, 237, 249
artists, 92, 123, 150
assertiveness, 83, 128, 141, 201, 202, 203,
    218
asthma, 195, 242
autonomy, 20, 28, 33, 36, 51, 92, 117, 124,
    171, 182, 228, 237, 251
  development of, 81–82
  see also self

beauty, personal, 19, 192, 202, 227, 245
  mothers and, 29, 73, 79, 101–107, 135,
    199, 200
bed-wetting, 109, 195
Be Here Now (Alpert), 173
belief vs. suspicion, 167
biological perspective, 233
blind spots, 33, 122–123, 191, 207, 221,
    258
body, 158–162
  criticism of, 79, 134, 169, 170, 180, 192,
    224, 227, 229
  of daughter, mother's mistreatment of,
    103–107
  feeling torn apart in, 161–162
  improper care of, 99, 160–161
  negative sensations in, 162
  nudity of, 169–170
  objectionable failings of, 194–196
  pain in, 159
  see also obesity

body image, 102
breast reduction, 107
Buddha, 174

camp, 150–151
car sickness, 195
character, 19
character traits, narcissistic, 11, 18, 23, 32, 116
charm, 21, 89
    public vs. private, 60, 80
children, 12–15, 21–22, 23, 116, 125, 132, 178, 201, 235–236, 244
    of adult children, 47, 52, 67, 76, 78, 82, 121, 122–123, 141–145, 164, 165, 190, 203, 214
    dependency of, denied by parent, 141–145
    as extension of parent, 12, 51, 52, 82, 165, 184, 251, 256
    grandiosity in, 20, 21
    healthy exhibitionism in, 22, 172
    idealized, 12
    identification with parents and, 15, 73, 109, 117, 157, 158, 218
    negative parental assessments believed by, 30, 61, 67, 91–95, 102, 149–151, 156, 228–229, 235, 253
    other people's, preference for, 61, 65
    parental approval sought by, 19–20, 79, 80, 81, 103, 115, 122, 127, 142, 149, 152, 162, 180, 233–234, 235, 237, 249
    parental identification with, 20, 224
    parental "improvement" of, 27, 29, 58, 102, 103, 105, 157, 182
    parental problems transplanted to, 29, 91–95, 102
    parents' personal ambitions fulfilled by, 58, 141–145, 162
    projections of, 14
    projections onto, 12–13, 27, 103, 107, 145, 193, 253
    rage of, 14, 126
    roles assigned to, 12–14
    separation anxiety in, 81–82
    see also adult children
cleanliness, compulsive, 114
codependency, 209, 232, 236, 259
competition, 160, 238
compromise, 236–237
conformity, submissive, 13, 30, 35–44, 83, 89, 92, 101, 115–116, 120, 135–136, 151, 201, 202, 203, 216, 228, 236, 237
conscience, 98, 244
constriction, functional, 111–117, 185, 203, 204–208, 243

control, need to, 38, 50, 51, 98, 100, 116, 133, 134, 137, 142, 143, 202, 204, 207, 208, 225, 227–228, 257
creativity, 23, 187–188, 253–255
    artistic, 92, 123, 150
criticism, 12, 13, 18, 22, 32, 53, 92, 97, 114, 150–152, 172, 180–182, 184, 185, 210, 229–235, 236
    by adult children, 100–101, 108–110, 154, 157, 176, 195, 199, 227–228
    appropriate reactions to, 229–232, 234–235, 259
    believed by adult children, 29, 134, 228, 229, 230, 233–234, 241
    of body, 79, 134, 169, 170, 180, 192, 224, 227, 229
    humor vs., 230–232, 238
    hypersensitivity caused by, 151–152, 171, 224
    ignored, 230
    love equated with, 31, 192
    by negative introject, 242, 253, 257
    noncombative firmness toward, 229–230
    public, 230–232
crying, 252
cults, 31, 165
cynicism, 74

Darjeeling, India, 174–176, 217
David Neel, Alexandra, 174
defensive mechanisms, 183
Delores (narcissistic mates), 57, 64, 71–90, 163–164, 190, 191
dependency, 52, 79, 92, 127, 198–201, 209, 249
    of children, parental denial of, 141–145
    of narcissistic mates, 75–76, 78, 83, 84–89, 199, 208, 210
depression, 23, 43, 46, 54, 79, 87, 98, 104, 117, 122, 138, 178, 206, 225, 242, 248, 258
    see also suicide
Diagnostic and Statistical Manual of Mental Disorders (Third Edition) (DSM 3), 18
dieting, 132
diet pills, 53, 99, 106, 107
Doryan (self-sufficiency), 198, 211–215
doubt, 12, 52–53, 72, 108, 121, 142, 182, 189
dreams, 73, 85, 112, 124, 126, 155, 200, 244
dress, style of, 105–106, 132, 134, 217–218
dukkha, 163
drug use, 52, 62, 75, 86, 87, 99, 107, 155, 225, 232
    in hospitalization, 247–248

Eastern religions, 75–76, 158, 173–174
    Zen Buddhism, 57, 67–68, 163, 164, 167
    see also meditation

eating, 99, 121, 132, 137, 162, 202–203,
    257
  compulsive, 102–103, 104, 105, 106,
    107, 225, 227
  controlled by mothers, 136, 202
  double messages about, 103, 105
  love equated with, 103
  procrastinated, 156
  as regression, 160
  see also obesity
emotional numbness, 51, 94–95, 115, 117,
    143–145, 183
empathy, 18
emptiness, inner, 21, 23, 94, 201, 236,
    252
entitlement, sense of, 18, 21, 51
exercise, 53, 99, 132, 161, 207, 224, 225–
    226
exhibitionism, 18, 22, 172

fairness, judgment of, 232–233
family, 57–58, 63, 64, 93–94
  abandoned by father, 60–61, 73, 75, 76,
    199
  dead member of, replaced by adult child,
    123
  narcissism in all members of, 37, 152–
    154, 195, 229, 237, 247–248
  of narcissists, 12, 20–22
fantasies, 30, 65, 73, 164, 178, 205, 221,
    238, 248
  grandiose, 18, 20, 21, 29, 144
  in healing, 148–149, 254, 257
father(s), 13, 20, 50–52, 75, 80–81, 123–
    125, 127, 148, 161, 187, 200, 204,
    210, 230–232
  abuse by, 50, 51, 59–60, 73, 74, 77, 112,
    115, 185
  of author, 36–44, 72, 91–92, 93–95, 120,
    122, 126, 128, 149, 151–152, 169,
    170, 171, 172, 176, 180–182, 183–
    184, 216, 218, 221, 223–229, 233–
    234, 249
  distant, 58–65, 73–74, 75, 83, 84, 89,
    164
  dreams of, 112
  family abandoned by, 60–61, 73, 75, 76,
    199
  incestuous feelings in, 50, 192
  Jewish, anti-Semitism of, 183–184
  in negative introject, 55–69, 111–117
  nonnarcissistic, 101–102, 103, 133, 141–
    142
  other people's children favored by, 65
  premarital vs. postmarital behavior of,
    80
  puritanical, 133, 135, 137, 138
  rigidly structured routines of, 38–39

fear, 252
  of abandonment, 49, 83, 92, 199
  of harm, 136, 154–155, 255–257
  of loss, 134, 193–194, 246
  of separation, 81–83
  of solitude, 82–83
  of unknown, 153, 176
firmness, noncombative, 229–230
French Revolution, 17
friendships, 31, 66, 113, 117, 150, 154,
    172, 174, 205–206, 209, 217, 232,
    245, 249
  codependency vs., 259
  narcissistic, 22, 25–26, 68, 115
  see also social isolation
fudge factor, 30
functional constriction, 111–117, 185, 203,
    204–208, 243

gaiety, surface, 49–50, 63, 82
geishas, 227
Giancarlo (traveling companion), 176–177,
    178
gifts, 21, 47
  other than requested, 26, 36, 87, 235,
    249, 250
God Speaks (Maya Baba), 174
Golomb, Elan (author), 91–95, 198, 215–
    218, 263
  father of, 36–44, 72, 91–92, 93–95, 120,
    122, 126, 128, 149, 151–152, 169,
    170, 171, 172, 176, 180–182, 183–
    184, 216, 218, 221, 223–229, 233–
    234, 249
  mother of, 38, 91–93, 94, 171–172, 180–
    182, 216, 226, 248–249
  Sara, aunt of, 37–44
grandiose self, 12, 21
grandiosity, 12, 13, 22, 23, 27, 73, 92, 127,
    153, 180
  in children, 20, 21
  in fantasies, 18, 20, 21, 29, 144
  of mothers, 20–21, 101
grandparents, 28, 32, 52, 58, 62, 80, 92,
    102, 185, 198–199, 237, 251
  nonnarcissistic, 25, 93–94, 133–134,
    135, 136, 137, 172, 225
group membership, 164–167, 244,
    262
group therapy, 51, 220, 245, 259
guilt, 98, 124, 126, 127, 223, 232
gullibility, 30–31, 259

hair, 103–105, 202
hallucinations, 103
handedness, shifting of, 58
harm, fear of, 136, 154–155, 255–257

hatred, 37, 55, 91–92, 93, 100–101, 108–110, 179, 205, 226, 255
see also self-hatred
healing, 54, 66, 68–69, 89–90, 109–110, 112, 117, 147–188, 203–204, 209–210, 218, 219–220, 261–262
acknowledging anger in, 151
creativity in, 187–188, 253–255
defensive mechanisms vs., 183
fantasy images in, 148–149, 254, 257
group membership and, 164–167, 244, 262
love of nature in, 92, 172–173, 174, 179, 180–183, 184, 212, 213–214
meditation in, see meditation
mistreatment and, 152–155
natural, 247
overcoming addiction in, 155–156, 159
redefining love in, 90, 177–179, 236
through sensitive people, 25, 183–186, 187, 219
travel in, 173–177, 178, 217
see also psychotherapy
health, 19, 48, 50, 243
of exhibitionism, 22, 172
of narcissism, 11–12
helpfulness, selfless, 198, 201–204, 207–210
Himalayas, 174–176, 178
hospitalization, 66, 246–249, 250
humiliation, 51, 61, 77, 114–115, 136, 185, 230, 243
humor, 245, 246, 255
criticism vs., 230–232, 238
hypersensitivity, 22, 44, 124, 127, 128, 170, 257
of adult children, 30, 32, 121, 128, 151–152, 153–154, 157, 162, 171, 172, 224, 229
criticism as cause of, 151–152, 171, 224

idealization, 12, 18, 68–69
identification, 50, 98–99
with aggressor, 111, 186
with child by parent, 20, 224
with parents, 15, 73, 109, 117, 157, 158, 218
self-love learned through, 20
identity, 121, 160, 201, 216, 221, 236, 261
sexual, 13, 80, 102
inarticulateness, 29–30
incestuous feelings, 50, 192
India, 173–177, 178, 217
infallibility, 32, 44, 107, 115–116, 128, 135, 228, 229, 237, 256, 257
inner child, 28, 109, 115
insensitivity to others, 123–124, 154, 157, 232
intellectual superiority, 30, 119–129, 132

grades and, 61–62, 64, 65, 67, 93, 97, 104
parental expectation of, 29, 32, 92, 122, 135–136, 160, 258
interrupting, 31, 124, 237
intimacy, 145, 198, 209, 214–215, 237
introject, 32–33
conscience vs., 98, 244
contents of, 97
development of, 49
external manifestation of, 138
negative, see negative introject
intrusiveness, 20, 116–117, 124–125, 127, 128, 141–142, 171, 212
irresponsibility, 60, 75–77, 84–86
isolation, social, see social isolation

Jewish culture, 125–127, 238
anti-Semitism vs., 183–184
symbiosis in, 125, 127
Jews for Jesus, 165
John (suicidal urges), 55–69, 73, 97, 98, 162–163, 164

Kali, 100, 108, 109–110
Kanchenjunga, Mount, 175
kundalini energy, 165

labeling, 27, 29, 31, 56, 158, 185
Lagkpa (Sherpa guide), 175, 178
learned errors, 148
lesbianism, 99, 102, 108, 231–232
Lorrie (selfless helpfulness), 198, 201–204, 207
loss, fear of, 134, 193–194, 246
Louis XIV, king of France, 17–18
love, 22, 29, 91–95, 98, 189–196, 206, 210, 235–236, 238–239
abuse equated with, 59–60, 74, 131
for animals, 184, 193–194, 211, 213, 246, 250
conditional, 14–15, 32, 79
criticism equated with, 31, 192
eating equated with, 103
fear of loss vs., 134, 193–194, 246
hated equated with, 55
manufactured from nothing, 192–193
of nature, 92, 172–173, 174, 179, 180–183, 184, 212, 213–214
negative introject vs., 250, 252–253
objectionable physical failings vs., 194–196
parental, futile expectation of, 20, 45, 49, 52, 71–72, 83, 93–94, 110, 115–116, 117, 125, 132, 136, 145, 177–179, 191, 199, 221, 227, 233, 236, 244, 252, 253
redefinition of, 90, 177–179, 236

love (cont.)
  sadomasochistic, 191–192
  self-, 19, 20, 160
  see also mates, narcissistic; romantic rela-
    tionships
lying, 249
  parental, 157–158, 248

McLuhan, Marshall, 129
manipulation, 20, 23, 30–31, 84, 97, 127,
  228, 229
Marie (obesity), 131–139
Marie Antoinette, queen of France, 17–18
Mark (heroic child), 141–145
Mary (dependency), 198–201
Marx, Groucho, 20
mask, social (persona), 12, 64, 66, 106,
  109, 151, 160, 170
mates, narcissistic, 53, 60, 71–90, 136–137,
  178, 203, 253
  abuse by, 74, 75, 77, 83, 84, 87–88, 89
  dependency of, 75–76, 78, 83, 84–89,
    199, 208, 210
  irresponsibility of, 75–77, 84–86
  sexual behavior of, 38, 84, 87, 177, 191,
    192, 208, 226–227
  see also spouses
Maya Baba, 174
meditation, 57, 68, 138, 163, 179, 217,
  253, 254, 255, 261
  teachers of, 165–167, 173–174, 256
"Me generation," 18
military school, 63–64
"mind fucking," 28
Möbius strip, 214
mockery, 32, 114, 148, 171, 185, 186
moral correctness, 124, 157
mother(s), 26–27, 32, 49–50, 78, 79–82,
  143, 151, 165, 214, 257
  abuse by, 50, 87, 134, 136, 258
  of author, 38, 91–93, 94, 171–172, 180–
    182, 216, 226, 248–249
  beauty and, 29, 73, 79, 101–107, 135,
    199, 200
  daughter's body mistreated by, 103–
    107
  dependency abetted by, 52, 198–201
  eating controlled by, 136, 202
  grandiosity of, 20–21, 101
  handedness shifted by, 58
  helpfulness demanded by, 201–204
  intrusive, 124–125, 127, 128, 141–142
  in negative introject, 97–110
  nonnarcissistic, 60, 62–63, 64, 66, 67,
    68, 76, 91–92, 116, 187, 198–199,
    210, 232
  obesity and, 133–136, 137–138, 139
  paranoid, 207–209, 235

narcissism, 11–15, 17–23, 48, 52–53, 106,
  174, 200, 233
  alleged shtetl origin of, 125–127
  in all family members, 37, 152–154, 195,
    229, 237, 247–248
  character traits of, 11, 18, 23, 32, 116
  external vs. internal, 157
  healthy, 11–12
  medical model of, 18, 22–23
  parasitic nature of, 125
  of society, 18–19
narcissistic character disorder, 18
narcissistic habits, acquired, 116–117, 143,
  157–158, 227–228, 245
narcissists, 11–15, 17–23, 31, 68, 114, 127,
  150–151, 152–153, 188, 192, 215,
  224–225, 235, 259
  admiration needed by, 12, 20, 32
  aging and, 53–54, 137–138, 225, 226
  agreement demanded by, 13, 35–44,
    119–120, 125–126, 158, 229, 236–
    237
  charm of, 21, 60, 80, 89
  cool indifference of, 18
  distorted reality perceptions of, 28, 36–
    37, 53
  family of, 12, 20–22
  friendships of, 22, 25–26, 68, 115
  happy occasions ruined by, 152–153
  hypersensitivity of, 22, 44, 124, 127,
    128, 170, 257
  infallibility of, 32, 44, 107, 115–116,
    128, 135, 228, 229, 237, 256,
    257
  injured self-esteem of, 18, 20, 27, 226,
    235
  insensitivity of, 123–124, 154, 157, 232
  interrupting by, 31, 124, 237
  manipulativeness of, 20, 23, 30–31, 84,
    97, 127, 228, 229
  mates chosen by, 22
  neediness of, 21, 232
  perfectionism of, 53–54, 114, 152, 171,
    254
  personal perfection of, 23, 32, 123, 125,
    165, 170, 219, 220, 228, 251, 258,
    259
  psychotherapy of, 23, 127, 205
  rage of, 19, 21, 22, 28, 50, 51–52, 87,
    92, 97, 125–126, 136, 157
  self-centeredness of, 17, 21, 32, 39, 53,
    60, 73, 83, 123, 192, 194, 200, 201,
    204, 235, 256
  sense of entitlement in, 18, 21, 51
  sense of specialness in, 11, 21, 22, 123
  sense of superiority in, 12, 122, 192,
    210, 234, 235
  separateness intolerable to, 51–52

sexual behavior of, 38, 84, 87, 177, 191, 192, 208, 226–227
social isolation of, 25, 60, 81, 127, 232, 237
social status desired by, 68, 79, 231, 255
see also mates, narcissistic
Narcissus, myth of, 18
nature, love of, 92, 172–173, 174, 179, 180–183, 184, 212, 213–214
Nazism, 185–186, 246
negative introject, 33, 45–54, 160, 161–162, 194, 241–259
criticism by, 242, 253, 257
development of, 244
eradication of, 139, 243–244, 249–259
love vs., 250, 252–253
maternal, 97–110
mobilized by events, 246–249, 250
in obesity, 138–139
outside information vs., 245–246, 253, 257
paternal, 55–69, 111–117
psychotherapy for, 244, 245, 258–259
negative reaction, 205
nervous breakdowns, 127, 160
Nick (self-denying negativism), 111–117, 132, 155, 198, 203, 204–208, 235
Nimcaroli Baba, 173–174
nonauthenticity, feelings of, 14
nosebleeds, 195
nudity, 169–170, 175
numbness, emotional, 51, 94–95, 115, 117, 143–145, 183

obesity, 53–54, 57, 102, 104, 105, 113, 131–139, 225, 227, 237
definition of, 132
dieting vs., 132
diet pills for, 53, 99, 106, 107
negative introject in, 138–139
sexuality vs., 53, 132, 135, 136, 137, 138
see also eating
open play, 182
orgasms, 38, 99, 108–109, 177
overachievers, 156

pacification, 236
paranoid tendencies, 30, 102, 207–209, 235
personalization in, 194, 255–256
parent(s), 11–15, 20, 50, 88, 98, 125, 147, 158, 164, 166, 170, 188, 197, 204–205, 213, 220, 221, 255, 256
addiction in, 155
ambitions of, fulfilled by children, 58, 141–145, 162
appropriate reactions to, 228, 229–232

children as extension of, 12, 51, 52, 82, 165, 184, 251, 256
child's love for pets as seen by, 193–194
compromising with, 236–237
consistent disapproval by, 49
controlling attitude of, 38, 50, 51, 98, 100, 116, 133, 134, 137, 142, 143, 202, 204, 207, 208, 225, 227–228, 257
creativity undermined by, 254
establishing new relationship with, 223–239
European, 133, 212
humiliation by, 51, 77, 114–115, 136, 185, 230
idealized, 68–69
identification with, 15, 73, 109, 117, 157, 158, 218
identification with children by, 20, 224
incomprehensibility of, 52–53, 105
intellectual superiority expected by, 29, 32, 92, 122, 135–136, 160, 258
intrusive, 20, 171, 212
judging fairness to, 232–233
love withheld by, 20, 45, 49, 52, 71–72, 83, 93–94, 110, 115–116, 117, 125, 132, 136, 145, 177–179, 191, 199, 221, 227, 233, 236, 244, 252, 253
lying by, 157–158, 248
"mind fucking" by, 28
mockery by, 32, 114, 148, 171, 185, 186
negative assessment by, 30, 61, 67, 91–95, 102, 149–151, 156, 228–229, 235, 253
negative predictions of, 30, 156
negative scrutiny by, 79, 114, 176, 184, 185, 242, 244
nonnarcissistic, 26
osmotic expectations of, 26–27
pacification of, 236
peculiar world view of, 26
personal problems transplanted by, 29, 91–95, 102
projections of, 12–13, 27, 103, 107, 145, 193, 253
rationalized self-interest of, 28
sadistic, 33, 111–117, 185–186, 204, 231
seeking approval of, 19–20, 79, 80, 81, 103, 115, 122, 127, 142, 149, 152, 162, 180, 233–234, 235, 237, 249
selflessness demanded by, 31
sexuality inhibited by, 99, 176
shaming by, 32
sharing activities with, 236–239
see also adult children; father(s); grandparents; mother(s); narcissists
Parker, Charlie, 224–225

passive-aggressive traits, 31
past-life regression, 149
perfection, personal, 23, 32, 123, 125, 165,
    170, 219, 220, 228, 251, 258, 259
perfectionism, 53–54, 114, 152, 171, 254
performance problems, 29–30, 46, 48, 67,
    107–108, 153, 156–157
persona (social mask), 12, 64, 66, 106, 109,
    151, 160, 170
personalization, 194, 255–257
phobia, 252
play, open, 182
positive reinforcement, 230
pregnancy, 193
procrastination, 113, 156
projections, 14, 151, 153
    of adult children, 151
    onto children by parents, 12–13, 27,
        103, 107, 145, 193, 253
psychosis, 21, 103
psychotherapy, 95, 99, 108, 117, 145, 162,
    170, 171, 173, 177, 179, 190, 197,
    201, 214–215, 219–221, 231, 232
    addicts in, 209
    formal, 220–221
    group, 51, 220, 245, 259
    inadequacy proved by, 150–151
    meditation vs., 163
    narcissists in, 23, 127, 205
    for negative introject, 244, 245, 258–259
    negative reaction in, 205
    parents threatened by, 14, 221
    silence in, 205, 211
    singing and, 148
    success as motive for, 217
    therapist's character important to, 67,
        167, 207, 220
    transference in, 205, 220

Rabbit Man, 184, 219
rage, 14, 68, 100, 114, 126
    narcissistic, 18, 21, 32, 28, 50, 51–52,
        87, 92, 97, 125–126, 136, 157
Ram Das (Richard Alpert), 173–174
reality, perception of, 31–32, 112–113, 233
    narcissistic distortion of, 28, 36–37, 53
rebellion, 55–69, 112, 116, 163, 165, 216,
    228, 257
regression, 35–44, 160
    past-life, 149
role-playing, 12–14, 33, 61, 81, 94, 116,
    170, 203
romantic relationships, 50–51, 60, 113,
    176–177, 210, 226, 227, 245–246
    commitment in, 74, 75, 83, 101
    critical attitude in, 100–101, 108–110,
        176
    identified with self, 98–99

intimacy restricted in, 198, 214–215
    see also mates, narcissistic; sexuality
rounded eye, 185

sadism, 33, 111–117, 185–186, 204, 231
sadomasochism, 117, 191–192
Sara, Aunt, 37–44
scrutiny, negative, 79, 176, 184, 242, 244
    rounded eye vs., 185
    self-consciousness caused by, 114
self, 14, 20, 28, 36, 94–95, 100, 106, 117,
    170, 186–188, 216
    acceptance of, 29, 186–187
    anti-self attitudes vs., 147–148
    grandiose, 12, 21
    healthy, 19
    personality vs., 162, 243
    recovery of, 147–168; see also healing
    romantic relationships and, 98–99
    sabotage of, 48, 108
    sadomasochism vs., 117, 191–192
self-censorship, 39
self-centeredness, 17, 21, 32, 39, 53, 60,
    73, 83, 123, 192, 194, 200, 201,
    204, 235, 256
self-consciousness, 114
self-doubt, 12, 52–53, 72, 108, 121, 142,
    182, 189
self-esteem, 13, 28, 92, 142, 156, 228
    of narcissists, 18, 20, 27, 226, 235
self-hatred, 80, 99, 102, 107, 132, 162,
    190, 194, 219, 225, 250
    experiential verification for, 149, 150–
        151
    suicidal urges from, 55–69
self-image, 12, 29, 58, 65, 109, 148, 149,
    164, 186, 194, 224, 245
    body image in, 102
    dual, 136
    positive, 133–134, 135, 136, 137
self-importance, sense of, 18
selflessness, 31, 51, 83, 244
    helpfulness and, 198, 201–204, 207–210,
        235
self-love, 19, 20, 160
self-presentation, 223–229
self-sufficiency, 21, 198, 211–215
self-worth, 19, 20, 29, 93, 98, 153, 154,
    155, 185, 198, 223, 257
sensitive people, healing through, 25, 183–
    186, 187, 219
separation, fear of, 81–83
separation anxiety, 81–82
sexual identity, 13, 80, 102
sexuality, 57, 101, 113, 176–177, 187, 210
    acting out in, 30
    child abuse in, 112
    incestuous, 50, 192

lesbian, 99, 102, 108, 231–232
narcissistic, 38, 84, 87, 177, 191, 192,
      208, 226–227
obesity and, 53, 132, 135, 136, 137,
      138
orgasms in, 38, 99, 108–109, 177
parental inhibition of, 99, 176
shaming, 32
shtetls, 125–127
siblings, 57, 59, 61–62, 64, 73, 76, 81, 103,
      136, 137–138, 160, 208, 211
signal anxiety, 98
singing, 134, 148, 212
social isolation, 134–135, 144
of adult children, 59, 66, 94, 174, 181,
      184, 194, 198, 210–211, 214–215,
      216, 219, 226
of narcissists, 25, 60, 81, 127, 232,
      237
see also friendships
social status, 68, 79, 231, 255
society, 57, 147
narcissistic, 18–19
solitude, fear of, 82–83
specialness, sense of, 11, 21, 22, 123
spouses, 37–39, 80, 91–92, 141–142, 208,
      210, 225, 227–228, 231
of adult children, 48–49, 53, 56–57, 75–
      76, 136–137, 142, 143–144, 151,
      214
behavior required of, 12, 13, 22
as exclusive possession, 101–102
self-censorship of, 39
treatment received by, 38–39, 60, 62,
      92, 116
stage fright, 170–172
strangling, 77, 88
strength linked to weakness, 162–164, 204,
      215, 216, 234
submissive conformity, 13, 30, 35–44, 83,
      89, 92, 101, 115–116, 120, 135–

      136, 151, 201, 202, 203, 216, 228,
      236, 237
suicide, 55–69, 73, 84, 98, 183, 248
motives for, 56
superiority, sense of, 12, 122, 192, 210,
      234, 235
see also intellectual superiority
surprise parties, 60, 153–154
suspicion vs. belief, 167
symbiosis, 28, 125, 127, 161

talkers, compulsive, 119–129, 237, 238
teaching, proper, 27–28
technology, 187
Tibet, 173, 174–176, 217
Tillie (selfless helpfulness), 198, 201, 204,
      207–210, 235
toilet training, 109, 194–195
transference, 31, 205, 220
travel, 173–177, 178, 217
truth-telling, compulsive, 157–158

unicorn, 89
unknown, fear of, 153, 176
unreliability, 53, 72, 78, 79, 82

values, 98, 148, 195, 235, 245, 255, 262
acquisition of, 13–14
of society, 19
Victoria (negative introject), 97–110, 125,
      132, 155, 158, 194–196

winning, 19
women, 74, 78
attitudes toward, 38, 44, 80, 87, 148,
      180, 226–227
crying by, 252
sexual identity of, 13, 80, 102
wounding, narcissistic, 19, 20

Zen Buddhism, 57, 67–68, 163, 164, 167

A NOTE ABOUT THE AUTHOR

ELAN GOLOMB earned her Ph.D. in clinical psychology and
her Certificate in Psychoanalysis and Psychotherapy from
New York University. Since 1972 she has been in private
practice in New York City. She lives part of the time in
Warwick, New York, where she writes a weekly column
called "The Mind's Eye" for the Warwick *Advertiser Photo
News*.